Modern Menu Planning in Hotel

Modern Menu Planning in Hotel

K.S. Gusain

CYBER TECH PUBLICATIONS
4264/3, Ansari Road, Daryaganj, New Delhi-110002 (India)
Ph.: 011-23244078. Fax: 011-23280028
E-Mail: cyberpublicationsdelhi@yahoo.com

MODERN MENU PLANNING IN HOTEL

K.S. Gusain

First Edition 2009

Published by :

G.S. Rawat for **Cyber Tech Publications**
4264/3, Ansari Road, Daryaganj, New Delhi-110002 (India)
Ph.: 011-23244078. Fax: 011-23280028
E-Mail: cyberpublicationsdelhi@yahoo.com

Printed at : Asian Offset Printers

Preface

Restaurants are encouraged — but not required — to provide complete nutritional information whenever possible. Operators only need to provide information about the specific nutrient for which a claim is made. For example, if your menu makes a claim about the sodium content of an item, you do not need to provide information about the item's calorie, fat or vitamin content — only the amount of sodium the dish contains. Operators do not have to worry about the format used to convey the information. It doesn't have to be set up like the "Nutrition Facts" labels seen on packaged foods. Nor does it have to be printed on the menu — it just needs to be readily available.

This book is about the Modern Menus and their planning in hotels all over the world, undersigned is hopeful that this work of him would be of immense help to the readers.

— *Author*

CONTENTS

1

Introduction

Each season has its food. And just as each season has its food, so too does each region. Creating a menu with ingredients that are not grown or readily available in your immediate area can not only increase food costs but may result in expensive but inferior dishes. So to help ensure your next seasonal menu is profitable and attuned to both local and competitive standards, HOTELS talked to consultants and hotel chefs from four continents who offer up some menu planning along with a few seasonal dishes of their own making.

Keep it Local

"The greatest advantage of a hotel is its location and its high visibility," says Tucker W. "Bill" Main, founder of Bill Main & Associates, a foodservice consultancy in Chico, California. "But its greatest weakness is its lack of local identity.

Nobody thinks of a hotel when suggesting a great regional restaurant." Main blames hotels' lack of local culinary regard on chefs, saying they "are more focused on what they want or what is easiest," as opposed to what is best for the guest. But even more challenging for hotel chefs are the demands of their international clientele. Foreign travelers often want foods that are familiar. But Main says if chefs just concentrate on foods from the local market, they cannot go wrong.

"Advances in food technology and transportation may have contributed to taking some of the 'specialness' out of local and regional foods," Main writes in an upcoming book titled Signature Solutions. "But foods that were once highly prized for their limited availability still hold substantial cachet as consumers become more concerned with product integrity.

"Seasonal, local foods have higher product integrity," Main writes. "Typically, this allows for simple preparations that save on labor and increase product turnover. All of these factors contribute to keeping costs down and in alignment with consumer expectations."

So when planning a seasonal menu, Main says, always keep in mind the global food expectations of the season. But more importantly, know the expectations of the local market. "I would keep my eye on the local climate because that's where a hotel is going to get its identity. And you can start by visiting the local grocery store."

To Market, To Market

It's that easy; take a trip to the local market. Actually, Main suggests visiting three grocery stores or food markets that cater specifically to the type of clientele the hotel restaurant is trying to attract. While there, note the types of produce and prepared foods available and talk to store chefs to learn what customers are purchasing and what products will become available in the near future.

Dean Zanella, executive chef of 312 restaurant in Chicago's Allegro Hotel, begins his seasonal menu planning at the local produce market. He talks to vendors about what's in season and which products are most plentiful. For example, "I love baby artichokes," Zanella says. "And I love to put them on the menu. But purveyors said this was a bad year in California for baby artichokes. So I'm not going to use them."

But just because a product is in season and popular doesn't mean it is always available. "Lobsters and mushrooms were very popular this past season, but I couldn't get my hands on them," Zanella says. So availability of seasonal products also is an important consideration when planning a seasonal menu. And don't forget to ask how long products will be in season. If a particular type of mushroom will be available for only a couple of weeks, you might want to feature it in a special as opposed to putting it on the main menu. And highlighting the product's limited availability will help ensure it's a top seller, regardless of price, Bill Main says.

Zanella's upcoming spring menu showcases fresh seafood, free-range chicken, and light sauces and broths.

- Farfalle Pasta with Shrimp, Tomato and Capers
- Seafood Stew with Lobster, Clams, Shrimp and Mussels in a Saffron

Broth

- Spit-roasted Chicken on Tuscan Bread Salad
- Sautéed Halibut on Braised Spring Vegetables with Green and Black Olive Oils

Menus for All Seasons

Some other ways Main suggests learning about local food expectations is by perusing regional cookbooks and talking to food writers and editors at the local newspapers. "Immerse yourself in the local market; find out what the people like to eat," he says. "You will find that what the locals like are foods special to that area."

Although Venezuela has a more tropical climate and does not experience changes of seasons like Chicago, Chef Hans Peter Hooft at the Gran Meliá Caracas still changes his menu every six months in order to maintain the culinary interest of his clientele. To cater to its international guests, the Gran Meliá houses five ethnic restaurants: Spanish, French, Mediterranean, Italian and Japanese. As such, Hooft's food budget is high and he can afford to order whatever foods his chefs require, regardless of season.

Nevertheless, Hooft agrees with Main on the importance of understanding local culinary traditions. For instance, Hooft uses a lot of cilantro, cumin and oregano in his dishes because these spices are prevalent in Venezuelan cuisine. Conversely, some foods can have negative connotations for certain cultures that could harm a restaurant's reputation. "Kidney may be a delicacy in other countries," Hooft says. "But in Venezuela, it is considered a poor person's food. The same is true for liver. So I would never put these foods on the menu."

Some of the foods Hooft will be featuring on upcoming menus include:

- Grapefruit and Avocado Salad
- Sole Fillets with Oyster Sauce
- Brussels Cabbage Cream
- Prune Terrine with Sabayon Cream
- Native Pride

Leslie Stronach, executive chef of the Peninsula Bangkok, also designs menus in a tropical climate, which he says is perfect for the discerning palate of the public he serves. When it comes time to design a seasonal menu, Stronach says, "First, research what is available in your market and try many varieties of each kind of food. Find suppliers who understand what you want and are willing to source or grow items for you." Once tronach finds what he's looking for, he marries the products in a "creative and healthy" menu that reflects the best foods of the seasons.

Stronach's spring menu features fresh seafood and tropical fruits and vegetables.

- Thai Spiced Gazpacho with Avocado Relish
- Pepper-crusted Tuna with Watercress, Spiced Prawn
- Toast and Wasabi
- Lamb Cutlets on Piadini Flat Bread with Lentils and Curry Oil
- Exotic Spiced Fruit Minestrone with Green Mango Sorbet

Chef Kenneth Healy from the Atlantic Hotel, located in Jersey on the British Channel Islands, takes a great deal of pride in offering locally grown produce and fresh seafood caught off the Jersey shores. "The use of local seasonal ingredients from nearby farms and waters," Healy says, "ensures a quality commodity and limits crowding the dish with too many flavors, which helps to make a balanced menu." On Healy's spring menu, locally caught fish, diver-gathered scallops and Jersey potatoes take center stage.

- Warm Griddled Scallops, Cured Salmon and Aromatic Vegetables

- Seared Jersey Lobster and Lemon Sole on Warm Jersey Royal Potatoes with Mayonnaise
- Pan-fried Turbot, Warm Jersey Royal Potato Salad, Tomato Fondue and Sauce Vierge
- Chocolate and Orange Tart with Cinnamon Ice Cream and Orange Confit And beyond the use of fresh, local foods in planning his seasonal menus, Healy also suggests, "keep your menu short, allow lots of time for mise en place, and use the best ingredients you can afford."

Farfalle with Shrimp, Olives and Capers

This light spring-time pasta dish comes from Chef Dean Zanella at 312 restaurant in Chicago's Allegro Hotel.

12 oz Farfalle pasta, cooked

24 Small- to medium-sized shrimp (26-30 count), peeled and deveined

1/4 cup Capers, drained

1/2 cup Dry cured olives, chopped and pitted

1/2 cup Oven-roasted tomatoes, sliced thinly

3/4 cup Extra-virgin olive oil

1/4 cup Italian flat-leaf parsley, chopped

Salt and Pepper

1. Place a large sauté pan over medium heat. Add extra-virgin olive oil to pan, and heat slightly.

2. Add shrimp and oven-roasted tomatoes to pan, sauté lightly.

Add capers, olives and half of the parsley. Let mixture simmer for 1 to 2 minutes.

3. Add precooked farfalle pasta to mixture, toss and let simmer 1 to 2 minutes.

4. Divide evenly among 4 bowls, making sure each serving contains 6 shrimp. Sprinkle with rest of parsley, and serve immediately.

Yield: 4 servings

Grapefruit & Avocado Salad

This refreshing fruit salad comes from Chef Hans Peter Hooft at the Gran Meliá Caracas.

Little head of American lettuce,

fine julienne cut

2 Rose grapefruits, sliced

1 Mature avocado

4 Big strawberries, sliced

6 Tbsp Sesame oil

3 Tbsp Dry sherry

1 Tbsp Wine vinegar

1 Egg yolk

1 tsp Dijon mustard

Salt and white pepper

1/2 Tbsp sesame seeds, lightly toasted

1. For dressing, combine sherry, vinegar, egg yolk and mustard. Mix well. While beating, add a spurt of oil. Season with salt and pepper, and add sesame seeds. Mix well.

2. Put julienne lettuce on 4 individual dishes.

Peel avocado, and cut into 4 parts. Then cut each part into slices.

Place avocado, grapefruit and strawberry slices on lettuce, and cover all with dressing.

Yield: 4 servings

Exotic Spiced Fruit Minestrone

This seasonal fruit medley comes from Executive Chef

Leslie Stronach at The Peninsula Bangkok.

300 g Watermelon, rind and seeds removed

80 g Tomato, vine ripened

140 g Sugar syrup

5 g Cinnamon powder

3 g Ginger powder

5 g Chinese all spices

50 g Yellow apple, diced

50 g Red apple, diced

50 g Green apple, diced

40 g Green grapes, halved

40 g Black grapes, halved

30 g Sun-dried cherries

40 g Strawberries, halved

40 g Blueberries

100 g Mango, scooped into balls

20 g Mint leaves, half deep-fried, half chiffonade

20 g Red basil leaves, half deep-fried, half chiffonade

1. Blend watermelon and tomato and syrup in a blender. Add spices, stir well, and strain.

2. Place fruits in a glass bowl. Top with fruit stock, and sprinkle with herbs.

Yield: 5 servings

Seared Jersey Lobster and Lemon Sole on Warm Jersey Royal Potatoes with MayonnaiseAtlantic Hotel Chef Kenneth Healy supplied this recipe as an example of the Atlantic's most popular spring-time offerings.

1 1-lb Cooked lobster

1 1-lb Lemon sole, skinned and filleted

2 tsp Fresh chopped herbs

2 tsp Chopped shallots

Extra virgin olive oil

2 Tbsp Mayonnaise Fresh ground salt and pepper

1 tsp Baby capers

1 lb Jersey Royal potatoes

Lemon Juice

1. Cook potatoes in salted water. Drain and keep warm

2. Portion lobster into 4, and cut sole fillets into

2 portions each. Place in a hot pan with oil, salt and pepper, and brown lightly. Deglaze with lemon juice.

Add herbs and more olive oil, seasoning to taste

3. Slice potatoes, and mix with mayonnaise, shallots and capers. Season to taste.

4. Place potato mixture in the middle of a warm plate in a cutter (press down). Stack lobster and sole on top, and pour over remaining dressing.

Yield: 4 servings

TRUTH IN MENU: IF YOU SAY IT SERVE IT

As a hospitality manager, you have a right to advertise your food and beverage products in a way that casts them in their best light. If your hamburgers contain 8 ounces of ground beef, you are free to promote that attribute in your advertising, your menu, and as part of your server's verbal descriptions. You are not free, however, to misrepresent your products. To do so is a violation of what has come to be commonly known as Truth in Menu laws. These laws, which could perhaps better be described as "accuracy in menus," are designed to protect consumers from fraudulent food and beverage claims. Many foodservice operators believe that Truth in Menu laws are a recent occurrence. They are not. In fact, the federal government, as well as many local communities, have a long history of regulating food advertisement and sales.

The various Truth in Menu laws currently in effect are overseen by dozens of agencies and administrative entities, thereby taking the labeling of food to much greater degrees of accuracy. Though these laws are constantly being revised, it is possible for a foodservice operator to stay up to date and in compliance with them. The method is relatively straightforward, and the key is honesty in menu claims, both in regard to the price that is charged and the food that is served.

Certainly, menus should accurately reflect the price to be charged to the customer. If one dozen oysters are to be sold for a given price, one dozen oysters should be delivered on the plate, and the price charged on the bill should match that on the menu. Likewise, if the menu price is to include a mandatory service charge or cover charge, these must be brought to the attention of the guest. If a restaurant advertises a prix fixe dinner with four courses and a choice of entrees, the guest should be told the price of the dinner, which courses are included, and the types of entrees they may choose from.

Accuracy in menu involves a great deal more than honestly and precisely stating a price. It also entails being careful when describing many food attributes, including the preparation style, ingredients, origin, portion sizes, and health benefits. Because this area is so complex, and because consumers increasingly demand more accurate information from restaurants, the National Restaurant Association (NRA) and many state associations have produced educational material designed to assist foodservice operators as they write and prepare menus. Called "A Practical Guide to the Nutrition Labeling Laws," this publication is written specifically for the restaurant industry; it outlines everything you need to know about nutrition claims you can make for your menu items. You can secure a copy for a modest charge from the NRA.

DECODING THE NEW MENU-LABELING REGULATIONS

Restaurants USA magazine's final issue was published in September 2002 but these archived articles remain available for our readers' convenience.

You had to know it was too good to last. Restaurateurs may have thought they had been conveniently overlooked when the Nutrition Labeling and Education Act (NLEA) including new menu-labeling regulation was finalized in 1990. But now the Food and Drug Administration (FDA) is leveling the playing field – and the reprieve for restaurant menus is over.

On July 30, in response to a decision by the U.S. District Court in Washington DC, the FDA amended its food-labeling regulations to remove the provisions that exempted restaurant menus from conforming to the standards for nutrient and health claims which appear on menus.

The new menu rules may look familiar to some – they are identical to the standards that have been in effect since May 1994 for claims on signs and placards in large and medium-size restaurants, and since May 1995 for smaller restaurants. Now, the

FDA has decided that all restaurant menus are subject to the same rules regarding claims, and if asked, by May 1997 restaurateurs must provide customers with backup nutritional information for claims made on menus. According to the government publication *Federal Register*, the FDA hopes that the extension of the regulations to include menus will help to "increase the awareness of the American consumer to the relationships between diet and health."

WHO MUST COMPLY WITH THE REGULATIONS?

Any restaurant (defined by the government as a place that serves food ready for consumption, including typical sit-down and carryout venues, as well as institutional foodservice, delicatessens and catering operations) that uses nutrient-content claims or health claims on its menu must comply with the regulations. Establishments that do not make those types of claims about their menu items do not have to follow the regulations.

Menus that utilize symbols – such as a heart or an apple – to signify healthful menu items are also covered by the regulations. So whether you use a symbol or words, if your menu has health or nutrient claims on it, you must follow the regulation.

What are nutrient-and-health claims? Basically, nutrient claims make a statement about a specific nutrient or food component of a menu item or meal. A nutrient claim typically includes such words as "reduced," "free" or "low." Claims such as "low in fat" or "cholesterol-free" are common nutrient claims. In addition, using the word "fresh" is considered a nutrient claim, because there is a strict definition of what constitutes a "fresh" food item.

A health claim links the food or meal with health status or disease prevention and usually mentions a specific disease. The government strictly regulates health claims and has approved only seven of them, for which it has determined that there is enough scientific evidence to support the relationship. Those are the same claims that food manufacturers use, so your diners should be fairly familiar with them.

Restaurateurs are not permitted to make up their own health claims or alter the approved health-claim statements in any way. For example, an operator could not claim that her carrot-raisin salad is high in antioxidants so it may help prevent cancer, because that is not an approved health claim.

What's Expected of Restaurateurs?

If your menu does not have any nutrient or health claims on it, and you do not use symbols to denote healthful items on your menu, then these regulations do not apply to your establishment. If you do use either type of claim, then the regulations require you to be able to demonstrate that there is a "reasonable basis" for believing that the food is qualified to make the claim.

Luckily, the regulations do allow restaurants some flexibility in establishing that reasonable basis. Nevertheless, restaurateurs must be prepared to show officials and customers – on demand – that their menu claims are consistent with the claim definitions established under the NLEA.

The National Restaurant Association's new publication *A Practical Guide to the Nutrition Labeling Laws for the Restaurant Industry* gives specific information about all aspects of complying with the regulations. Donna Shields, author of the guide, characterizes it as a "working manual for restaurateurs and chefs." She adds that "providing lots of examples, as the book does, makes it easier for restaurateurs to understand how the regulations' technical jargon relates to their menu and business."

Before you decide to make a claim on your menu, you should consult reliable references, such as the Association's guide, or discuss the regulations with a knowledgeable professional. According to Nancy Chapman, a registered dietitian and consultant to the Association, "Restaurateurs who don't want to do the work themselves, or who are unsure about the regulation, should probably seek assistance from a dietitian who is familiar with the rules."

Backing up Menu Claims

When the FDA published the final rules for health-and-nutrient-content claims in January 1993, the agency concluded that if claims on restaurant foods are to be useful, they must be valid – as they must be for processed foods. And although restaurant foods must comply with the same standards as processed foods in order to bear a claim, the way in which a restaurant determines the nutrient content of a food item or meal may be different – yet still be considered valid.

FDA spokesman Arthur Whitmore says, "Because there are no exemptions from the regulation – no matter how small the restaurant is – we've made the rules fairly easy to comply with." For example, although processed-food manufacturers must have their foods analyzed by a lab and use computer-generated labels that contain information produced in a strictly enforced format, restaurants may determine nutrient levels using computer databases, cookbooks or some other reasonable source that can provide assurance that the food or meal meets the requirements for the claim.

Whitmore says operators may use a wide variety of reference information when documenting claims. "One need not have a computer analysis performed. In fact, calculations by hand using a reliable source such as the *USDA Handbooks*; government *Home & Garden Bulletins*; or analyzed, published cookbook recipes are perfectly acceptable," he says.

Showing that your menu item was prepared using a recipe from a recognized health-professional association or dietary group is also permitted.

COMMUNICATING NUTRITION INFORMATION

Once you've got the nutrition information you need to back up your menu claims, you need to decide how best to communicate that information to customers. Again, the FDA offers operators a number of ways to present this information to diners – the most important part is making sure the information is correct and reliable.

Restaurants are encouraged – but not required – to provide complete nutritional information whenever possible. Operators only need to provide information about the specific nutrient for which a claim is made. For example, if your menu makes a claim about the sodium content of an item, you do not need to provide information about the item's calorie, fat or vitamin content – only the amount of sodium the dish contains. Operators do not have to worry about the format used to convey the information. It doesn't have to be set up like the "Nutrition Facts" labels seen on packaged foods. Nor does it have to be printed on the menu — it just needs to be readily available. You may decide, for example, to compile the information for your menu claims in a notebook or folder, print it in a brochure (if your menu doesn't change frequently), write it on a poster or display it on a bulletin board.

When a customer asks for the information, you can present him or her with the notebook or handout, or deliver the information orally. You are covered as long as you have printed backup material that your staff can refer to quickly.

Follow Through

Having all of your nutrient-claim information on paper doesn't do customers any good if the food served doesn't consistently conform to the recipes analyzed. To make the process of strictly adhering to recipes easier to control, Shields has the following recommendations for restaurateurs: "Start out with just one or two items for which you're going to make menu claims until you've established a workable protocol within your kitchen."

Operators must also realize that adjusting to the new regulations will take time and practice. "Reviewing ingredients, cooking methods and perhaps most importantly, portion size, will be an ongoing effort until kitchen staff is well-trained," says Shields.

The good news is that there are resources to help operators come into compliance with the FDA regulations. Find a professional, either a dietitian or another expert with restaurant-consulting experience, to assist you. The Association can also provide guidance. "There are many people available around the country who can take a look at your menu, your recipes and your claims and make suggestions to help you comply," says Chapman. "You don't have to go it alone."

GUIDANCE FOR COMPLYING WITH MENU GUIDELINES

Here are some sources to help you comply with the Food and Drug Administration's (FDA) food-labeling regulations.

A Practical Guide to the Nutrition Labeling Laws for the Restaurant Industry. This 60-page guide, authored by registered dietitian Donna Shields and published by the National Restaurant Association, provides detailed coverage and examples of the types of claims allowed and how to comply with the regulation. Call (800) 424-5156, ext. 5375.

Food Labeling Questions and Answers, Volume II: A Guide for Restaurants and Other Retail Establishments. This FDA publication on food labeling provides information from the government's August 1995 regulations dealing with claims on restaurant signs and placards. Copies of the document can be obtained by calling the office of the Superintendent of Documents, U.S. Government Printing Office, in Washington DC at (202) 512-1800.

American Dietetic Association (ADA). The ADA will provide you with referrals to professional registered dietitians with experience in menu planning, recipe development and restaurant consultation in your area. It is the restaurateur's responsibility to determine whether the dietitian is familiar with the menu-labeling regulations, because the ADA will not have information of that specific nature. To request a professional referral, call the ADA at (800) 877-1600.

SYMBOLIC OR NOT, HAVE DOCUMENTATION ON HAND

You need to have documentation if your menu uses any of the following words or symbols representing these words:

- Free
- Low
- Reduced
- Light/Lite
- Provides/Contains/ Good Source of
- High/Excellent Source of/ Rich in
- Lean/Extra-Lean
- Fresh
- Natural
- Healthy

2

Health and Nutrition Claims on Restaurant Menus

INTRODUCTION

For many people, restaurant dining is no longer reserved for special occasions. It is a daily event. In fact, nearly half of all food dollars is spent on food eaten away from home. That food represents one-third of all calories in the average American's diet.

While people are eating out more than ever before, many are also concerned about health and disease prevention. To appeal to health-conscious patrons, restaurants have begun offering an expanding array of "light" or "low fat" foods. More and more menus contain special "healthy" sections with names like "The Lighter Side," "Heart Smart," and "Guiltless." Do these foods live up to their claims? Not necessarily.

Unlike claims on food labels, claims on menus were not regulated by the Food and Drug Administration (FDA) until May 2, 1997. Since then, restaurants that make claims, like "light," "low fat," and "heart-healthy," have had to comply with definitions established by the FDA.

We've written this pamphlet to inform you about the FDA's new truth-in-menu requirements and to suggest some strategies to help you choose more healthful foods when eating out.

WHAT THE LAW REQUIRES

- Claims must meet FDA standards. Restaurants that make health or nutrition claims, like "heart-healthy" or "low fat," must meet FDA standards. For example, if a restaurant claims its mashed potatoes are "low fat," a typical serving of the food must contain no more than 3 grams of fat.

- Nutrition information. must be provided upon request. Nutrition information need not appear on the menu, but must be provided upon request. It may be provided in writing, such as on a flier, brochure, poster, or notebook, or may be provided orally by a statement from a waiter or other employee.
- Full nutrition information is not required. Restaurants only need to provide information that pertains to the particular claim. For example, a restaurant that makes a "low sodium" claim must tell consumers who ask that the food contains no more than 140 mg of sodium in a typical serving. However, the restaurant is not required to provide information about calories, fat, or other nutrients.
- Laboratory analysis is not required. Nutrient levels do not need to be determined by laboratory analyses or certified by third parties. Instead, the levels may be calculated from nutrient data bases or cookbooks. However, restaurants are required to explain how nutrient levels are determined upon request.
- Only menu items for which claims are made are affected. Restaurants are only required to rovide nutrition information for foods for which health or nutrition claims are made.

"DINER BEWARE" – CLAIMS TO LOOK OUT FOR

"Low fat": Most foods may be described as "low fat" if there are no more than 3 grams of fat in a standard serving. Standard servings have been established by the FDA to reflect the amount of food that is typically consumed. Since restaurants often serve foods much larger than the standard serving, a "low fat" food may actually contain large amounts of fat.

For example, ice cream may be called "low fat" as long as there are no more than 3 grams of fat in a standard half cup serving. However, restaurants may offer portions several times larger than the standard serving size. So a 2-cup serving of "low fat" ice cream may contain up to 12 grams of fat!

Also, keep in mind that even a small-sized serving of "low fat" main dishes like hamburgers, pizza, or sandwiches, can have more than 3 grams of fat per serving.

And remember, "low in fat" does not always mean "low in calories."

"Light": "Light" is commonly used to mean many different things. It may describe a food's taste, color, or texture, or it may indicate that the food's calorie, fat, or sodium content has been significantly reduced. Menus must clearly indicate what "light" is intended to convey. If the meaning is not clearly explained, diners should ask for clarification. If "light" is used to indicate a reduction in calories, fat, or sodium, information about those nutrients must be provided upon request.

"Cholesterol free": "Cholesterol free" claims are very popular on restaurant menus, but can also be very misleading. Keep in mind that:

* "Cholesterol free" does not mean "fat free."
* Foods like meat, poultry, and seafood contain cholesterol – even if they are fried in "cholesterol free" oil.

Also, saturated fat and trans fat can raise the level of cholesterol in your blood:

* "Cholesterol free" foods may contain saturated fat. The FDA only allows foods that are low in saturated fat to be described as "cholesterol free," but watch out – many restaurants may not comply with this requirement.
* The FDA allows foods with significant amounts of trans fats to be called "cholesterol free." To avoid trans fats, limit foods prepared with vegetable shortening or partially hydrogenated oils.

"Sugar free": Some foods, especially desserts, may be described as "sugar free." But keep in mind that "sugar free" does not mean "calorie free" or "fat free." If a food described as "sugar free" is not low-calorie or reduced-calorie, the menu must say so.

"Healthy": Food described as "healthy" must be low in fat and saturated fat and may not be high in cholesterol or sodium. However, there are no limits on the amount of sugar or calories that a "healthy" food may contain.

- "Heart" claims: Claims like "heart-healthy," "heart smart," and "heart" symbols imply that a food may be useful in reducing the risk of heart disease. When such claims are made, the food must be low in fat, saturated fat, and cholesterol, and must not be high in sodium. But keep in mind that restaurants may not always comply with these restrictions.

MAKING HEALTHFUL CHOICES

- Ask for nutrition information: When menus make claims like "healthy," "light," or "heart smart," ask for nutrition information. This information must be provided upon request. However, keep in mind that the law does not require that the food be tested in a laboratory, so the numbers may not be precise.
- Watch out for large serving sizes: Serving sizes on food labels are required to reflect the amount of food that is normally consumed. But restaurants are free to determine their own serving sizes. A CSPI survey found that restaurants often serve from two to three times more than food labels list as a serving.

For example, the official serving size of a tuna salad sandwich is 4 ounces and it contains 340 calories. The typical restaurant serving is 11 ounces and it contains 720 calories.

- Keep in mind that restaurant foods are probably fattier than you think: The nutrient content of restaurant meals is extremely difficult to assess. A survey conducted by CSPI and researchers at New York University found that trained dietitians underestimated the calorie content of five restaurant meals by an average of 37%. They underestimated fat content by 49%.

For example, the dietitians estimated, on average, that a tuna fish sandwich provided 374 calories and 18 grams of fat, while the sandwich actually contained about 720 calories and 43 grams of fat!

If well-educated nutrition professionals consistently and substantially underestimated the calorie and fat content of restaurant meals, it's clear that ordinary consumers also have trouble guessing what's in their meals.

Request that your food be specially prepared: Most restaurants want to please their customers and are usually willing to satisfy specific requests.

- Order sauces and salad dressings on the side, or ask for low-calorie dressings.
- Request salsa, mustard, or flavored vinegars to get fat free flavor.
- Request half-portions at a reduced price or take home half the meal in a doggie bag.
- Ask that foods be prepared with olive or canola oil instead of butter, margarine, or shortening.
- Request that foods be broiled or grilled instead of fried.

Make Healthful Substitutions

- Substitute skim or 1% milk for 2% milk, whole milk, or cream.
- Choose baked, broiled, or grilled (not fried) chicken, turkey, or seafood instead of red meat.
- If you eat red meat, select leaner cuts, like sirloin steak or filet mignon (instead of most steaks), or pot roast (instead of hamburgers or meat loaf).
- Substitute a salad, vegetables, or a baked potato for french fries or a "loaded" baked potato.
- Add just a tablespoon of sour cream instead of butter on your baked potato.
- Request whole-grain breads and rolls.
- Substitute fresh fruit for sugary, high-fat desserts.

THE RESTAURANTS

Besides the seven large restaurants supplied by the Main kitchen of the Bailey Catering Company there were numerous smaller and specialized eateries preparing and serving food for expositon visitors and workers. The more expensive establishments were located in such areas as the Pergolas and the Electric tower. Ethnic foods could be found throughout the Midway, and even the Indian Congress Restaurant boasted a "First class meal and all kinds of refreshments." Exposition visitors were not limited to dining on the grounds proper as many Buffalo establishments promoted and advertized their restaurants as viable alternatives to the often overpriced meals found on the Pan-American grounds. This section exhibits some of the restaurants and food choices available to Exposition-goers. In addition, the Menus and Advertisements section allows viewers to compare food prices at the exposition to the annual income/expenditures of families of the period.

Pabst on the Midway

This crude poem appeared in the *Journal of American Industries* 3, no. 9 (February 1901) and was followed by a description of the Pabst concession. Graced with colored lights and 150 x 10, the restaurant cost over $30,000 to build and employed upwards of 100 people. Mueller and his family were veterans of other fairs and he was assisted at Buffalo by his three sons.

"Gesundheit!"

Pabst on the Midway – Frtiz Mueller the Host

Eat, Drink, and Be Merry

When the sad tourist is tired out with sights,

When he is thirsty and needs rest, by rights

There's Pabst on the Midway, with Fritz in command;

Step over and see him and get the glad hand!

Eat, drink, and be merry. Forget every care.

Have a good time as long as you're there!

The big exposition will tire out the best

And all will need a place they can sit down and rest
And sip a good beverage such as Pabst makes
And Mueller dispenses. Such a place takes!
Yes, Pabst on the Midway is just the right thing.
Here say me "Gesundheit." Pabst's praises we'll sing.

SOME ADVICE ON HOW TO GET THE MOST FROM AN EXPOSITION MEAL

In the *Everybody's Magazine* special Pan-American issue, Mary Bronson Hartt offered the following advice to the thrifty:

"The problem of dinner at the Pan-American is one of grave importance. If you are careless of expense it is easy to be happy; you dine at Alt Nürnberg, or up in the Tower, or at the American Inn. But if you want your money for something more lasting than viands the case is complicated.

There are two fifty-cent dinners offered on the grounds: one at the restaurant beside the Philippine Village, the other in the Dairy Building. There is even a thirty-five-cent dinner to be had beside the East Amherst gate. For this I cannot vouch. In general the low-priced places furnish as good service and as desirable a menu as would be expected with Pan-American prices prevailing at the markets.

The Nebraska Sod House used to be an exception. It furnished, and still furnishes for that matter, a meal of fricasseed chicken, coffee, and bread and butter for thirty cents. And it was good. But unfortunately everybody knows about the Sod House now, and unless you go at eleven o'clock in the morning it is always full and closed. The Rice Kitchen is another reasonable place, but too popular for comfort.

There is a moderate-priced restaurant with entrance from the street in Fair Japan. " Streets of Mexico" serves both native tamales and *chili con carne* and American food well cooked, at prices below that of the dearest places. Sandwiches and such unstaying trifles can be had at lunch counters everywhere, but they are not cheaper than more substantial dishes – that is, if you buy enough to sustain life.

Habitues of the Exposition get their most substantial meal at noon at one of the cheaper places, and sup lightly at Alt Nürnberg to the music of the fine band or up on the colonnade of the Electric Tower with the whole sunlit spectacle spread out before them."

MAIN KITCHEN OF BAILEY CATERING COMPANY, ENORMOUS IN EVERY WAY

The Exposition's main kitchen was located in the northwest corner of the Pan-American grounds, near the Midway. In the "Maps to the Essentials" section, see Major Restaurants on the Exposition Grounds to find the location of the Main Kitchen (section A-3) in relation to the larger dining facilities. A more detailed map of the Softdrink Vendors, Restaurants and Toilets Located on the Exposition Grounds shows many of the smaller restaurants and refreshment stands.

The main kitchen's design is described in this *Buffalo Courier* article of 7 March 1900:

> "Construction work was begun this morning at the Pan-American grounds on the immense kitchen upon which will devolve the task of preparing food for the millions of people who will visit the Exposition next summer.

The plan is to have the Kitchen apart from the restaurants which it will purvey for, in order that the odors of the flower beds may have a chance against the redolent tornadoes of cooking smells that are bound to escape form the pie-foundry that is to be built with a capacity of 50,000 pies of these pastries every day, and which will enthrone Buffalo for one season at least, as Queen of the Pie Belt. It is deemed wise, too, to have the roaring furnaces that will furnish power in the manufacture of eatables apart from the Exposition buildings.

For these reasons the Kitchen, the size of which entitles it to be pronounced with a capital initial, is being built in the north side of the grounds near the power house. . . When the north wind blows the aroma of the baking Boston beans will be wafted through the Beautiful Orient and Dreamland. At other times they will regale firemen in the firehouse. The Kitchen will be 200 hundred feet long, 150 deep and two stories high. It will be devoted exclusively to cooking with the exception of rooms in the second story, which will be set apart for the chef and scullions. Although the Kitchen is not designed as an exhibit, it will be open on all three sides for inspection. To this end the lower story will consist largely of windows, through which visitors may watch the odorous transformation of strange substances into mince pie.

It has not been decided yet how to get over the difficulty of serving hot meals in the restaurants that top the kitchen when the institution will be nearly a half mile away. The problem is one that involves rapid transit. A system of overhead trolley lines similar in principle to that used for transactions of cash in department stores has been considered seriously.

The plan provides for large baskets mounted upon trolley wheels. One strong objection is the birds of the air, who might levy toll upon the baskets en route. The gravity of the danger will be realized when it is stated that the feathered population of the grounds will be reinforced next summer with 500 more pigeons direct from Venice."

Portions of an *Enquirer* article of 28 March 1900 add some details:

> " ... The kitchen is a long, two-story affair lying behind large square buildings which will screen it from ordinary sight. Visitors will be welcome, however, large giant windows and convenient platforms being provided of a view of operations within. It's size is 250 x 75 feet.

On the west end is a large bakery, with two immense ovens, capable of baking 1,000 loaves of bread every hour. These ovens rotate and have swinging shelves like the cars on the Ferris wheel. Cake, crackers, or cookies may be baked instead of bread. North of the bakery is a laundry for table linen, and east of that an ice cream room.

Next is a store room and then a wine room, which is supplemented across the walk by a deep recess, fitted with a complete refrigerating plant for beer and wine. On the south side are a butcher shop, a room for vegetables and fish, one for butter and eggs, one for grocer's supplies, a cold storage box and an immense receiving space, 50 x 75 for stores and supplies.

Grand View from Gates

In addition, there are eight lunch rooms in various convenient places. The most popular will probably be those in the Pergolas, each seating 600 persons. These will be open with a view to the Esplanade to the north and to the south over the triumphal bridge to the State buildings. Another delightful dinning room will be in the Temple of Music. ... There will be sandwiches, ice cream, and cake and similar light refreshments. The company is counting on an average of 50,000 meals a day from the start. They can take care of 100,000 in a pinch. There are to be 6,000 chairs. The big rush, however, will not come until after the Fourth of July.

Sleeping Room for Employees

Upstairs are the offices for officials, a large dining room for employees, of which there will be about 1,000 ... the paymaster's room and twenty-eight sleeping rooms for officials and cooks.

The kitchen will supply the seven large restaurants. There are four in the main buildings, two on the stadium side and two on the opposite side, each capable of seating 750 persons. One in the northwest corner will accommodate 700 and one in the Dairy building 250. The most exclusive, both in price and quality, as well as in location, will be the electric tower, overlooking the great fountain and the main feature of the Expo. The prices here will be about those charged at first class cafes. "

Waiters and Waitresses Wanted!

The restaurants on the grounds of the Exposition, and in Buffalo, presented good employment opportunities for waiters and waitresses. From as far away as Chicago they came. Some came so early they arrived before employment was available.

The *Enquirer* of 1 March 1901 described this problem:

> "It is estimated that something like 300 bartenders and waiters are in Buffalo unable to find work. They have come here in an anticipation of the Pan-American Exposition.
>
> Throughout the country many are making their way toward the city – they will arrive in time to discover what a cold place a beautiful city with a glorious expo-

> sition can be just in the heyday of its marvelous summer until the visitor has the wherewithal to satisfy the lunch counters or an acquaintance with the Director-General.
>
> Local proprietors in seeking help are giving preference to home men. They will continue to do so, and though there will be a demand for extra labor after May 1st, the material to satisfy it will be way in excess of demand.
>
> Buffalo unions have issued warnings to the waiters and bartenders stating that they will make a big mistake by getting here before May or June, and that if they continue to arrive in the next three months, as they have of late, hundreds of them will be walking the streets hungry and homeless."

And there was some effort to organize cooks and waiters, as reported in the *Enquirer* of 12 March 1901:

> " The organization, it is said, contemplates demanding $100 a month as a minimum for all good cooks or persons employed as head cooks. The minimum salary for waiters is said to be fixed at $2 a day. "

A Few Restaurant Menus and Advertisements

The first menu (click on the image) is that of the American Inn, one of the hotels located in the immediate vicinity of the Exposition grounds. The second is a menu of the luncheon held for President William McKinley during his visit to the Pan-American. This luncheon was held in the New York State Building on September 5, 1901, the day before the president was shot in the Temple of Music.

The Food Timeline

Ever wonder what foods the Vikings ate when they set off to explore the new world? How Thomas Jefferson made his ice cream? What the pioneers cooked along the Oregon Trail? Who invented the potato chip...and why?

Welcome to the Food Timeline! Food history presents a fascinating buffet of popular lore and contradictory facts. Some people will tell you it's impossible to express this topic in exact timeline format. They are correct. Most foods we eat are not invented; they evolve.

BEGINNINGS

water & ice————————
salt I & II————————
shellfish & fish————————
eggs & mushrooms————————
insects ————————
rice I, II & III————————
emmer grain—17,000BC——
einkorn grain—16,000BC——
almonds—10,000BC——
sheep —9,000BC——
apples & lentils—8,000BC——
pork —7,000BC——
beans: old world & new—7,000BC——
walnuts old & new—7,000BC——
pistachios—7,000BC——
cattle domestication—6,500BC——
wine—6000BC——
maize & tortillas—6000BC——
spelt —6000BC——
dates & broccoli—6000BC——
honey—5500BC——
chickpeas & lettuce —5500BC——
olives & olive oil—5000BC——
cucumbers & squash I & II—5000BC——
chilies, avocados & taro—5000BC—
potatoes I & II—5000BC—
milk & yogurt—5000BC—
grapes—4000BC—
citrus: oranges & citrons —4000BC—
watermelons—4000BC—

popcorn – 3600BC –
chicken domestication – 3200BC –
butter & palm oil – 3000BC –
barley, peas & carrots – 3000BC –
onions & garlic – 3000BC –
spices I, II, III, IV & – 3000BC –
figs – 2900BC –
soybeans I & II – 2838BC –
tea – 2737BC –
rhubarb – 2700BC –
duck – 2500BC –
muskmelon – 2400BC –
peach palm – 2300BC –
pasta & noodles – 2000BC –
radishes – 2000BC –
purslane – 2000BC –
marshmallows & liquorice – 2000BC –
carob – 2000BC –
peanuts I & II – 1500BC –
chocolate – 1500BC –
horseradish – 1500BC –
raisins – 1490BC –
sugar – 1200BC –
pickles & peaches – 1000BC –
oats – 1000BC –
tomatoes & tomatillos – 900BC –
celery – 850BC –
cinnamon – 700BC –
cabbage – 600BC –
sausages & artichokes – 500BC –
pastries & appetizers – 5th century BC –
vinegar – 5th century BC –
peppercorns & garden cress – 5th century BC –

beets & bananas – 4th Century BC –
turkeys & asparagus – 200BC –
quinces – 65BC –
Devon cattle – 55BC –
chestnuts – 1st Century –
lobster, crab & shrimp – 1st Century –
French toast & omlettes – 1st Century –
truffles – 1st Century –
strawberries & raspberries – 1st Century –
capers, turnips & kale – 1st Century –
ice cream – 62 –
lemons – 3rd Century –
pretzels – 5th Century –
eggplant – 6th Century –
Spinach I & II – 7th Century –
coffee – 9th Century –
cod – 9th century –
loquats – 10th century –
baklava & filo – 11th century –
corned beef & lychees – 11th century –
breadfruit & okra – 12th century –
hamburgers I & II – 13th century –
Mexican limes – 14th century –
kebabs – 14th century –
gingerbread – 1395 –
coconuts – 15th century –
Japanese sushi & sashimi – 15th century –
pork & beans – 1475 –
hot dogs – 1487 –
pineapples I & II – 1493 –
Cows in America I, II & III – 1493 –
marmelade – 1495 –
rissoto & teriyaki chicken – 16th century –

pecans & Cornish pastys-16th century—
papayas—16th century—
turkeys in Europe—16th century—
cashews introduced to Old World—16th century—-
tempura in Japan—16th century—
Texas Longhorns—16th century—
sweet potatoes in Europe—1517—
vanilla in Europe—1529—
tomatoes in Europe—1544—
Camembert cheese—1554—
Brussels sprouts & kohlrabi—1587—
pot luck—1592—
doughnuts in America—17th Century—
treacle—17th Century—
pralines & coffee cake—17th Century—
cream puffs & eclairs—17th Century—
maple syrup I & II—17th Century—
modern ice cream—17th Century—
cranberries in America—17th Century—
Jerusalem artichokes—1605—
bagels—1610—
coffee in Europe—1615—
rum—1650—
Kosher food in the U.S.—1654—
cowpeas in America—1675—
cranberries in New Jersey—1680—
rice in South Carolina—1690—
French fries I & II —18th Century—
coffee in America—18th Century—
muffins & crackers-18th Century—
root beer & tapioca —18th Century—
Montelimar nougat—1701—
casseroles—1708—

Stilton cheese–1722–
caramel & Welsh Rabbit–1725–
Hereford cows–1742–
sugar beets–1747–
grapefruit–1750–
Swedish meatballs–1754–
Newtown Pippin apples–1755–
mayonnaise–1756–
Tartar sauce–1756–
sandwiches–1762–
oysters in America–1763–
Baker's chocolate–1764–
Bartlett pears–1765–
soda water–1767–
grapes in California–1769–
Tofu in America–1769–
Jersey cows–1771–
New Zealand spinach–1771–
tomatoes in America–1781–
lollipops–1784–
potash–1790–
Mandarin oranges/Europe–1805–
Bosc Pears–1807–
ice cream cones–1807–
McIntosh apples–1811–
taffy, toffee & butterscotch–1817–
lady fingers–1820–
chicken-fried steak–1824–
A1 Steak Sauce–1824–
fondue–1826–
Macadamia nuts–1828–
soft drinks in America–1830–
bouillabaisse–1830s–

Hopping John—1830s—
Worcestershire Sauce—1835—
Michigan mint—1835—
Idaho potatoes—1837—
Key limes—1839—
Poland Spring water—1845—
Chinese food in America—1847—
Necco Wafers—1847—
Trenton crackers—1848—
Concord grapes—1849—
berries in Oregon—1850—
modern marshmallows —1850—
cherries in Michigan—1852—
potato chips I & II—1853—
Condensed milk —1856—
Peek Freans—1857—
Rumford Baking Powder—1859—
fish & chips—1860—
cranberries in Wisconsin—1860—
Vernor's Ginger Ale—1862—
breakfast cereal—1863—
Conversation Hearts—1866—
Underwood Deviled Ham—1867—
synthetic baby food—1867—
Tabasco sauce—1868—
Fleischmann's Yeast—1868—
Campbell's Soup—1869—
margarine—1870—
Paragon tomatoes—1870—
California raisins—1870s—
Philadelphia cream cheese—1872—
Long Island duck—1873—
summer pudding—1875—

Heinz Ketchup – 1876 –
Wheatena – 1879 –
Saccharin – 1879 –
candy corn & passion fruit – 1880s –
French dressing – 1880s –
salt water taffy – 1883 –
milk shakes & Dr Pepper – 1885 –
evaporated milk – 1885 –
Coca Cola – 1886 –
malted milk & Georgia pecans – 1887 –
Barbados cherries – 1887 –
pizza – 1889 –
ice cream sundaes – 1890s –
Fig Newtons & Knox Gelatine – 1891 –
Cracker Jacks & Postum – 1893 –
fudge & Good and Plenty – 1893 –
Hershey bars & Sen-Sen – 1894 –
peanut butter & Salisbury steak – 1895 –
Chop suey – 1896 –
Corsicana fruitcake – 1896 –
oatmeal cookies – 1896 –
Jell-O & tangelos – 1897 –
1000 Island dressing – 1897 –
cotton candy& Melba toast – 1897 –
jelly beans & candy corn – 1898 –
Pepsi & Texas sweet onions – 1898 –
Cottolene – 1900 –
peanut butter & jelly – 1901 –
Nabisco's Animal Crackers – 1902 –
Karo syrup – 1902 –
Mt. Clemens Flakes & Marmite – 1902 –
Club sandwiches – 1903 –
canned tuna – 1903 –

banana splits & Ovaltine—1904—
New Zealand kiwi —1904—
New York pizza —1905—
submarine sandwiches—1905—
Kellogg's Corn Flakes—1906—
Muffoletta sandwiches—1906—
Crisco & Junket—1911—
Oreos—1912—
Mallomars—1913—
Fettuccine Alfredo—1914—
hush puppies—1915—
Moon pies—1917—
Marshmallow Fluff—1917—
Fortune cookies—1918—
Chase's Cherry Mash—1918—
Eskimo Pie & Good Humor—1920—
Yoo-hoo—1920s—
Wonder Bread & Wheaties —1921—
Gummi Bears & Clark Bars—1922—
Vegemite—1922—
Girl Scout Cookies—1922—
popsicles —1923—
frozen foods—1924—
pineapple upside-down cake—1924—
Texas hot weiners—1924—
ice cream sandwich—1926—
Kool-Aid & Pez—1927—
Gerber's baby food—1928—
Heath bars & It's It—1928—
Twizzlers & Karmelkorn—1929—
Po'Boy & hot Italian sandwiches—1929—
Twinkies & Jiffy biscuit mix—1930—
dry soup mix—1930s—

Bisquick & Vidalia onions – 1931 –
tacos in LA – 1931 –
refrigerator biscuits – 1931 –
Fritos – 1932 –
Marshmallow Sandwich cookies – 1932 –
Hawaiian Punch & Rutgers tomatoes – 1934 –
sloppy joes – 1935 –
Kashering of Coca Cola – 1935 – -
Dagwood sandwich – 1936 –
SPAM & Krispy Kreme – 1937 –
canned soda – 1938 –
chicken & waffles – 1938 –
Spiedies & Ugli fruit – 1939 –
York Peppermint Patties – 1940 –
M & Ms & Cheerios – 1941 –
Corn dogs & Pronto pups – 1942 –
Irish coffee & nachos – 1943 –
Chicago-style pizza – 1943 –
Nutella – 1946 –
Betty Crocker's cake mix – 1947 -
frozen french fries – 1948 –
seedless watermelon – 1949 –
Jolly Ranchers – 1949 –
Whoppers – 1949 –
Loco moco – 1949 –
American Tex-Mex – 1950s –
smoothies – 1950s –
frozen pizza – 1950 –
diet soda – 1950 –
Maypo – 1953 –
Jello-O instant pudding – 1953 –
Marshmallow Peeps – 1953 –
TV Dinners I, II, III & IV – 1953 –

ranch dressing—1954—
Broasted chicken—1954—
Oregon Marionberries—1956—
Tang & Beefalo—1957—
Rice-A-Roni & Diet-Rite—1958—
instant ramen noodles—1958—
brown rice in USA—1960s—
Life cereal—1961—
instant mashed potatoes—1962—
Buffalo Wings & Pop Tarts—1964—
Gatorade & Slurpees—1965—
Ramapo tomatoes & Space Food Sticks —1968—
gyros—1970s—
Lactaid—1974—
Pop Rocks & Jelly Bellies—1976—
Kobe beef & wagyu —1976—
portobello mushrooms—1980s—
Yukon gold potatoes—1981—
Gardenburgers—1982—
Red Bull energy drink—1984—
Orangetti spaghetti squash—1986—
Flavr Savr tomatoes—1994—
grape tomatoes—1998—
Flat Iron steak—2002—
tear-free onions—2002—
Deep fried Coca Cola—2006—
trendy foods—2007—
New product introductions—2008—

RECIPES

—10,000BC—-Agriculture begins I & II
—10,000BC—- bread, beer & soup
—4000BC—-yeast breads: pitta & focaccia
—2300BC—-Ancient Egypt

—1700BC—-Mesopotamia banquets & recipes
—1000BC—-Jerusalem, Labeneh
—1st Century—-Bible era foods
—1st Century—-Ancient Rome I, II, III & IV
—1st Century—-fried chicken & foie gras
—1st Century—-Italian wedding soup
—1st Century—-rice pudding
—1st Century—-flan & cheesecake
—1st Century—-The Haggis
—70—-challah bread
—3rd Century—-Roman Britain's cuisine & recipes
—3rd Century—-De Re Culinaria (in Latin) & De Opsoniis et Condimentis, Apicius
—4th Century—-Jerusalem, White kidney bean salad
—5th-9th century—-Anglo-Saxon foods
—7th century—-Jerusalem, Coriander & pine nut salad
—7th century—-kimchi
—8th century—-Ancient Maya
—8th-12th century—-Crusader cuisine in Jerusalem
—8th-12th century—-Viking era food I, II, III & IV
—9th century—-halva & goulash
—10th-15th century—-Medieval food
—10th century—-Peking duck
—13th Century—-ravioli & lasagne
—13th Century—-pancakes & waffles
—13th century—-*Viandier de Taillevent*
—13th century—-couscous
—14th century—-guacamole & kolache
—14th century—-Humble pie history & recipe
—14th century—-*Le Menagier de Paris*
—1303—-pie
—1381—-apple pie & crumpets
—1386—-Chaucerian Cookery, feasts!

–1390-- *The Forme of Cury*
–1390--applesauce
–1393--Pipefarces (fried cheese sticks)
–15th century--Italian risotto & English marzipan
–15th century-- borshch
–15th century, Netherlands *Wel Ende Edelike Spijse*
–1492–Christopher Columbus old world cuisine
–16th century--salsa
–16th century--quiche
–16th century--puff paste
–1514--*Een Notabel Boecxken Van Cokeryen,* in Dutch
–1520--*Libre...de coch,* Robert de Nola (Catalan) & English
–1545--*A Proper newe Booke of Cokerye*
–1590--Shakepeare's food
–1593--*Cocboeck,* Carolus Battus (in Dutch)
–1596--English trifle
–1597--potato salad
–1599--hasty pudding
–17th Century--corn bread, hoe cakes, spoonbread & hominy
–17th Century--chess pie & shortbread
–17th Century--authentic recipes, transcribed
–17th Century--French onion soup
–17th century-- Salad I & II
–1604--Raspberry jelly & modern version
–1605--Guy Fawkes' menus I & II
–1607--Jamestown settlers ate pottage (p. 20)
–1612--*Koocboec oft familieren keukenboec,* Magirus (in Dutch)
–1615--*A New booke of cookerie*
–1616--*Koge-Bog* (first printed Nordic cookbook)
–1621--Pilgrim Thanksgiving
–1651--*Le Cuisinier Francois,* La Varenne (en Francais)
–1653--pumpkin pie & lemonade
–1661--*Les Delices de la Campagne,* Nicolas de Bonnefons

—1669—-*De Verstandige Kock,* in Dutch

—1672—-*A Queen-Like Closet,* Hannah Wooley

—1675—-Gervase Markham's *English House-Wife*

—1683—-*De Verstandige Kock,* colonial Dutch recipes

—1685—-Robert Mays' *Accomplisht Cook*

—1686—-croissants

—1691—-lemon meringue pie

—1691—-*Bill of Fare of Seventy-Five Noble Dishes of Excellent Food,* Thomas Tryon

—18th century South Africa—-Dutch cuisine

—18th century America—-Colonial & Early American fare

—18th century America—-crab cakes

—18th century Canada—-French Canadian fare, Fortress of Louisbourg

—18th century—-English muffins & chowder

—18th century—-sticky buns (aka cinnamon buns)

—1706—-croquettes

—1717—-Massialot's *Le Nouveau Cuisiner Royale et Bourgoise* I & II

—1720—-*Receipts of Pastry and Cookery for the Use of his Scholars,* Ed. Kidder

—1727—-Hasty pudding, *The Compleat Housewife* E. Smith

—1728—-mushroom ketchup

—1740—-pound cake & cupcakes

—1747—-Yorkshire pudding & sweet potato pie

—1747—- Salmagundi, Hannah Glasse

—1750—-Francois Marin's *Les Dons de Comus* I, II & III

—1754—-Colonial Williamsburg food

—1756—-Welsh rabbit

—1758—-*Nuevo Arte de Cocina,* Juan Altimiras

—1764—-*English Houswifery,* Elizabeth Moxon

—1765—-apple butter

—1769—-ice cream & beef a la mode , *Experienced English Housekeeper*

–1769––Eccles cakes

–1770––Colonial wedding cakes

–1771–– Election Cake

–1771––Colonial Day Menu, Turkey Run VA

–1775––Dried apples from Paul Revere's kitchen

–1777––Firecakes & pepper pot from Valley Forge

–1780s––Martha Washington's Great Cake

–1780s––Thomas Jefferson's ice cream (manuscript) & muffins

–1780s––Martha Jefferson's cream cheese

–1782––souffle

–1785––*Kokebok,* from Norway

–1786––deviled eggs

–1787––toad-in-a-hole

–1789––Moravian sugar cakes

–1790s––California Missions Atole & pozole

–1796––pompkin pudding & federal pancakes, Amelia Simmon's *American Cookery*

–1796––Charlotte & Charlotte Russe

–1796––Jumbles, Fort York Ontario

–1798––Voyageurs ate pemmican

–1798––*American Cookery,* Amelia Simmons

–1798––turnovers

–19th Century––Frontier foods from Missouri

–19th Century––New England seafood & Chile con carne

–19th Century–wedding cake & Sally Lunn

–19th Century–Napoleons & Linzertortes

–19th Century–ammonia cookies & Cape Breton pork pies

–19th Century– shepherd's pie & pickled peppers

–19th Century– canapes

–1800––Regency English recipes [Jane Austen]

–1800––Napoleon's Chicken Marengo

–1803––Gumbo

—1803—-*Frugal Housewife,* Susannah Carter

—1805—-Charbonneau's "white pudding" recipe

—1807—-*A New System of Domestic Cookery,* Mrs. Rundell

—1808—-Lucy Emerson's *New England Cookery*

—1810—-Kentucky Burgoo

—1817—-Remoulade, *Le Cuisinier Royal* (en Francais)

—1818—-Mulaga-tawny soup, Dr. William Kitchener

—1821—-Tomata catsup & orange marmelade, Frederick Accum's *Culinary Chemistry*

—1824—-gazpacho in America

—1826—-Jean Anthelme Brillat-Savarin's Physiologie du Gout

—1826—- *Cook and Housewife's Manual,* Margaret Dods (Scotland)

—1828—-Duck a l'Orange

—1828—-Dr. Creed Haskins' Brunswick stew

—1828—- Vermont common crackers & Philadelphia Apee cookies

—1830—-*Frugal Housewife,* Lydia Maria Child

—1830—-Washington Cake & other recipes, Old Sturbridge Village

—1830—-Reform Club chef Alex Soyer's Dessert gelatin

—1830—-Mrs. Isaac Cocks' Long Island corn bread

—1830—-Cornmeal mush, early Texas cuisine

—1831—- *The Cook Not Mad,* Watertown NY

—1832—-*Seventy-five Receipts for Pastry, Cakes and Sweetmeats,* Eliza Leslie

—1832—-*The Cook's Own Book,* N.K.M. Lee

—1836—-Wedding menu, from America's heartland

—1837—-Sylvester Graham's *Treatise on Bread and Bread Baking*

—1838—-*The Virginia Housewife,* Mary Randolph

—1839—-*The Good Housekeeper,* Sarah Josepha Hale

—1839—-cobbler

—1840—-*La Cuisiniere Canadienne* (en Francais)

—1840—-*Directions for Cookery,* Eliza Leslie

–1840—-Oregon Trail pioneer foods
–1840s—-Sam Houston's recipes
–1840s—Irish soda bread & French Savarin
–1843—-Washington cake, *Old Sturbridge Village Cookbook*
–1844—- Cornish pastys in UP
–1845—-roly-poly pudding & tipsy parson
–1846—-*Jewish Manual*, Judith Montefiore
–1847—-Utah bound!
–1847—-peanut brittle
–1848—- *Skilful Housewife's Guide*, Montreal
–1848—-pesto
–1849—-Eliza cookees, Mrs. Hubbell
–1849—-California sourdough bread & Hangtown fry
–1850s—Western sandwiches
–1850s—Eliza Leslie's Strawberry shortcake
–1850—-anadama bread
–1851—-*Great Western Cook Book*, Anna Collins
–1853—-Maryland beaten biscuits
–1855—-Boston cream pie
–1857—-Hanna Winsnes' cookbook (in Norwegian)
–1857—-Country captain chicken
–1857—-Eliza Acton's *English Bread Book*
–1860—-Cakes & plum puddings, *Godey's Lady's Book*
–1860s—-Baked Alaska & ice tea
–1861—-Charles Elme Francatelli's Baked Goose
–1861—-*Mrs. Beeton's Book of Household Management*
–1861—-Beef Stroganoff & popcorn balls
–1861-1865—-hardtack
–1863—-*Confederate Receipt Book*, Richmond VA
–1863—-fruit salad
–1864—-Sanderson's *Complete Confectioner* & *Complete Cook*
–1864—-Apple Crisp & Apple Brown Betty
–1865—-Mrs. Goodfellow's *Cookery as it should be*

–1866—-*The National Cookbook,* Hannah Peterson

–1868—-*The Dominion Home Cookbook,* Toronto

–1869—-parfait & Chateaubriand

–1869—-*Wright's book of 3000 practical receipts*

–1869—-Pickled limes, *Little Women*

–1870s—-Parker House rolls

–1870—-*Jennie June's American Cookbook,* Jane Cunningham Croly

–1870—-New Orlean's King cakes

–1870s—Neapolitan ice cream

–1871—-groom's cake & marble cake

–1871—-Wild Turkey

–1873—-American cuisine, from *Miss Beecher's Housekeeper and Healthkeeper* cookbook

–1875—-*Breakfast, Luncheon, and Tea,* Marion Harland

–1875—-*Young Housewife's Counsellor and Friend,* Mary Ann Mason

–1876—-*Practical Cooking and Dinner Giving,* Henderson

–1876—-popovers & ground nut cakes

–1876—-Lobster Newburg

–1877—- ambrosia

–1877—-*Buckeye Cookery,* Estelle Woods Wilcox

–1877—-Cowboy cooking

–1878—-Army bread from Ft. Laramie, WY

–1878—-*Directions Diverses,* Montreal

–1879—-funnel cakes

–1879—-Crimean Tatars ate Chee-Borek & Kobete

–1880—-*Miss Parloa's New Cookbook,* Maria Parloa

–1880s—-angel food & meatloaf

–1881—-*What Mrs. Fisher Knows About Old Southern Cooking,* Abby Fisher

–1883—-Christmas pudding

–1884—-*Mrs. Lincoln's Boston Cook Book*

–1885—-*La Cuisine Creole,* Lafcadio Hearn

—1886—-*Woman's Suffrage Cook Book,* Mrs. Hattie A. Burr

—1886—-*Miss Corson's Practical American Cookery,* Juliet Corson

—1886—-pecan pie

—1887—-Cherries jubilee

—1887—-*White House Cook Book,* F.L. Gillette

—1889—-*Aunt Babette's Cook Book: Foreign and Domestic Receipts*

—1889—-bundt cake

—1890—-Corn oysters

—1890s—-*Gems of Fancy Cookery,* Ontario Canada

—1892—-*Science in the Kitchen,* Ella Eaton Kellogg

—1893—-*Art of Living in Australia,* Philip Muskett

—1893—-*La Cuisine Francaise: French Cooking for Every Home...*

—1893—-*Favorite Dishes,* Carrie V. Shuman

—1894—-Ranhofer's *The Epicurean*

—1894—-Terrapin, from Delmonico's in NYC

—1894—-Eggs Benedict

—1894—-*Recipes Tried and True,* Marion Ohio

—1896—-Waldorf salad

—1896—-*Boston Cooking School Cook Book,* Fannie Merritt Farmer

—1896—- *The Cook Book,* Oscar Tschirky (of the Waldorf)

—1896—-Military field bread, *U.S. Manual for Army Cooks*

—1896—-*Henriette Davidis' Practical Cookbook,* 35th German edition (in English)

—1897—-*Swedish-American Cookbook* (Swedish and English)

—1897—-Sweet potato croquettes, *Practical Vegetarian Cookery*

—1897—-*Steiger's Deutsch-Amerikaniches Kochbuch* (in German)

—1898—-*New Galt Cook Book,* Ontario Canada

—1898—-Lane Cake

—1900s—-cioppino

—1900's—-*Culinary Wrinkles, or how to use Armour's extract of beef*

—1900—-*My Pet Recipes...,* St. Andrews Church, Quebec

—1900—-Pensacola Souvenier Cook Book

—1900—-Banbury tarts, *The Stonington Cookbook*, CT

—1900—-*Enterprising Housekeeper*, Pan-American Exhibition

—1900—- *Food for the Sick and How to Prepare It*, Edwin French

—1901—-*Pan American Cookbook*

—1901—-*Settlement Cook Book*, Mrs. Simon Kander

—1902—-Devil's food cake

—1902—-*Mrs. Rorer's New Cook Book*, Sarah Tyson Rorer

—1903—-U.S. Senate Bean Soup

—1903—-Baked stuffed cucumbers, *Landmarks Club Cookbook*

—1904—-*Dr. Price's Delicious Desserts*

—1904—-*Cooking in Old Creole Days*, Celestine Eustis

—1904—-*Blue Grass Cook Book*, Minnie Fox [Kentucky cookery]

—1905—- *Los Angeles Times Cook Book*

—1905—-Lady Baltimore cake

—1905—-Tomato gravy & Tamale pie

—1905—- *Finnish-American Cookbook*, Kaleva Michigan (with English translation)

—1906—-brownies

—1906—-*Inglenook Cook Book*, Elgin IL

—1906—-*Refugee's Cook Book*, (San Francisco earthquake)

—1906—-One Hundred and One Mexican Dishes, May E. Southworth

—1907—- Divinity fudge

—1908—-Steak Diane & Lobster fra diavolo

—1909—-*Good Housekeeping Woman's Home Cookbook*, Isabel Gordon Curtis

—1909—-*Washington Woman's Cook Book* (Seattle)

—1909—-*Reform Cookery Book*, Mrs. Mill

—1909—-shrimp cocktail

—1910s—-Popular U.S. foods & menus

—1910's—-*Jell-O: America's most famous dessert*

—1910—-*Home Helps: A Pure Food Cook Book*

—1910—-Chipped beef, *Manual for Army Cooks*

—1910—-Charles Fellows' *Menu Maker*

—1911—-*Good Things to Eat,* Rufus Estes

—1911—- *Paper Bag Cook Book*

—1911—-*Kitchen Encyclopedia,* Swift & Company

—1912—-Chicken a la King

—1912—-Thousand Island dressing

—1912—-*Mary Frances Cook Book,* Jane Eayre Fryer

—1912—-*Standard Paper-bag Cookery,* Emma Paddock Telford

—1912—-*War Time Cooking,* Lydia E. Pinkham

—1913—-*Chinese Cook Book,* Chong Jan Co.

—1913—-*Choice Recipes: Chocolate and Cocoa,* Walter Baker & Co.

—1913—-*Dishes and Beverages of the Old South,* Martha Williams

—1913—-Coq au vin

—1914—-*Chinese-Japanese Cook Book,* Sara Bosse

—1914—-*Neighborhood Cook Book,* Council of Jewish Women

—1914—-ANZAC biscuits I II & III

—1914—-Fruit recipes, *Encyclopedia of Practical Horticulture*

—1914—-Clarence Edwords' Celery Victor

—1915—-*Dainty Desserts for Dainty People,* Knox Gelatin Co.

—1915—-*Healthy Life Cook Book,* Florence Daniel

—1915—-*Pan-Pacific Cookbook,* Exposition fare

—1915—-*Economical Cook Book,* Ottowa

—1916—-Field bread, *Manual for Army Bakers*

—1917—-Icebox Cake (aka Refrigerator Cake)

—1917—-Donuts from the Salvation Army

—1917—-Vichyssoise, Louis Diat

—1917—-*55 Ways to Save Eggs & Best War Time Recipes*

—1918—-*Rocky Mountain Cookbook: For High Altitude Cooking,* Caroline Trask Norton

—1918—-World War I recipes from the *Doughboy Cookbook*

—1918—-*Foods That Will Win the War,* Goudiss & Goudiss

—1918—-Fannie Farmer's *Boston Cooking School Cook Book*

—1919—-*International Jewish Cook Book,* Florence Kreisler Greenbaum

—1919—-*The Hotel St. Francis Cookbook,* Victor Hirtzler

—1919—-*Italian Cook Book,* Maria Gentile

—1919—-chocolate truffles

—1920s—-Popular U.S. foods & menus

—1920s—-egg creams

—1920—-*Fleischmann's recipes*

—1920—-*School and Home Cooking,* Carlotta C. Greer

—1922—-Chiffon pie

—1922—-Jell-O recipes

—1923—- *Food for the Diabetic,* Mary Huddleson

—1923—-*Svensk-Amerikansk Kokbok* (Wisconson)

—1924—- *Mrs. Allen on Cooking, Menus, Service,* Mrs. Ida C. Bailey Allen

—1924—-Caesar salad

—1925—-George Washington Carver's peanut recipes

—1925—-Lemon sponge cake from *800 Proved Pecan Recipes*

—1927—-*Electric Refrigerator Recipes,* General Electric

—1927—-s'mores

—1928—-Nellie Aldridge's orange recipes

—1928—-Springfield's Horseshoe sandwiches

—1930's—-Popular U.S. foods & menus

—1930s—-Pavlova cake

—1930s—-Philly cheese steak (Pat's!)

—1930s—banana bread

—1930s—Cajun fried turkey

—1931—-souffle, *Joy of Cooking*

—1933—-Ruth Wakefield's Toll House cookies

—1933—-peanut butter cookies & refrigerator pie

—1936—-Chef's salad & no-bake cookies

—1936—-Dr. George Washington Carver's 115 tomato recipes

—1937—-Dr. Carver's sweet potato recipes

—1937—-Reubens & Chicken Kiev

—1937—-*Specialita Culinarie Italiane,* Boston MA

—1937—-Old Dutch Recipes, Pella IA

—1937—-Green goddess dressing, Palace Hotel

—1937—-Cobb salad, Brown Derby

—1939—-Colonel Sanders' secret recipe

—1940's—-Popular U.S. foods & menus

—1940—-British rock cake & syrup biscuits

—1940—-Recipes, Britain's Ministry of Food

—1941—-Lord Woolton Pie & sugarless sponge cake

—1941—-Rice Krispies treats & Monte Cristo sandwiches

—1941—-carpetbag steak

—1942—-MFK Fisher's Tomato & War cakes

—1943—-99 ways to share the Meat, USDA

—1945—-chicken Francese

—1946—-city chicken

—1948—-chiffon cake & chicken vesuvio

—1948—-Mr. Truman's recipes I, II, & III

—1949—-Pillsbury Bake-Off Contest Theodora Smafield's *No-Knead Water-Rising Twists*

—1949—-Wacky cake

—1950's—-Popular U.S. foods & menus

—1950's—-Mexican wedding cakes

—1950's—-Nesselrode pie

—1951—-Bananas Foster

—1953—-Mrs. Eisenhower's Million Dollar Fudge & Ike's Vegetable Soup

—1954—-California onion dip

—1955—-Chex mix

—1956—-Panini

—1957—-Poutine from Quebec

—1957—-German's Sweet Chocolate cake

—1958—-Navy bean soup & other U.S. Navy traditions

—1960's—-Popular foods & menus

—1960's—Beef Wellington & Grasshopper pie

—1960s—-Digger bread, San Francisco
—1960—-Green Eggs & Ham, Dr. Seuss
—1962—-Minced beef, *Navy-Marine Corps Recipe Service*
—1963—-Texas sheet cake
—1963—-lemon bars
—1963—-Ladybird Johnson's recipes
—1964—-Hot Dutch Tuna Buns & pita bread, NYC World's Fair
—1966—-Tunnel of Fudge Cake
—1968—-Taco salad
—1969—-Creamed ground beef, *Armed Forces Recipe Service*
—1969—-Flower Pot bread
—1970's—-Popular U.S. foods & menus
—1970's—-California rolls
—1970's—Tiramisu
—1975—-Pasta primavera
—1978—-hummingbird cake
—1980's—Popular U.S. foods & menus
—1980's—Mud pie & Dirt cake
—1980's—monkey bread
—1980s—Panzanella & pasta salad
—1981—-Watergate salad & cake (pistachio)
—1983—-Penne alla vodka
—1991—-Ohio Stadium Cake
—2007—-Kool-Aid pickles

3

The Art of the Menu

Ample thought Goes into How a Restaurant Lists its Offerings

You walk into a restaurant, sit down and pick up the menu. And, whether you realize it, that piece of laminated cardboard or leather-bound collection of parchment already is doing its job.

It may have been the reason you walked into that particular restaurant in the first place. It may be prompting you to select a particular dish the restaurateur wants you to select. It's conveying to you, subtly and almost subliminally, the memory you'll have of your dining experience.

And, it might even make you spend a bit more for your meal than you'd planned to.

It's a pretty good day's work, really, for an item most diners would consider a utilitarian, albeit sometimes fancy, book of gastronomic lists.

A menu actually is "a very important marketing tool," says Theresa LeClerc, marketing assistant for Big Dog's Hospitality Group, which currently operates six Las Vegas-area restaurants. A menu is "the first thing people see and study," she notes, "so (a menu must) make a good first impression."

A menu serves, first, as a sort of miniature billboard for a restaurant. That function is particularly significant at restaurants that post menus outside in an effort to turn idle passers-by into actual customers.

"You want to appeal to as many potential customers as possible, and when I say `potential,' the first key is to get the customer in the door," explains Frank Rigley, vice president of food and beverage at Bally's. A menu, he adds, often is key to that go/no-go decision.

Once you're inside the door, the menu's job is to capture "the whole feeling of the place, whether it's casual or elegant," says Van Heffner, president of the Nevada Restaurant Association. "The menu tells a story. It's like the passport to your dinner."

So, in designing a menu, says Steve Arcana, corporate food and beverage director for Station Casinos Inc., "we look at the theme of the restaurant – what type of feel are you trying to give?"

The trick then becomes conveying that theme – that feel – in a two-dimensional way through artwork, typefaces, colors and prose.

"There are some certain expectations you have of various menus," Arcana says. "An Italian menu would probably have more red or green print or traditional, Italian-style (art). For a steakhouse, you're going to have, perhaps, a leather-bound menu and bolder printing, because steakhouses are big and masculine and bold."

Menus for Mexican restaurants tend to be longer than other menus because "there's a tremendous amount of items that are necessary to have on a Mexican menu," Arcana says. "And, you'll see a Mexican menu broken up with different Mexican-style print and Mexican-style borders."

Despite any culinary commonalities, a good menu will be unique to the restaurant it serves. LeClerc says that, while menus at all Big Dog's Hospitality Group properties share common elements, each contains minor variations that help convey each restaurant's identity.

For instance, at Big Dog's Cafe & Casino, she says, "we carry out the (canine) theme with bone-shaped headings for appetizers and little comments – `Doggone good' – just to keep it fun and light and happy and comfortable."

However, such canine elements obviously aren't suitable at Holy Cow! Casino, Cafe and Brewery, or even the Wisconsinthemed Draft House Barn & Casino, two other Big Dog's Hospitality Group outlets.

The same holds true at more upscale restaurants. Al Dente, the Italian room at Bally's, was designed to have "a bright, cheerful, contemporary, upbeat atmosphere, and we needed to reflect that in the menu," Rigley says. "So, on the menu cover, we've got sharp, bright colors. The design is very modern, very contemporary."

In fact, the al Dente menu cover features an overt link to the room's design – a computer-enhanced image of a stained-glass panel in the restaurant. Similarly, Rigley says, the cover of Bally's Steakhouse menu features an image of a copper medallion based on the real medallions situated throughout the restaurant.

Dan Lankford, vice president of sales for Kenyon Press Inc., a Hawthorne, Calif.-based menu design firm, says that, in creating a menu for a new restaurant, his company examines everything from carpet swatches to the lighting fixtures a restaurant will have in an effort to "get a feel of what they want to do with the restaurant."

Kenyon Press has worked for a number of hotel properties, too, Lankford says, and, in those cases, "I even go and check into a hotel to get a general feel of the hotel and what you want me to feel when I check into your hotel."

Practicality is also important. Because coffee-shop menus receive so much use and abuse, Arcana says, they're typically fashioned "in laminated form or in a holder – like a booklet that lets you slide pages in and out."

And, LeClerc says, "the color of the paper is important. We do (Big Dog's menus) on white, because we are a bar-restaurant sort of setting and (inside lighting is) a little dimmer. It's easier to read."

Designing menus is a science as well as an art. Lankford says there's actually been "a lot of research" done to figure out, for instance, "exactly where your eye goes to first" when opening a menu.

"Nine times out of 10," he notes, "a person's eye is going to go to the upper right corner, then follow a (specific) pattern."

Arcana says that he usually will put to the middle-right side of a menu page "any item I'd like to sell more than something else – an item I'd like to make a highlighted item," because "that's the most natural place for the eye to go."

Menus usually list categories of dishes "in the order the customer would order, because customers would eat an appetizer before the main course," Rigley says. "It's like writing a book – the conclusion would come only at the end of the book, so dessert comes at the end of the menu."

Arcana generally favors listing the items within each menu category from least complex to most complex. "For instance, if you deal with the breakfast section, you do all of your egg items – all of your steak and eggs, and ham and eggs, and bacon and eggs – then work in some more complicated stuff, like eggs Benedict. Then you might do skillets, huevos rancheros or a lox platter."

Rigley says it's generally best to "start off a section with a lower-priced item," so that a diner does not suffer sticker shock that might force him to skip the entire menu section and move on to the next one.

"It's important to get the customer's attention to the entire menu," he explains. "And, with the prices, I believe it's important to list the item, then the description and then the price. And the fonts that you use shouldn't highlight the price or give more attention to the price than to the item."

Lankford says some restaurants list a dish's price in the body of its description, rather than letting the price stand alone to the right of the page. Diners still may price-shop among the items, he explains, "but what we've done is force your eye to look at the description first. And, hopefully, by the time you've read the description you'll say, `What the heck, what's another dollar or two?' because we've sold you on the description before the price."

In writing descriptions of dishes, "you want to clearly describe your items, but you don't want to lose the attention of the customer," Rigley says. "If you write a book, chances are customers are not going to have time to read the menu."

Approaches do differ, Arcana says, and "different people have different philosophies. But I think there's definitely got to be some creativity in whatever you do." In June, many of Nevada's best restaurants entered their menus in a design competition sponsored by the Nevada Restaurant Association and Kenyon Press. It was the first such event held here and Lankford says about 100 Nevada restaurants participated.

The quality of entries "really exceeded our expectations," he adds. "You have such a wide range of variety in Las Vegas, it's tremendous."

Most diners probably don't realize – and may not even appreciate – the thought, effort and money that goes into creating the basic restaurant menu.

"But you know what? I don't think it really matters," Rigley says. "We put the effort into designing a menu to sell the restaurant and to project the identity of the restaurant, not to get recognition for the effort. So if we've captured the customer and make them happy, then we've achieved our objective."

DESIGNING MENUS THAT SELL

There are many factors that could bring customers to your restaurant. A strong reputation may pique their curiosity. An advertised promotion may spur them to visit. A striking exterior may grab their attention. Or the scents from the kitchen might draw them from down the block. But even with all of the marketing opportunities there are to persuade a customer to try your restaurant, once customers have come to you, the most concise outline of your marketing plan is the menu.

"There are only four tools inside the walls of your restaurant to build your business. The menu is the No. 1 tool," says Tom Feltenstein, CEO of Feltenstein Partners located in Palm Beach, Florida. The menu comes before employees, before point-of-purchase promotions and before data capture (getting the names, birthdays and addresses of every person who walks through the door). "Of all those tools, menus are the place to begin. Menus are the purest form of your restaurant's strategic marketing plan," says Feltenstein.

"An effectively designed menu will entice guests to buy the items you want," he says. You achieve that by strategically engineering the menu's layout, design, graphics, format and price points to stimulate selection of highly profitable items. The most powerful menus are those that successfully, but subtly, weave those important factors into a pleasing presentation that can drive home your restaurant's message in just minutes.

Pricing for Power

Although customers spend only a brief time with a menu, it's important to recognize how menus drive profit and cash flow by guiding the guests to what to select, not just showing them what selections you have, says Feltenstein.

Careful pricing is a vital step to marketing with full force, so be sure to cost out your recipes and don't just put random prices—or the same prices as your competition—on the menu, he says. Carefully go through the recipes and cost out all the ingredients to reach accurate prices.

Feltenstein feels that one of the biggest obstacles to success in the restaurant industry is "Percentage Target Myopia (PTM), or restaurateurs trying to work on percentage as opposed to working on the money in the bank." The cause of PTM, he says, is a historical reliance and focus on menu pricing based on percentages rather than on gross-profit dollars generated. "That is when operators develop menus, they use the conventional cost/multiple 'formula pricing' method of multiplying the raw cost of a menu item by a preset factor, i.e., 3 times to attain a 33 percent food cost to establish a retail menu price. The fundamental flaw inherent in this method is that it grew from a cost-control mindset rather than a marketing perspective," he says.

There are remedies for PTM. Feltenstein suggests using the "rounding strategy." "The proper pricing must always be based on the value perception of the guest, not a pre-established formula," he says. Feltenstein explains that pricing increments of less than $1 do not change the value perception of an item that is more than $5. For instance, the perceived value of a New York strip steak priced at $11.95 will be identical to that of the same item priced at $11.50.

Price points based on 50-cent or 95-cent increments will help you maximize your profits.

Spreads that Sell

With strategic prices in place, the next step is to decide how to lay out the menu items to reinforce the layered messages of the marketing plan—from pricing to presentation. An effective presentation mingles artful nuances such as placement, sequence and size to capture the guests' attention and lead their eyes to important items.

"Because people don't read menus—they scan them—you need to put the biggest-contributing items in the places where the eye goes first," Feltenstein says. "Profit is always driven by marketing—selling your target customers your most profitable items." The eye follows a certain critical path in the brief time that a guest holds the menu, so position and placement of the most profitable items in eye-catching spots are critical to merchandising them effectively.

For instance, on a one-page menu, Feltenstein says, the category you want to sell the most should be in the center, where the eye would naturally fall. For a two-page menu, the eye would first fall on the top of the first page and then to the top of the second page.

Since most customers order sequentially—appetizers, salads or soups first, then entrees—it makes sense to place the items in a traditional sequence, Feltenstein says. Bigger items on the second page, after your appetizers, in the visual "sweet spot," will get the most attention.

Size is another factor used to grab attention and subtly affect your customer's impression of the menu. A small menu—anything that isn't 81/2 inches by 11 inches—may catch people's attention, says Ellen Bailey Dickson, lead designer of Bailey Edward Design in Chicago.

A larger menu, on the other hand, may be harder to handle—on several fronts. "There's more work for the kitchen and little focus for the customer," says Linda Lipsky, consultant/owner of Linda Lipsky Restaurant Consultants, Inc. in Broomall, Pennsylvania. She advises restaurateurs to go with smaller menus and use more white space to cut down on the time the customer has to spend reading, the time they spend at the table and the cost spent on printing.

Signaling Specials

Strategic placement of items can draw attention to special attractions, but there are still other ways to use graphics to grab the eye and lead it to featured items, says Charles Polonsky, president of Associates Design in Northbrook, Illinois. Colors, boxing, typefaces, icons, artful illustrations or photos are all ways to help the reader find his or her way through the menu, like legends on a map, Polonsky says. Photos, however, are expensive, take time to produce and may imply a visual guarantee. "You make a promise that your kitchen better be able to keep," says Lipsky.

Dickson suggests two ways to draw attention to important items. One way is with images—icons, pictures, boxes or colors; the other way is with copy. Creative descriptions, bold headlines or titles can explain what an item is and why it should be noticed.

A story, Dickson suggests, can be used to give that special item a context to boost sales. Are its origins exotic? Is it rooted in history? "It starts conversation, it welcomes people into the culture or history of the restaurant and brings some special attention to an item," she says.

Not all of those devices are appropriate for every restaurant, warns Dickson. Be careful of visual overload, she says. "It's like choosing jewelry. You would want to go out wearing some pieces, but maybe not every single piece you own."

Delectable Descriptions

The creativity and detail you put into the menu reflect the care you put into your food. It's the first contact you have with the customer and the only thing in the restaurant, besides the staff, that uses language to impart a message to the customer, says Lisa Cherkasky, food stylist, author and a judge in this year's National Restaurant Association Great Menu Design Contest.

The descriptions of the menu items—the message of your marketing plan—need to be crystallized, Lipsky says.

To get to the point, she suggests limiting descriptions to 10 words or fewer. But make sure to leave some room for imagination, Cherkasky advises, "because food is about imagination." If there are questions, an educated staff can help fill in the gaps. Besides knowing the details about the items on your menu, staff members should also be able to identify key sales opportunities, Lipsky says. For instance, it helps when servers know which items are profitable.

An educated staff also ensures that your menu is being fully utilized. For example, servers can cite the use of brands in explaining items to customers. Brand names – which have primarily been used to promote beverages – are being used more and more in other categories, says Judi Radice Hays, author, designer and a judge in this year's Great Menu Design Contest. Using a brand name in describing a product quickly tells the customer that the product is high quality, notes Radice Hays. "It justifies a higher price point by the customer's recognition."

When describing exotic or unusual items, be aware of your word choices – especially when using certain culinary terms. "No one wants to be insulted, especially when they're paying for the privilege," says Lipsky. The same is true of a wine list. Offering customers the option of ordering by bin number provides an easy solution, and it helps in terms of organization, too.

Sometimes word choice can influence a customer's decision. Lipsky says avoid the word "extra." She gives the example of "add cheese – 50 cents extra." Instead, she advises, use the word "just" or "only," as in "add cheese for just 50 cents."

It is especially important to spell menu-item ingredients correctly, says Lipsky, whose company sells "The Official Food and Beverage Spell Checker." If you can't spell an item, how can a customer trust that you will know how to prepare it?

Finally, while the mechanics of spelling and word choice need to be considered, the artistry of the description can't be ignored. Items need to be described so they sound physically attractive, says Polonsky. An experienced copywriter is essential for writing a description that is creative, accurate and attractive, he says.

The Importance of Image

Even if every detail is attended to, the menu's place in the overall scheme of the restaurant cannot be overlooked.

"Presentation on the plate is important; the presentation on the menu should be just as important–it shows the concept, it sets the mood–essentially it sets the table," says Polonsky.

For fine-dining restaurants, the importance of the menu's image goes beyond an artistic presentation to validating the restaurant's expertise and authority. "The menu has to be able to command the price of the food," says Dickson. Once the server has walked away with the menu, something that bears the name of your restaurant should remain on the table, says Polonsky. "A nice clean look is good for your image, but the repetition of a theme also reinforces the name of the restaurant into the customer's memory." If you're going to have matchbooks at the bar, take the extra step of having your name put on them, he suggests. The same is true for coasters, beverage napkins or table tents.

The Grand Design of Good Communication

A menu is just one part of the whole atmosphere of the restaurant. "It's worth your while to put money into the design of your menu," says Polonsky, "but the most important thing that should go into the planning of your menu is thought–it doesn't have to cost an arm and a leg." Good designers welcome input from restaurateurs, Polonsky says. A good designer can take a restaurateur's ideas, put them to paper and assemble them in a format that will be an economical and attractive fit with the image of the restaurant, he says.

Experts say it is important to solicit thoughts and ideas from others, but if you have a vision, go with it. "There's no real right or wrong, as long as it's done tastefully. And there's no one solution for any restaurant–only guidelines," says Polonsky. "The most important characteristic a menu should have is it should be reader-friendly and not too cute." Don't get carried away with concept, he advises – menus still have the big responsibility of selling your food as well as your image.

MENU DESIGN: MENU PSYCHOLOGY

Menu "psychology" is about making suggestions to customers through category layout, menu item placement, menu merchandising and rounding strategies – all of which are based on consumer research. Keep these five tips in mind when designing your menu, and for more helpful menu design information, contact your Food Services of America Sales Associate.

Be Selective

Take the time to find out what your customers want and add it to the menu, but don't get spread too thin. "Less is always more," says Julie Kalkowski, Restaurant Operations Consultant for Food Services of America in Seattle, WA. "When you have too many items it can be overwhelming to your customer. Focus on what you are good at and stick to that."

Be Objective

"Be sure to make your decisions based on data, not hunches," says Kalkowski. Too many restaurateurs will pull items from the menu because they think it is not selling, but you need to know it's not selling. Do your homework and be objective. Identify the items that create the greatest gross profit and focus on them, not on items that have the best profit percentages.

Placement is Important

Put your most important and profitable items where they will get noticed. "Research shows us that customers have a particular way in which they look at a menu," says Kalkowski. "At Food Services of America we offer operators detailed instructions to design their menus based on the gaze patterns of customers." The most important items should be placed centrally on the menu. Also, based on consumer research, diners tend to make their selections more often from the top and the bottom of a category. So, logically, you want your highest gross profit items at the top and bottom of a list.

Highlight Important Items... but not Every Item

Use creative and complete descriptions to tempt your customers, and considering using a box, shading, different font, or your logo to help special items stand out. But beware of overdoing it. Julie Kalkowski notes, "Menu Merchandising should be used on no more than 1-3 items per category. Over-use causes the strategy to be wasted since too much causes it to become common and will not be noticed."

A Picture is Worth a Thousand Words

"Diners can easily be persuaded to buy based on sight," notes Rene Englert, Marketing Manager at FSA Boise. "Advertising your signature item or a seasonal special by adding a picture to the menu or a specially designed table tent can increase your sales." Food Services of America will assist operators in designing appealing plate presentations and can even shoot photos of actual plated items. Please contact your local Food Services of America Sales Associate for details.

Use Rounding Strategies to set Prices

There are certain ways that consumers think about money. When items are prices under $5, we think of money in $.25 increments. Over $5 and we begin to think of money in a bit bigger increment, so rounding should be up to the nearest $.50. Cross that $10 barrier and you round up to the nearest dollar. Food Services of America offers a rounding calculator to help operators set their prices in a manner that will appeal to customers. Kalkowski adds, "If rounding strategies are not utilized, your customers are literally leaving change on the table."

Think Beyond the Menu

"Table tents and special inserts are also a great way to test new items in a restaurant before committing them to a menu," says Englert. "It also offers you the ability to rotate items for seasonal and house specials." Many operators have found the best way to increase their dessert sales is by placing table tents on their table for diners to see prior to ordering dinner. A quick reminder by servers to "save room for dessert" will start their taste buds watering.

READING BETWEEN THE LINES: THE PSYCHOLOGY OF MENU DESIGN

Restaurants USA magazine's final issue was published in September 2002 but these archived articles remain available for our readers' convenience.

The menu handed to customers at Chi-Chi's restaurants these days is a far cry from its predecessor. The old, standard rectangular menu was replaced this spring with one that features a jagged edge, warm earth tones and lively drawings of fresh fruits and vegetables. The bill of fare was designed to better showcase 25 new items.

"The new menu has a fun-looking, new-wave shape," says Robert Carl, a spokesman for the Louisville, Kentucky, company, which has 148 units nationwide and is a subsidiary of Irvine, California-based Prandium. The new menu is part of the repositioning message Chi-Chi's is trying to send consumers. "You can tell this is not the same old food," he says. "It's a hip, awesome-looking menu."

Like Chi-Chi's, many restaurants realize that their menu's appearance sends out subtle signals that can affect how customers perceive their operation. "The menu is part of your brand identity," says Bill Main, founder of Bill Main and Associates, a Chico, California, foodservice management and training company. "It's a reflection of who you are in the marketplace. If you have a dirty menu, it sends out a message that you probably have a dirty kitchen. If it's a bright, clean, sharp menu, it looks like you're a bright, clean operation." A bill of fare can also subtly direct customers to order higher-profit items.

A menu redesign can improve sales an average of 2 to 10 percent, according to restaurant consultants interviewed by *Restaurants USA*. For an operation that brings in $1 million a year, that amounts to an additional $20,000 to $100,000 annually. "Restaurateurs should view menus as an investment not as a cost," says Main. "The driving force behind profits is the menu."

Is your menu as effective as it could be? Chances are there is room for improvement. "One of the things I've found is that 90 to 95 percent of menus can be improved," says Bill Paul, founder of Cincinnati-based The Menu Advantage, a company that helps restaurants develop their menus.

Subliminal Messages

If you think customers decide on their own what to order, think again. "A menu should tell a customer what you want them to buy," says Steve Miller, who teaches a menu-design seminar and is president of the Miller Resource Group, in Grafton,

Massachusetts. The placement of menu items, the graphics and the item descriptions all send messages about what you want customers to order. For example, in a four-page menu – including front and back covers – Miller says the "power position" is on the inside right page above the center. Menu designer William Doerfler identified this as an optimum position in the November 1978 issue of *The Cornell Hotel and Restaurant Administration Quarterly*.

"The placement is very important," agrees restaurant consultant Isidore Kharasch, president of Chicago-based Hospitality Works, citing the example of a microbrewery that came to him for help with its menu. "They were selling mostly hamburgers and sandwiches, and the chef wanted to sell more of the higher-end items," Kharasch recounts. He recommended that the restaurant place the high-end specialties on the inside right page, toward the middle, and move the burgers and sandwiches from that spot to the back page. "We increased the font in that area [with the specialties]. Then on the back, we reduced the font for the burgers and sandwiches. It was a very subtle thing. In the first week [after the change], the average check went from $16 to $21. It's not that people were looking to order sandwiches and burgers, but people were being forced to order them."

A menu item's position within a list can also affect sales. People tend to remember the top two items on a list and the bottom item, says Miller. "Nothing goes in those spots by accident," he says.

Because all locations are not equal on a menu, restaurateurs need to prioritize what they want to sell, says Paul. "That's sometimes difficult for restaurateurs to do. You rarely hear them prioritize what they want to sell. Instead, they say everything on the menu is good."

What items should restaurateurs put in the high-profile spots? "Items that have a high margin and appeal are strategically placed to produce the highest margins," says Lowell Petrie, senior director of brand marketing for Denny's, headquartered in Spartanburg, South Carolina. Of course, logic also plays a role in arranging a bill of fare. For example, appetizers tend to go in the top of the left panel – a high-profile position that also makes sense sequentially. "It's a combination of logic tempered with strategy and doability," says Paul.

"The same item on a menu will sell differently if placed differently," says Andy Lansing, president and chief operating officer of Levy Restaurants, a Chicago-based restaurant group with 17 restaurants, ranging from the casual-dining Mrs. Levy's Delicatessen to Spiaggia, a fine-dining Italian restaurant. He notes that the same basic placement principles apply – no matter the type of restaurant concept – but he adds a couple of caveats. "Nothing is going to sell if it's not good," he stresses. And servers play an important role in determining what customers will order. "The menu helps steer people in the right direction," says Lansing, "but the servers are the ones who close the deal."

Avoid a Split-personality Design

"The font you use, the size of print, boxes, shading – all those things help [draw attention to an item]," says Lansing. "But you don't want to go overboard with all of that; it still needs to look elegant and concept appropriate. You don't want to have a starburst in the margin that says 'Buy this.' . . . But that's what you want to say subliminally."

Menus should be graphically exciting, but first and foremost they should be functional, says Lansing. "We want our menus to be spectacular, but we also want them to be good business tools," he says. "Some people want to create the coolest menu that ever existed." In their quest to be creative, "they forget that people might not be able to read the menu." In other words, forget about winning design awards; concentrate on winning customers.

"By using things like borders, illustrations, symbols and heavier type, you can bring attention to things," says Miller. But he cautions not to overdo it. "Use an easy-to-read typeface in 12-point size. . . . If I had to trade off between selling power and beauty, I'd pick selling power."

At Denny's, photos liven up the menu and sell items. The latest menu, released this spring, "has bigger pictures and more pictures, because we know that pictures sell," says Petrie. "You've got to show it to them to sell it." Kharasch says photos seem to be effective for casual restaurants like Denny's as well as for restaurants where customers might not be familiar with the foods—such as sushi operations. But photos aren't for everyone; good alternatives include pencil or color drawings of fresh fruits and vegetables.

Word Association

Customers won't find any descriptions on the menu at the 15th Street Fisheries in Fort Lauderdale, Florida. In addition to traditional seafood, the restaurant offers more distinctive items, such as "Bugs," an Australian crustacean that's similar to lobster. "We want the customers to be talking about the items, rather than reading flowery descriptions," says owner Michael Hurst, past chairman of the National Restaurant Association and immediate past chairman of its Educational Foundation. He depends on his servers to give customers the details. The strategy works great, says Hurst, but he admits that it might not suit every operation. "It depends on the type of restaurant and the distinctiveness of the food."

As a general rule, Miller says, a menu should not describe common, familiar items. "People know what roast beef is," he says. "You don't need to create an ode to roast beef."

Kharasch agrees. "The customer is very sophisticated today. Some items don't need to be described." But if you're offering something special or unusual, it's worth a mention, he says. For example, if your salad features locally grown arugula, radicchio and endive, you'll want to list that. "That way customers will know you're not asking them to spend $8.95 for just a bed of lettuce," he says. But don't give the entire recipe. "The customer doesn't need to know every ingredient. The customer just wants to be enticed to order the item."

And certain words have more selling power than others. For example, "marinated," "roasted" or "cooked in our wood-fire oven" have more allure than "fried," says Kharasch. What if the item is fried? "Then you can say that it's hand-battered. That way you've told the customers the item is fried, without telling them the item is fried."

You'll also want to direct customers to high-profit, high-quality items by making the descriptions of those dishes more appealing than others, says Paul. "You should have a continuum of appeal. Not everything should sound equally delicious. . . . Having everything sound equally attractive doesn't help the guest any more than having everything sound equally bland."

That's not to say that anything should sound unappealing. "If you want to sell something, make it sound as delicious as possible," says Lansing. "Even the ones you don't want to sell should sound good and taste great — they just shouldn't sound as good as your signature dishes."

And once you've written your bill of fare, take the time to proofread it. Spelling errors and typos are two items that shouldn't appear on any menu, says Kharasch. "It says a lot about a restaurant. If the restaurant can't spell hamburger or salad, it makes me wonder how good they are at making those items," he says.

Number Neuroses

The final critical element of a menu is the pricing. All too often restaurants arbitrarily select a price for an item without analyzing whether they'll profit at that price, says Kharasch. He recommends that restaurants cost out each menu item before setting the price. "I've heard people say, 'We just don't have the time to cost out our menu.' What that means to me is that you don't have time to make money. People could be putting in 15 hours day, bringing in $1 million, but losing money, because they didn't take the time to cost out items."

Of course, knowing the food cost is just a starting point. Restaurateurs often take their cost and multiply it by three or so to set their menu price. In other words, they aim for a food-cost percentage of about 33 percent. Using this philosophy, an operator might be more apt to push an item with a 25 percent food cost than one with a 40 percent food cost. But that's just one ingredient to pricing. Another aspect is the actual profit margin on each item.

"I focus on the profit, not the food-cost percentage for determining what to sell," says Paul. Take the example of a restaurant that sells a $15 steak with a 40 percent food cost, netting a $9 profit, and a $10 chicken with a 25 percent food cost, netting a $7.50 profit. Even though the steak has a higher food-cost percentage, it still brings in $1.50 more per order.

Denny's also concentrates more on the profit margin than on the food-cost percentage, says Petrie. "When it's a low-cost item to produce, if you only look at food-cost percentage, you won't be making much," he says. "You take the margin to Mr. Banker. Mr. Banker isn't interested in food-cost percentages."

Another factor to examine is what your competition charges, says Hurst. "You don't want to be too far off for an item. If others are charging $12, you don't want to be charging $20." In setting prices, he also considers the value customers place on an item. The price consumers are willing to pay doesn't always correlate with an item's actual cost, notes Hurst. "Some things cost so much compared to their visual impact, that they're not worth selling," he says. Other times, customers will be willing to pay $5 for a drink that costs only 50 cents to make. Items on a menu also should have a relative value, says Hurst. "For example, you shouldn't be charging more for chicken than for shrimp," he says.

And at times, it might make sense to forfeit a profit on an item in order to attract customers. For example, Kharasch recounts that one of his clients was known for its steak special. With a 60 percent food cost, steak brought in a minimal profit, but it attracted a lot of customers – many of them who brought companions who purchased high-profit items. "Designing a menu is like playing chess against the customer," he says. "You have to be very strategic about what the customer is going to order."

Not everyone believes that the loss-leader strategy works. "You should make money on every item you sell," says Miller, noting that each customer is only going to purchase one entree.

In most cases, restaurateurs can round up their menu prices. The practice puts some extra change in their pockets while eliminating odd prices. Paul recommends rounding up items to the nearest 25 cents. "Using other numbers looks bogus and doesn't have an impact. If it's $3.45, that's no different to the guest than $3.50," he says. As an exception, he recommends using numbers that end in 95 cents, rather than rounding up to the next dollar – a point at which customers tend to perceive an item as more expensive. Of course, none of these rules are set in stone. There's also an art to presenting menu prices. Among the mistakes Kharasch has seen are menus that align prices in a column on the right, leading customers to use the "shop-by-price method." "No matter how nice the descriptions, it forces customers to look at the prices first. The eye tends to go straight to the prices," he says. "And don't put the prices from most expensive to least expensive. People figure that out quickly."

Paul agrees that the placement of the price is critical. "I like to position the price at the end of the description, in the same type, the same boldness and without a dollar sign. This approach helps the reader focus on the product — not the price. Even the dollar sign makes the guest a little more aware of the price."

Analyzing your Menu's Strengths

Customers spend less than two minutes perusing a bill of fare, estimates Main. If a menu is designed correctly, it can have a significant impact during those few critical minutes. "The menu is the purest expression of marketing," he says. "It's your blueprint for profitability."

MAXIMIZE MENU MERCHANDISING POWER

Menu designs vary as much as the restaurants they serve. The chic downtown bistro spotlights its signature espressos and cappuccinos on a large single sheet punctuated by bold graphics and garnished with copper-foil trim. The family-style restaurant showcases its value-priced dinner entrees on a laminated trifold menu sprinkled with mouth-watering food photography. The popular theme restaurant highlights its specialty burgers and sandwiches on a die-cut, hand-lettered menu.

Every year, the National Restaurant Association recognizes some of the nation's most effective and creative menus in its Great Menu Contest. The hundreds of entries present a veritable smorgasbord of styles, but — outward appearances aside — all of the menus are designed to accomplish the same objectives, beyond simply listing the food available: define the concept and operation, align the customer's expectation with the experience, and perform as a powerful marketing tool. How well a restaurant's menu carries out those functions can determine customer satisfaction, a restaurant's profitability and even an operation's ultimate success or failure

Nonetheless, what many menu-design-and-development specialists most often see when they visit restaurants are menus that don't quite make the grade, which translates into a multitude of missed marketing opportunities. "The average customer spends about three minutes with your menu," says Robert Welcher, president of Restaurant Consultants Inc., a fullservice consulting company based in Columbus, Ohio. "How much is comprehended during that three-minute contact with your in-house marketing tool depends on how well organized it is, how readable it is and how well it conveys the tone of the operation."

"The average person does not express disappointment with a menu, but a poorly designed menu does reduce a restaurant's opportunity to reinforce the idea that this is a special place and worthy of the customer's investment," says Ginger Parker Riley, director of graphic communication for Shook Design Group Inc., located in Charlotte, North Carolina.

Mixing it Up

Obviously, the first step in putting together a winning menu is developing your food-and-drink offerings. The quality and variety of a restaurant's food certainly helps determine whether it is worthy of a customer's investment. To whet diners' appetites and keep quality standards high, restaurateurs and chefs search for that perfect menu mix that maintains the delicate balance between innovation and tradition, healthfulness and indulgence, delicacy and robustness – all the time keeping a close eye on America's fickle dining public with its constantly changing tastes and trends.

Naturally, the most successful restaurants are those that keep up with the current food trends and America's eating habits. For Welcher, the complex puzzle of menu development reduces to one uncomplicated principle: keep attuned to what's selling and what's not selling, and then make the necessary adjustments. He advocates running a detailed analysis of all menu items to track declining or increasing sales. Welcher recommends using focus groups to get a better handle on customer response to a restaurant's menu.

"Ask people what they want, what they like and what they don't like. Find out how much they're willing to spend, how large portion sizes should be and how value is perceived," says Welcher. "A good menu mix requires solid research and creativity. You have to have options for your guests – and by talking to them, you can achieve the proper mix." When items clearly appear to be poor sellers, unprofitable or unpopular with consumers, be ready to delete them promptly from your menu. Be equally ready to add new items that customers crave.

The trend toward trying to appeal to all customer tastes is one that troubles Welcher. "I'm disappointed and concerned by the homogenization of the American restaurant menu. Restaurants have the obligatory spaghetti, steak, stir-fry, pizza and burgers," says Welcher. "They want to be something to everybody, which is a hard thing to do. I think it's critically important that these restaurants find out what their segment wants. I look at a menu and wonder, "Did the chef develop this menu? Who did he talk to? And why does he think the guests like this menu?' " Specializing in certain styles and dishes can make your menu – and your restaurant – stand out in a crowded field.

For Mark Cupolo, chef at Victor Grilling Company in Victor, New York, finding a workable balance between old and new menu items to satisfy his customers' preferences and maintain the restaurant's profitability is a perpetual challenge that has required him to make some adjustments to his original concept. "I had intended my menu to be small – approximately eight to 10 main courses – and I found that from the start I was dedicating three or four of those main courses to beef to meet customer demand," he says. "That bothered me a little bit, and I tried to fight that tendency, but I finally gave in to it." Now, the menu at Victor Grilling Company features straightforward beef dishes supplemented by poultry, seafood and game meat.

Creating a successful menu can mean more than appealing to customer tastes, however. Chefs often face other factors that determine the desirability of certain dishes. Over time, Cupolo has refined his menu mix to rely on five ingredients: seasonal availability of produce, cooking methods, sales, price and labor. Even physical space can affect the items offered on a menu. For example, the limitations of the kitchen compelled Cupolo to rethink his concept and his menu. "A grilling restaurant wasn't what I wanted, but the setup of the kitchen dictated it," says Cupolo. "Grilling is faster, and more items can come off a grill than a saute station. There are a lot of dishes I want to do, but I know I can't because of the kitchen design. Your kitchen often dictates your menu mix."

Cupolo's menu mix – although not what he originally intended – effectively deals with the unique needs of his customers and the restaurant – and establishes the restaurant's identity by refusing to try to be all things to all people.

Menu Moneymakers

Once you've discovered your customers' menu preferences, it's time to decide what to feature on your menu. An attractive menu with appealing dishes by itself will not automatically boost sales. To do that, you need to determine how much a menu item – for example, a grilled-cheese sandwich – costs to make. "You need to know how much those two pieces of cheese, those two pieces of bread and butter for that grilled cheese cost. So you have to count bread slices, cheese slices and tablespoons of butter. When you're finished, you'll know exactly what the butter in that grilled cheese costs," says Gregg Rapp, a Seattle-based menu consultant.

"I've found that 95 percent of independent and chain restaurants have not done their food costing because it takes so long to do," says Rapp. "But when you start guessing about food costs, there will be holes in your pricing" – holes that can cost you money. Once you know your restaurant's food costs, you can begin maximizing your menu's profit potential.

When working on a menu, Rapp begins by conducting a profitability-and-popularity analysis of each menu item. This rather sophisticated system divides the menu items into four categories: "stars," "puzzles," "plowhorses" and "dogs." "A star is a highly profitable, highly popular item. A puzzle is a highly profitable but not very popular item. A plowhorse is a highly popular but not very profitable item. And a dog is an unprofitable, unpopular item," explains Rapp. "Once you know the profitability of the items on your menu, you can design it to enhance puzzles or stars and downplay dogs or plowhorses."

Turning puzzles into stars and softening the bite of the dogs requires applying some basic principles of marketing and salesmanship as well as some crafty design tricks. "To draw attention to an item, put a box around it, include an illustration of it and write lengthy copy about it. Place the item in a menu 'sweet spot' – either the top of a column or the top right-hand side of the menu. The more you bring attention to that item, the more important it looks and the more you sell," says Rapp.

Other subtle techniques restaurateurs can use to boost menu profitability include removing leader dots if your menu uses them to guide a guest's eyes to prices. Rapp says leader dots compromise a menu's profitability by encouraging customers to order solely on the basis of price. He recommends putting the price at the end of the copy instead.

Don't be too quick to shoot those less-profitable plowhorses or chase those dogs off your menu. Downplay them instead. "To minimize an item, remove boxes, remove copy and place it in a not-so-sweet spot," Rapp suggests. "The item is still on the menu, but the customer has to search for it. We don't want to take it off the menu, because we might lose that customer."

Quick-change Artists

A quick response to changing seasons, fluctuating food prices and vacillating customer taste buds requires that menus themselves be flexible as well as the dishes they list. "To keep the attention of a trendy, capricious customer base, you have to keep the menu fresh and new," says Restaurant Consultants' Welcher. Thanks to the proliferation of personal computers, menu-making software and laser printers, flexibility is easier than ever to achieve.

Chef Mark Cupolo appreciates the freedom that in-house menu-making provides. "The Victor Grilling Company is a small restaurant and reflects my very personalized taste," he says. "We print our menus using a personal computer. I can change things overnight, and I often do." It's this quick-change aspect of in-house menus that appeals to many restaurateurs who are trying to stay ahead of the competition and satisfy fickle palates.

Professional menu designers, however, warn restaurateurs to proceed with caution. Even though do-it-yourself menu software can slash design and printing costs, it does not replace expert design advice. Inexpensive clip art, borders and spot color do not necessarily build a good foundation for an effective or professional menu, according to Welcher. "If you don't have an eye for design, a grasp of proper layout principles or an understanding of the psychology of a menu, software won't help you," he explains. "Use a professional designer to establish a basic design template, even if you want to keep the menu simple." A designer can offer invaluable guidance on paper color and weight, typefaces, and graphics — subtle adjustments that give any menu a professional look and boost its effectiveness.

Menus Set the Mood

Maximizing the impact of your menu during those three precious minutes that guests typically spend with it begins by understanding the greater function of a menu. A truly effective menu can sell much more than just the dishes you serve — it can promote your entire operation. Your menu is part of an ensemble of ambience-enhancing elements that act in concert to achieve the right atmosphere for a restaurant and draw customers in.

At a time when the typical household income has diminished and competition has intensified, all operators need to be looking for advantages in their marketplaces. One such advantage is giving restaurant customers more entertainment value for their dollar. A 1995 National Restaurant Association consumer survey indicated that 44 percent of adults agree that they like a restaurant environment that is stimulating and active. A well-designed menu can augment a stimulating and active atmosphere. "I think the most important function of a menu is to offer information in an entertaining manner," says Shook Design's Riley. "People are going to be very particular about how they spend their money. They are going to go to a restaurant where they can have an entertaining experience instead of just a meal."

Restaurant owners striving to create entertaining dining experiences begin their efforts by building customer anticipation even in the parking lot, observes Riley. Ideally, the architecture, the decor and the tabletop design continue this anticipatory build-up, which culminates in a menu that fully expresses the style of the restaurant. Because the menu is the first thing restaurateurs give customers that definitively says "This is what we are," Riley cautions operators against doing anything on the menu that upsets the operation's self-congruity. "You want everything about the menu to relate to the restaurant and the environment you have created," she says. "You don't want to create an upscale restaurant, and then hand guests a plastic-sleeved menu."

Conversely, a gold-embossed, hand-lettered menu on fine linen paper would seem impractical and out of place at a midscale family-style spot – especially one frequented by tiny tots with messy fingers.

"Look at the menu as an extension of who you are and what you are about," says Welcher. "If the menu is not properly designed and developed, it can have a detrimental effect on the overall impression guests have of your restaurant."

Utilize the Full Power of the Menu

Despite the power menus can have, Rapp says he is still dismayed by the laissez-faire approach many restaurateurs take toward menu engineering. "Most restaurateurs think, "Who cares about the menu? Guests have to order something anyway.' "

That may be true, but Rapp and other designers agree that every effort should be made to ensure that the item ordered is the most profitable one on the menu and that the menu itself shows your food – and your restaurant – in the best possible light. According to Rapp, "A good menu will sell, it will make patrons hungry, and if they can't decide among three different items, you have a better chance of getting them to return."

4

Menu Development and Analysis

The industry experts have long sought to establish the right 'pedigree' of menu analysis for foodservice operators and educational guidelines. Currently, there are plenty of theoretical alternative approaches to menu analysis available published in professional hospitality journals. Although all of these menu analysis approaches advocate different tactical solutions for analyzing the menu items, performance, they all share the same objective, which to improve (or to provide a solution for) the current menu items performance. However the question that poses a great dilemma for the foodservice operators is which approaches or methods are suitable for practical application? A recent research indicates that none of the theoretical approaches of menu analysis is totally embraced by the foodservice operators when a menu analysis is conducted. This paper is to ascertain how is the foodservice operators conduct their menu analysis and what criteria are they based on?

INTRODUCTION

Menu is one of the important aspects for the success of any foodservice establishment. Perhaps it is arguably the soul of the restaurant. Menu infers several interpretations for both the buyers and sellers. Khan (1991) suggests that "menus are statements" of the food and- beverage items provided by a foodservice establishment, primarily based on consumer needs and/or demands and designed to achieve organisational objectives" (p. 40). Mooney (1994) and Kreck (1984) note that menu can be interpreted as a list of product range that a restaurant offers and the same time it can be a piece of literature or display used to communicate the product range to the customer. However, a recent study argues that "menus are more than the conventional function of a communications and selling tool but also a research and experimentation device that can be studied to increase restaurant profit" (Seaberg, 1991).

An interesting point is that the battle for pre-eminence menu offered to the consumers is an endless task faced by most foodservice operators. The model of new menu development advocated by Mooney (1994) which is illustrated in Figure 1, shows how critical it is to have thorough research and analysis of the various elements from the restaurant's objectives and strategies to the bureaucratic processes of menu planning, selection, design, pricing and analysis.

A matter of fact this process is actually an endless cycle of research and analysis because once a new menu is developed that menu is periodically reviewed for its effectiveness. Quite simply, the research process is crucial to find out what is going on in the market and the analysis process determines which dishes need further assessment. It is this periodical review known as menu analysis that determines the success of the menu performance.

In broad terms, menu analysis can be defined as a range of techniques and procedures that enable more effective decision making both with respect to marketing and operating the menu (Atkinson and Jones, 1994). Various tactical solutions to menu analysis have been sought in endless attempts by many restaurant operators to improve menu performance. One of the notable approaches that has gained enormous momentum both from the hospitality literature and educational curriculum is Boston's matrix technique (Morrison, 1996) also known as the 'portfolio analysis' or menu engineering'. Jones (1994) defines this approach as the "systematic evaluation of a menu's cost and/or sales data for the purpose of identifying opportunities for improved performance" (p. 205). One of the specific Boston's matrix techniques known as menu engineering made popular by Kasavana and Smith (1982) has taken a step further with the introduction of the computer software packages (Dougan, 1994; Kasavana, 1996, 1997 and 1998). However, the irony is many scholars and menu planners have criticized the imperfection of these matrix approaches including the Kasavana and Smith's menu engineering approach (Hayes and Huffman, 1985; Atkinson and Jones, 1994; Beran, 1995).

Subsequently more tactical solutions to menu analysis have emerged. The issue of non-material variable costs, which is claimed being ignored in the previous menu analysis approaches, becomes prevalent of its important in the works of Hayes and Huffman (1995), Bayou and Bennett (1992) and LeBruto et. al. (1995 and 1997) respectively. Other approaches such as the micro-marketing mix (Atkinson and Jones, 1994) and economic approach (Beran, 1995) have each advocated their own method of tactical solutions to menu analysis.

Although all these menu analysis approaches advocate different tactical solutions for analysing the menu items' performance, they all share the same objective, which to improve (or to provide a solution for) the current menu items performance. However, the question that poses a great dilemma for the foodservice operators is which approaches or methods are suitable for practical applications?

Recent research indicates that menu analysis is not purely on the "process of analysing costs and sales data in order to manipulate.. products on the menu [but understand] in-depth customers' need and perceptions" (Jones, 1994, p. 214). Jones (1994) in his article entitled Menu Analysis highlights three main approaches. One of the approaches he suggests is "based on intuition and experience rather than detailed quantitative analysis" (p. 206). Another recent survey conducted by HOTELS reveals that there are alternative approaches to menu analysis that can build revenue and keep repeat customers (Hensdill, 1998). According to this survey, the positioning and descriptions of the menu item on the menu can influence its popularity. In addition this survey also points out that creative menu design with the use of tasteful product pictures and the size of the menu are an integral part of menu planners' menu analysis.

To sum up, this summary reveals that there is no definite evidence of what actual/or dominant method(s) of menu analysis are adopted by menu planners in the global foodservice industry. The industry experts have long sought to establish the right "pedigree" of menu analysis for the foodservice operators and educational guidelines. In order to achieve this, further research is required to examine and understand how menu analysis is conducted by menu planners.

METHODOLOGY

In this research, a qualitative approach was undertaken to ascertain chain foodservice attitudes in the menu analysis decision-making. Although the acceptance of qualitative research methodology is less prevalent than the quantitative research (Maykut and Morehouse, 1994; Brotherton, 1999), it is argued that the choice of qualitative research would fulfil the needs of the purpose of this research project. Quite simply, the interest of this research is a phenomenological approach, an approach to understanding how menu analysis is conducted by foodservice operators rather than the use of a positivist approach, which is largely based on measurable variables and provable propositions (op. cit., 1994).

This qualitative research approach to inquiry also involved a case study approach, where people and setting were explored in-depth and described in a series of mini-case studies reports. It is believed that a series of mini case studies reports would enhance the body of knowledge in understanding the intended research objectives. Thus, personal interviews were deployed to explore the phenomenon of interest from the foodservice operators with the use of a semi-structured questionnaire, which was composed based on the secondary research and piloted in predetermined sampling settings.

Undoubtedly, a large-scale population would make this qualitative case study research more valid and reliable. However, to conduct in-depth personal interviews in a large-scale survey would be too costly and time consuming. This to a large extent answers why a case study approach was adopted in this qualitative research. A list of twelve UK chains companies (See Table 1) with over 25 restaurants brands was compiled. The reason behind the selection of chain restaurants was as followed: Restaurants that have a chain affiliation are known to be more standardised and organised in their overall operations. Mass financial capabilities and diversification of divisions and departments provide huge advantage in making the operations more efficient and effective. Furthermore with the increased numbers of outlets, a need for better menu analysis methodology is surely crucial apart from being competitive in the market.

Table 1. Major UK Chain Restaurants, 1994-1995

Company	Key Brands	Outlets
Allied Domecq*	Big Steak, Wacky Warehouse, Exchange	270
Bass*	Toby, Harvester	278
Bright Reason PLC	Pizzaland, Bella Pasta, Pizza Piazza	190
City Centr Rest. PLC	Deep Pan Pizza, Garfunkels, Chiuita, Caffe Uno, UK Diner, Raja Mama's, Nachos	205
Granada	Happy Eater, Little Chef, Welcome Break, Granada	400*
Grand Metropolitan	Burger King	380
McDonald's	McDonald's	650
Pelican	Cafe Rouge, Dome	100
Pepsico	KFC	367
Pizza Express	Pizza Express	94
Scottish & Newcastle*	Chef & Brewer, Old Orleans	1,600
Whitbread	Beeffeater, T.G.I Friday's, Pizza Hut+, Brewer Fayne	875

+ Pizza Hut in the UK is a joint venture between Whitbread and Pepsico

* Restaurant operators within public house estates, including many outlets also serving food

Source: Davis, et.al., (1998) Food and Beverage Management, 3rd Ed. Oxford: Butterworth Heinemann, p. 239 (After Keynote 1996 Market Report: restaurants)

To a large extent, the variables that needed to be measured were quite complex and subjective because most of the different approaches to menu analysis advocated different criteria and each of them function differently. Some of the menu analysis approaches have incorporated tangible and intangible elements to advocate their menu analysis techniques. Because of this, 'statistical generalization' or enumerate frequencies' were considered unsuitable, instead 'analytical generalisation' or 'expand and generalise theories' was a more appropriate selection of measurement.

MENU ANALYSIS: QUANTITATIVE APPROACH

The findings show that the obvious equipment used by the chain operators to analyse the menu performance is the Electronic Point-of-Sale (EPOS). Almost all of these chain companies have an advance computer system, which is linked with the EPOS. Because of this the menu analysis is entirely conducted in the head office and such analysis from the EPOS at the restaurant outlets are no longer applicable.

Quantitative data analysis is predominantly the main method to assess the menu mix sales volume popularity) and gross profit profitability/ contribution margin). The findings imply that once the new menu is launched in the market, the first criterion used to review the menu effectiveness is the menu sales mix reports (quantitative data). Daily sales mix reports are accumulated for a period of one month to produce a monthly sales mix report. Every menu item sales volume and gross profit are analysed and the outcomes of what actions should be done for the menu items are decided in several ways.

However, this quantitative data analysis is not the sole determinant to decide what actions should be done to the menu items. Other criteria such as based on intuition, experience and company's financial policy are also taken into considerations for appropriate alternative approaches. This seems to confirm Jones's (1994) propositions where he argues that 'menu changes.. .are based on strategic decisions rather than simply on analyses of operating performance (and) the addition and removal of a new menu item is often based on competitive and market analysis" (p.. 213). Details of these alternative approaches are explained under sub-heading: alternative approaches to simple and complex menu analysis.

MENU ANALYSIS: QUALITATIVE APPROACH

Qualitative analysis approach is indeed equally important as the quantitative data analysis for the chain operators when a menu analysis is conducted, specifically deciding what actions should be done for the menu items. Endless research projects are carried out to analyse customer trends in food preferences and acceptances.

These research projects are vital to supplement information for menu development so that improvement for new and current menu items in term of its value and nutritional acceptances, taste, ingredients and presentation can be enhanced.

The analysis of customer trends is obtained in many ways. The findings reveal that market analysis is the common method used to obtain the plausible answers of customer trends. Analysing the target market disposable income and age population, competitors menu and awareness of current issues in food preferences and acceptances is the main areas of concern in the market analysis. Apart from this market analysis, travelling to Italy and French, which known of their gastronomic expertise is visited regularly to seek popular dishes that suitable for UK market, particularly in London market.

Based on intuition and experiences rather than relying detailed quantitative analysis are also played crucial part when a menu analysis is conducted. It should be remembered that most of these chain companies have been established for many years therefore, decision on how to analyse, amend and develop the menu items is largely based on previous experiences. Because of this, many of the chain operators analyse their menu items by advertised its on the black board menu, popular radio channels, and relevant magazines.

Customer feedback such as complaints, suggestions and compliments about the menu items are crucial for the success of the menu efficiency. Sometimes low popularity and profitability of menu items may not cause by diminishing of customer demands but poor control of the food production is likely be the culprit. Because of this, mystery shoppers are assigned to analyse the menu performances in term of its quality, presentation, taste, and the waiting period after the order taken. The accumulative of this crucial information is indeed the 'source of aspirations' for the chain operators to act what amendments and developments should be done for the menu items.

THE FINDINGS OF HOW MENU ANALYSIS IS CONDUCTED

The findings appear to disclose that the prevalent methods of how menu analysis is conducted by chain operators are combination of qualitative and quantitative analyses. Because of the complexity of the menu analysis procedures, the author uses a diagram shown in Figure 3 to the present the findings so that understanding of how menu analysis is conducted can be enhanced. Figure 3 demonstrates how menu analysis is conducted using both the qualitative and quantitative analyses. Each step of the menu analysis procedures is explained according to the given numbers shown in the Figure 3.

Figure 3 indicates that chain operators analyse their menu effectiveness after the menu is launched. These findings can be linked to Mooney's (1994) model of new menu development, where he argues that the review of menu effectiveness (menu analysis) is performed after all the menu development processes are thoroughly analysed and implemented.

Figure 3 Menu Development and Analysis

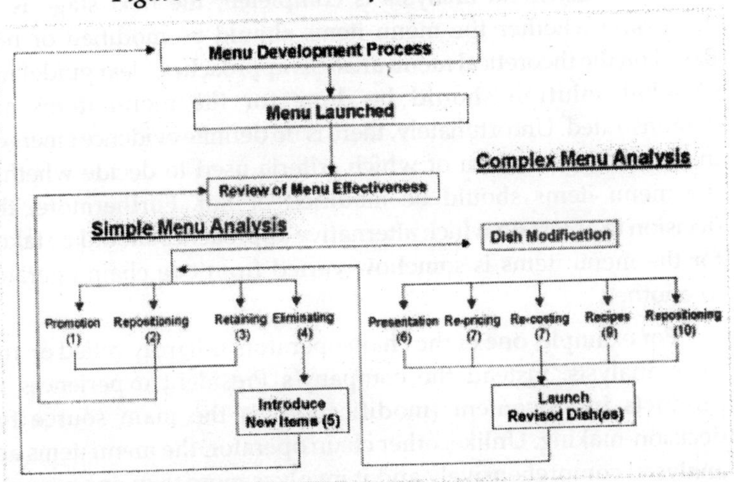

The Review of Menu Effectiveness

Notably, quantitative data analysis is the dominant approach used by chain foodservice operators when analysing the menu mix. The use of sales mix reports generated by EPOS is the main source of inputs to analyse the menu mix performances. Sales volume popularity) and gross profit profitability / contribution margin) are the common criteria under investigation for every menu item. In addition, the use of gross profit percentage (GPP) is also found to be adopted. Although different methods are used to measure menu effectiveness, some of the methodologies used by the chain operators to analyse the menu item popularity and profitability seem corroborated with the theoretical menu analysis approaches. Nevertheless, none of the theoretical methodologies of menu analysis are totally embraced by the chain operators.

Apart from using the quantitative data to analyse the menu performances, the use of mystery shoppers is also adopted to analyse the menu performances in term of its quality taste, value and overall presentation. Additionally, periodical inspection of food production processes are also conducted by the chain operators for making sure all standard procedures are followed according to specification. The finding implies that these analyses are indeed very essential so that the generation of the sales analysis produces more accurate and reliable information.

After the menu analysis is completed, the next stage is to determine whether the menu items should be modified or not. Based on the theoretical menu analysis approaches, clear guidelines of what solution should be done for the menu items are demonstrated. Unfortunately, there is no definite evidence emerged in the findings in term of which criteria used to decide whether the menu items should be modified or not. Furthermore, the decision to ascertain which alternative approaches should be taken for the menu items is somehow varied from one chain operator to another.

For example, one of the chain operators is hardly relied on the sales analysis, instead the company's President experiences in products improvement (modification) is the main source for decision-making. Unlike, other chain operator, the menu items are analysed comprehensively and it involves more than one person/ department. Yet, the decision to ascertain which alternative approaches should be taken for the menu items is still pending on the market research and customer trends. Thus, the decision making to decide which appropriate approaches to be done for the menu items is quite complex and it involves various persons / departments. Nevertheless, regardless of which decision the chain operators decide to base on, several alternative approaches are highlighted based on the findings of the case studies, which can be the ideal solution. Detail explanations of each of these alternative approaches are presented below.

Alternative Approaches to Simple Menu Analysis

There are four alternative approaches, which fall under the 'simple menu analysis'.

1. Promotion,
2. Re-position,
3. Retention and
4. Elimination

are the notable findings used by the chain operators when they decided not to do anything to the menu items regardless of what results obtained from the sales analysis. It should be remembered that in the theoretical menu analysis, especially the Boston's matrix approaches, any menu items that are categorised 'problem items' will be modified its composition in order to change the items to 'star' or 'prime' category. However, in reality this is no the case. From the analysis, it is found that the main reasons why the foodservice operators are declined to modify the menu items composition are because of the following criteria:

Menu Promotion (1)

Promotion is used to analyse further the menu effectiveness because experiences and marketing strategy indicated that lack of awareness from the public eyes may be the caused why the menu items are low in demand. This strategy is adopted because the result of low popularity obtained from the sales analysis may not be necessary due to loss of customer demands. This strategy correlate with Bowen and Morris (1995) definition that highlights the advertising maxim, "unseen is unsold". Sometimes the demand of the menu items is still alive but lack of public attentions can cause the faith of the menu items in jeopardy therefore, every precaution should be observed before the menu items undergo such modifications. Menu promotion involves both internally and externally. Black board menu and mini table standing menu, which highlights 'problem dishes' only, are the example of internal promotion.

On the other hands, using popular radio channels, posters and fliers in busy places such as cinema, hybrid places, etc. is the notable findings in their external promotions.

Menu Repositioning (2)

Changing the presentation and layout of the menu design is quite essential for boosting the menu sales. A matter of fact, this is one of the dominant approaches used to boost the sales of low popularity menu items by placing them at the strategic location known to be in the centre of the menu. These findings can be linked to the works of Miller (1980), where, according to him, menu items that most want to sell should be placed above the middle on a one-page menu.

The analysis carried out on respondents' responses has revealed that placing the items at the wrong position can cause an adverse effect of its demand. Because of this, the result of the sales analysis to some extent can provoke incorrect decision on what solutions should be taken for the menu items. Additionally, proper choice of words uses to describe the dish ingredients and methods of cooking also played a part for improving the menu popularity.

Menu Retention (3)

Undoubtedly, successful menu performances in term of its popularity and profitability should be retained. There is nothing to do with these menu items except to maintain or/and improve its quality in order to increase the popularity. However, an interesting finding obtained is that any menu items, which are known as 'problem items', are still being retained in the menu. Nonetheless, the composition of these items is subjected to be reviewed and modification is likely to be implemented.

Subsequently, once these three options are finalised and implemented, the menu items will undergo to menu analysis again. In fact, the review of menu effectiveness is an ongoing process mainly because of the changes in customer demands. It is these changes in customer demand, which make the menu items to be reviewed periodically. Needless to say, the ultimate aim is to detect the 'shadow of customer demands' (which either be high or low) before it happened. Thus, the use of sales analysis to measure the menu effectiveness to correlate with the alternative approaches as to improve the item performance is insufficient. A matter of fact, using market analysis and customer feedback to detect customer trends and correlates with the alternative approaches as to improve the items performance is more convincing than the sales analysis. These findings probably answer the reason why the theoretical menu, which uses hard data to analysis menu item performance as to improve the item popularity and profitability, is problematic.

Menu Elimination (4)

There are several reasons why decision is made to eliminate the menu item. Menu items that are no longer popular properly due to menu fatigue and changes of customer preferences and acceptances such as healthy foods are the real caused why the menu items are eliminated. Limited supplies and escalating in product prices are also found to be the caused for menu items to have been eliminated. An interesting point emerges that decision making to eliminate menu items is predominantly based on qualitative analysis rather than from the sales analysis.

Introduce New Menu Items (5)

Decision to introduce new menu items is mainly because of customer demands. The most common sources referred by the chain foodservice operators when considering to add menu items into the menu are company's research and development department (R&D), market information from Mintel and Keynote reports and Henley Data, professional hospitality journals and customer feedback.

It should be remembered that the addition of menu items can only be materialised after thorough analysis from market demands.. Moreover, current kitchen equipment and personal expertise about the new dishes are also due consideration in the internal analysis. Finally, the new menu items are launched in the market and the process of measuring the menu items effectiveness begins again.

Alternative Approaches to Complex Menu Analysis

There are five alternative approaches, which fall under the 'complex menu analysis'.

1. Presentation,
2. Re-price,
3. Re-costing,
4. Modify recipes and
5. Reposition

are the notable alternative approaches used by the chain foodservice operators to modify the menu items composition. The finding reveals that most of the chain operators make the decision to modify the menu items based on the actual performance against the predetermined criteria and allow the menu items to be further developed as appropriate.

In this case, menu items which fall below acceptable level are bound to be undergone such modifications. Unfortunately, details of the 'acceptable level' are somehow quite ambiguous. It appears that there is no definite time period when the menu must be changed or modified after the launched of the menu. Regardless of how frequents the menu items are modified, here are the alternative approaches adopted by chain operators as to improve the current menu items performance.

Menu Items Presentation (6)

The main references that are used to decide the modifications of the menu items presentation are mystery shoppers and the customers. Customer feedback such as complaints and suggestions are essential for improving the menu items presentation. However, what form of research instrument are used to seek customer feedback is not mentioned.

The author suggests that an "informal procedure" is likely to have been adopted where such feedback is reported on a random basis based on the recollection of staff experiences. Unlike the mystery shoppers, there are more formal and standardised, and independently performed by outside foodservice consultant. Depending on this feedback analysis, the presentation of the menu items may be modified either one or combination of these elements: taste, garnishing, saltiness, colour, texture, etc. Nevertheless, the use of chefs artistic expertise in food presentation also plays a part in decision making for menu items presentation.

Menu Re-pricing (7)

Usually, such decision to re-price the menu items is caused by several factors. The finding indicates that inflation is the main caused why chain operators re-price the menu items. Another factor that contributed to menu re-pricing is because of over-pricing the menu items.

For example, one of the operators says that over-pricing the menu items could be the main reason why the demand of such items declined and not because of the deterioration of the foods quality or demand. When the selling price is changed to slightly low than the former one, the popularity of the menu items has increased by 5 percents.

In addition, unavoidable factors such increase in distribution costs and liquor tax imposed by the Government also lead to re-pricing the menu items. Of course, other considerations such as company financial policy, food costs and pricing strategies are also contributed to the changing of the selling price. For instance, the psychological pricing method where by all the menu prices end with either 5 or 9 number, which can be associated with the theory of 'magic numbers or costless approaches' highlighted by Pavesic (1989) and Carvin & Norkus (1990) also found being used by these chain operators.

Menu Re-costing (8)

An obvious finding show that the cause of re-costing menu items is highly correlated with the change of the product specifications. Any changes on products purchase price from the suppliers therefore, leads to the change of the standard specifications.

Notably, the standard specifications are designed by the menu planners which than becomes the control tools for menu recipes and portion size. Simply put, any modification on the items' presentation is indirectly caused its recipe specifications to change.

Thus, any changes involve between these factors will lead to menu re-costing. Apart for that, the change of the item portion size also leads to menu re-costing.

Above all, many chain operators have allocated a budgeted food costs by the Finance department for every chain's outlet for cost control purposes. Hence, any chains' outlets that are found to have been exceeding the budgeted food costs that outlets' menu items cost will be reviewed and menu re-costing is subsequently followed.

Recipes Modification (9)

Recipe modification is basically linked with the menu re-costing.

Menu Re-positioning (10)

Unlike the menu repositioning discussed earlier, this part discusses those menu items that involve several modifications from its name, recipe, selling price and presentation. The findings reveal that after the menu items undergo several modifications (depending on how many menu items are modified) new menu design is developed with high probability of changing the menu layout and general presentation of the menu card, since the former menu card is no longer applicable with the modifications being made. Thus, the applications of the menu repositioning discussed earlier are being used again. However, if only a small proportion of the menu items undergone such modifications than the menu items may go for promotion or repositioning.

Launch Revised Menu Item(s)

Subsequently, after the menu items undergone such modifications regardless of which alternative approach is used these revised menu items are reviewed of its effectiveness again. Similar procedures of menu analysis discussed above are applied and the processes of how menu analysis is conducted begin again.

CONCLUSION

The analysis of the case studies reveals that the common methodologies adopted by the chain operators when engaged in menu analysis are qualitative and quantitative analyses. However, the finding indicates that the quantitative analysis is insufficient to generate pertinent information for decision-making in improving the menu items performance.

Instead, the qualitative analysis is notably regarded as the 'source or guidelines' in decision-making. Subsequently, it is observed that the main focus of the menu analysis is to detect the trends of customer demands before it actual occurred. Thus, using the quantitative analysis for measuring the menu effectiveness as to improve the menu items performance is actually incomplete simply because there are other reasons that can cause the decline of the menu items sale, which can not be explained from the sales data.

5

Critiquing Restaurant Critics

It is fact: When dining at a restaurant, if you were to clandestinely listen in on most conversations at the tables around you, I guarantee that at some point during their discourse, patrons topics would ultimately fall upon the restaurants they have recently visited, followed by an extensive elaboration and evaluation of each. My wife and I dine out very frequently and I admit that I do my share of eavesdropping when the subject I overhear is the culinary adventures of others. Not long ago, the commentary from a four-top next to us had me fascinated:

Wife #1: "We had dinner at that new place - that Pan Asian spot that just opened in Old City."

Husband # 1: "I loved it but she hated it and..."

Wife # 1: "That's not true dear. I liked the food very much, I just didn't care for the fact that I was being served by young people in what looked like their pajamas. If a restaurant expects me to look fashionable then I want the waitstaff to look somewhat dressy as well."

Wife #2: "Oh, we had that happen at a place in Chinatown. Honey, what is the name of that restaurant?"

Husband #2: "I don't remember but I'll never forget that they put chili peppers in everything. I thought my tongue would burn off! Even the desserts were spicy. I had heartburn for days!"

Wife #2: But never mind that. We had the best dinner ever last month with Herb and Sarah at the Four Seasons..."

Husband #2: "The best ever! And we've been to Guy Savoy - in Paris!"

In the span of about a minute, the four of them had succinctly reviewed three different dining establishments!

The public as a whole is an armchair restaurant critic, and as much as we enjoy chatting about our own dining experiences, we have always appreciated the good, the bad and the ugly, dished out each week by the savvy, legitimate restaurant reviewer. It is this salient fact that has made names like Mimi Sheridan, Ruth Reichl and Elaine Tait, renowned throughout the world of journalism.

Never mind the veiled advertisements written by "critics" at smaller local papers, the real thing fulfills a niche that is pervasive throughout American culture. Whether it is the new Bruce Willis movie, an entertaining Broadway show, our town's professional football team or the latest sport sedan from Chevy, the public as a whole lives by and trusts in the all-important critiques we read in print; those that categorize and measure most every product and service we may consider using at one time or another.

And just because "Consumer Reports" has given your electric razor a fair to midland review, it doesn't mean that no one will ever buy that particular model ever again. It's just good sense in knowing how it rates compared to the others out there on the market.

The same may be said for restaurant reviews. They serve as a true and valid evaluation of a property and ultimately, can serve in the overall improvement of a site being focused upon. From the honest dining report, management will glean perceptions of their establishment from the viewpoint of the everyday patron, as reported through the eyes of the critic. Hence, one can better understand the positive and negative variables of his or her site and work to amplify or correct them.

A good example of this is the fairly recent review of one of Philadelphia's top French restaurants. The critic had great praise for the chef and his gastronomic masterpieces, but he harshly and repeatedly criticized the service staff for a series of inexcusable gaffs. From that column, the general manager now surely realizes where to further initiate training procedures and what is needed to rectify the problems he may never had known before.

Ultimately, the public enjoys and expects to read and hear the truth about a restaurant - warts and all. And for all the arguments stated against dining critics, especially from the restaurateurs themselves, the proverbial proof is in the pudding: People swear by the stars, diamonds, bells, numbers or spoons the reviewer bequeaths upon an establishment. Just ask Nina and Tim Zagat. The covers of their survey guides may be red, but you can bet it has put them well into the black.

COUNTERPOINT/THE DETRIMENT OF RESTAURANT REVIEWS

Rather than elucidate on the many pitfalls produced by the food critics critique, I relate a true story regarding such; one that I feel illustrates the title of this piece perfectly. The counterpoint here is in the very last line, so please bear with me as I give it due buildup:

This past July, I decided to tour several dining operations in and around the Wilmington, DE area. The region was a bit foreign to me and as a concierge, I felt it was high time I became more familiar with that culinary territory, so that I might feel more comfortable with my Delaware dining suggestions. Besides, with the advent of the popular Nickolas and Alexandra exhibit, I knew my clientele would soon be bombarding me with queries on where to eat before or after the exhibit.

I visited five different yet thoroughly enjoyable restaurants during my two trips down to the area, but it was my last stop that captivated me most of all. It was there I met with the owner and general manager of a highly rated, very popular and wildly successful restaurant along the outskirts of town. Being my first visit to the property, I entered without too many preconceived notions regarding the site.

The food was fabulous. It was creative, satisfying and affordable without being too haute, or in contrast, simple or basic in taste and preparation. The decor was convivial yet sophisticated, but most of all, comfortable and relaxing. The service, while not formal by any means, was friendly and genuine and I noted that my server, along with most of the others present that evening, knew a great many of the patrons by name. It was a very enjoyable experience. More importantly though, literally everyone dining there that night seemed to be having a really good time. And while I surely did not go to tables taking polls of people's own impressions of the place, I believe that the consensus would have been unanimously positive which is why, on a hot Tuesday evening at 9PM during the slow summer season, the restaurant appeared to be booked solid. Through all the revelry that night, I spotted a man who looked vaguely familiar to me. "I know you." I remember saying to myself, but couldn't quite place a name with the face. I forgot about this until a couple weeks later when I opened the Sunday paper, turned to the Dining Out section and read the abysmal headline and following commentary that basically annihilated every aspect of this same restaurant. I realized then that the man I could not recognize was this very same critic, mercilessly relating his own experiences from that Tuesday night.

Three thoughts went through my mind at that moment: 1. If a restaurant is that popular and successful, shouldn't it mean that people are, for the most part, quite happy with their overall experience there? 2. Literally everyone seemed most content that night. Whose reviews should I believe; the praises sung to the owner by dozens of his clientele that night, or the lone remonstrations from the man with the food column? 3. I was there too, sampled many of the same dishes as he and enjoyed them all. Am I that uneducated a diner or did he simply stumble upon a singular kitchen lapse compounded by a server who had an hours worth of bad mood in him?

Fast forward now to a convention and visitors bureau food show. Staffing a booth there, representing his restaurant was the affable general manager of this aforementioned property. I had not seen him since that infamous evening, over two months prior.

"Nick" I said, " I'm sorry to have read such a negative review of your restaurant." "Oh that's okay Ken." He replied cheerfully. "It really didn't hurt us. If anything, business has been better than ever!" "Maybe" I retorted, "but what if you were a brand new restaurant just starting out, with no prior allegiances built up with clientele over the years?' He looked at me solemnly, his voice lowered. "Then I would probably not be here talking at this show with you right now"

SHIFTING GEARS

I suppose I should fess up to something. It's not that it's a secret, or something I don't want to talk about. It's just been a little hard to have to do, and sad to talk about. I put my notice in at Veil.

It's not really a surprising move, to those that know me well. My schedule at Veil had been minimized from a salaried full time position to an hourly paid two days a week, and my focus had begun to shift to my internship and the ice cream shop.

My internship, I have been hesitant to write about at all, due to some threatening non-disclosure agreements and stern warnings not to write about it. But I believe I am safe in mentioning that the powers that be are putting together a comprehensive cookbook on modern techniques. I am beyond lucky to have been brought on as the first of many interns, to see the lab form, and watch the project grow. So when people ask, "Is there a textbook, or some kind of guide to molecular gastronomy?" I smile and say all I am allowed to, "soon...."

As for the ice cream shop, it's a shift I never expected to make. I have focused on plated desserts so long, made choices in my career to foster my growth in that area, and always worked in small artisanal restaurants. I pushed everything out of the way that distracted me from developing creatively, including learning the business side of things. One can only add so much to their life at once, only hold so much in their brains. (I heard a professor once say, "for every students name I have to remember, there goes the Latin name for a butterfly.")

But as I come of age in the kitchen, and watch friends launch their own endeavors, it has become clear that the time to begin learning about business is here. Without this knowledge, I am powerless. I used to say that I never wanted to worry about owning a restaurant. I just wanted to cook. While this still holds true, it's become clear that if I ever want to make my expression, free from any restriction, I have to build myself a forum. What that is, I don't yet know. I think about little treat shops, dessert only restaurants, tiny 6 table dinner houses, wholesaling dessert components and complete menu's to restaurants that can't afford full time pastry chefs, custom cakes, a culinary retreat with classes build on my in law's amazing deep forest property in Oregon, little coffee shops with baked yummies, taking over The Frontier, (a real country restaurant on the outskirts of the Willamette Valley decorated with John Wayne posters and past members of the live exotic bird exhibit housed at the restaurant,) and reviving the 1950's drive-in I worked at in high school.

But it's become clear for the first time in my life, that knowing how to make perfect food won't keep a business alive. My innocent and naive belief over the years has been, "If I make perfect food, every day, people will come and I'll be successful, the business will fall into place." But watching friends and employers struggle it's become clear that my lack of business knowledge could take any dream of mine down quickly, breaking my heart with it.

Working for Molly, I am in part exchanging my culinary know how for her business knowledge. This lady has put as much effort into developing herself as a businesswoman, owner, and employer, as I have into developing myself creatively. Just as I would take a stage, she took a seasonal job at J-Crew because she wanted to learn their reputable motivational tactics to better lead her own staff one day.

As I help develop new flavors, and standardize the production as the company grows from one store to many and possibly into the wholesale market, she will mentor me through the process of opening a business and running it successfully. I am proud to be a part of Molly Moon's, as I look up to her business ethics and practices, leadership qualities, and believe in her and her company wholeheartedly.

As I was plating my new and last menu last week I felt a great sadness. I love plated desserts with everything in me, and being in a small intimate restaurant like Veil. Giving them up is painful, especially just as fruit comes into season! But if I ever want something of my own, it's a sacrifice I need to make.

Besides, making ice cream all day sure does make me happy. You wouldn't think it, but ice cream is pure science, and I look forward the years of learning attached to this discipline. My last day at Veil is this coming Tuesday, and my final menu should run for at least another week or two. If you have been meaning to come in and try my desserts, hesitate no longer. Otherwise, come find me at Molly Moon's ice cream shop in Wallingford, and try our flavors and some of my hand crafted toppings!

LARGE AND IN CHARGE

Summer pulls everyone this way and that. I myself have two more out of town trips planned, all the while balancing a schedule of classes to teach, demonstrations, and my 3 jobs.

At Veil, we are running on a skeleton crew with our sous chef working "off site" on a yacht for two weeks, and our owner/ executive chef at home these past weeks with Jack, the newest member to his family. Tonight our chef de cuisine is also off site.

This leaves no one above me in the pecking order, thus I am in charge. I have had a management title for some time now, "pastry chef", but never has there been anyone but myself in my department. Save the rare intern under my wing, like the outstanding Jasmine, I am really only in charge of myself.

Sure, I holler at the boys when I find things out of place, and offer guidance when applicable. But it's been since the day I left Lampreia that I have managed the kitchen.

My reign begins tonight, and runs through the two brunch services this weekend. With all the authority of a substitute teacher, I am using it to do just one thing, run a brunch special.

I tested this dish a while ago, and it's absolutely delicious. It needed but one thing, strawberries to be in season. This dish could have made it to the dessert menu, but here in the States, where we like to start our day off sweet, it is perfect for a summer brunch.

The dish is composed of warmed disks of cream of wheat, little patties that behave much like polenta. Once warmed, they are served with a mound of fresh strawberries, strawberry sauce, and a billowy cloud of malted whipped cream.

When testing recipes, the plates are left for the staff to taste, who usually pick at it, and leave some politely for those busy with other things. When we put this dish up, I made it 3 times, watching the staff devour it each time. This was fine with me, I improved the pick up and plating each time, and took the compliment.

(The "Pick up" is the steps a cook takes to prepare the food for your dish, from the moment the order is called to them to the time the food is completely plated. This covers everything from how you store the prepared components, to the manner in which you cook and hold them, and the process of putting the food on the plate. A good line cook will constantly watch their pick-up techniques looking for ways to streamline the process and improve quality.)

If you cant make it into Veil this weekend for the first of the season strawberries, and one of our stellar bloody mary's or my preference the dirty caesar, then try making it at home.

Cream of wheat

3 cups milk

3/4 cups cream of wheat

1/2 cup brown sugar

2 tbsp butter

1/2 tsp cinnamon

1/2 tsp salt

1. Bring the milk and brown sugar to a simmer and whisk in cream of wheat. Whisk constantly to avoid lumps, and cook over low heat.

2. Stirring constantly, cook until the cream of wheat is thickened, about 5 to 8 minutes. When the mixture has thickened, stir in the butter, cinnamon, and salt. Pour this into a greased or plastic lined pan, roughly 9 by 9 inches. You can use any pan you have around, it will effect only the thickness of the patties.

3. Allow the cream of wheat to cool and set, and cut it into your desired shape. At Veil we will cut disks, which produces a little waste. To avoid this you can cut squares or triangles that utilize every bit of your cream of wheat.

Malted Whipped cream

2 cups cream

1/2 cup malted milk powder

1/4 cup sugar

1/2 tsp vanilla

1. Whisk the malted milk and sugar together, until even. Add the cream and vanilla and whip to medium peaks

Strawberries....

4 pints of berries, or what the heck, get the half flat!

Separate the best of the strawberries, reserving them for slicing. If you are short on time, take the B-list berries and immediately puree them with a little sugar in the blender, using as much or as little sweetener as you like. Strain the puree of seeds and serve in a pitcher or bowl with ladle. Slice the remaining berries and toss them with just enough sugar to gloss them.

If you have a little more time on your hands, follow the following process for making strawberry puree. It is worth every extra step you take, and makes for a remarkable puree.

Strawberry puree

To Serve

Reheat the cream of wheat by frying them in a thin layer of butter, or alternately warm them on a greased cookie sheet in the oven. You can serve this family style, but the patties are delicate, and do better the less they move, so you might want to take them directly from reheating to the individuals plates.

Serve the berries and whipped cream family style, so each person can take as much or as little as they like

QUESO FRESCO

I withstood the rain today, meandering through the University farmers market in desparate hopes of a sign of a coming summer, and found it in two baskets of strawberries and a pound of cherries. The first of the year!

The cherries aren't great, and let me tell you they certainly weren't cheap! And I'll bet if I counted, each strawberry ran me upwards of a quarter a piece. It wasn't only my desperation for anything besides rhubarb that led me to these purchases.

Tomorrow, at noon, I will be the chef demonstrator at the farmers market on the street outside the pike place market. I have been a little nervous, you see. It's really hard to demonstrate a dessert with out fruit! Last resort, I could have shown off my favorite rhubarb compote. But really, it's June already, and rhubarb is like, so last season.

Thankfully I spied a table with my strawberries, which disappeared in a matter of minutes, myself taking two of the last four pints. The crates of cherries were going just as fast, but with a truck load carried over from Chellan I wasn't at risk of missing out. They aren't yet as sweet as I know they can be, bursting with the intense sunshine they absorb, so they will be treated to a pickle with balsamic and sugar , or a stewing of sorts with their pits.

Ironically, after all this hullabaloo over some fruit, that isn't the focus of my demonstration tomorrow.

I will be demonstrating a technique for queso fresco. Nothing fancy, but this humble cheese is something I find incredibly impressive each time I do it. This cheese I have seen under many an alias. At Veil we call it Fromage Blanc on our menu, I have often seen it as Farmers Cheese, and the New York Times even featured a similar recipe under the name Ricotta. Press this cheese for a couple of hours, and you have Paneer.

This easy and quick cheese is a product of curdling milk at 170 degrees with an acid and straining the curds from the whey. This preparation varies from most other cheeses by using an acid rather than rennet to cut the casein's, and break the curds from the whey, but that is a different post, waiting for myself to become better informed. Because an acid is so readily available, and this cheese is meant to be eaten as quickly as you can, it is the most accessible, and therefor humble of cheeses.

My introduction to this process was last summer at Veil, where we traded the milk for half and half laced with tarragon, rosemary, and thyme. This sat between a mascarpone enriched risotto and a veil of shaved parmesan surrounded by a thin drizzle of truffle oil. I have seen it stuffed into all manner of pastas, layered in lasagna's, used in spreads, and of course in desserts like cheese cakes.

To apply this method to dessert, we will steep the milk with lemon balm before we break it, and serve it sweetened with a drizzle of honey, a scattering of toasted nuts. I chose this recipe because it is the perfect foil for summer fruit. While the New York

Times called it bland in a good way, I prefer to think of it as subtle. Either way, it is definately a blank canvas, and can be dressed up or down, being paired with something simple like sliced strawberries tossed with a bit of sugar and black pepper, or something a bit more involved like peaches roasted with honey and chamomile. It could be scattered with fresh raspberries still warm from the sun they collected on the vines in your back yard minutes before, or pickled sour cherries. Sliced nectarines dusted with turbinado and burnt with a torch wouldn't mind sharing the plate with this cheese, and a sautee of plums and cherry tomatoes a la Claudia Fleming would find a spot next to this cheese just as comfortable.

I am still formulating a dish to feature queso fresco at Veil, although I am sure we will call it Fromage Blanc as we always do. To take this simple summer dessert from the back yard to the white table cloth, I'll add textural components, fruit components, force the cheese into an obedient shape with two spoons, and then design a beautiful plate to make this as much a feast for the eyes as the palate. Already I see a honey sauce stenciled on the plate, a proud white quenelle of queso fresco broken from sea breeze fresh raw milk, raspberries, crystallized ginger, shards of a cookie of some sort, and petite green leaves of lemon balm scattered.

But who knows where this dish will be by the time the rest of the fruit arrives. I do know that this delicious and amazing fresh cheese will help me and my menu welcome summer and her fruits into Veil.

Queso Fresco

Queso Fresco, or farmers cheese

½ gallon whole milk

2 to 4 oz lemon juice

1 tsp sea salt or kosher salt, or ½ tsp table salt

A handful of lemon balm or lemon verbena, or other fresh herbs

Equipment:

A fine mesh strainer

Cheese cloth

A large bowl

A large slotted spoon or slotted utensil

A thermometer that reads up to 180 degrees Fahrenheit

A large pot

A whisk

1. Prepare the mesh strainer by lining it with 3 layers of cheese cloth large enough to drape over the sides, and set it over the bowl.

2. Place the milk and salt in the large pot with the herbs, and scald. Remove from heat and allow to steep for 10 minutes. Insert the thermometer. Bring the milk back to 170 degrees, and begin whisking in the lemon juice, starting with 2 oz and adding more if needed. Whisk until the milk curdles, let it sit undisturbed for a few minutes.

3. Carefully transfer the solid curds to the cheese cloth lined strainer, removing the herbs, and allow to drain for 10 minutes. Alternately, you can carefully pour the contents of the pot into the strainer, slowly and with much caution.

4. When the whey has drained from the curds, remove them from the cheese cloth and transfer to a storage container. Chill for an hour or two before serving.

THE EASY BATTLE

Sometimes I forget myself. I forget that I am good at what I do, do it every day, and have a solid lump of experience under my belt.

Hmmm.... that's not quite right.

Sometimes I forget you. I forget that you aren't me and don't have the experience and daily handling that I do.

I am reminded of this occasionally when I am teaching a class and say things like, "it should be the texture of pastry cream." You blankly stare at me, and I remember that you came to a beginners baking class today and may not have even heard of pastry cream, let alone know what it's texture is like.

Molly Moon laughed at me a couple of days ago, saying, "Dana, I just love that you talk to me like I know what the heck you are talking about." I thought we were discussing the hydration properties of the pectin in her stabilizer, but she just asked if I had put it in yet.

But often, my forgetfulness shows most when I make the statement, "oh this recipe is really easy."

Then proceed to rattle off a dish that is easy to me in the professional kitchen I work in, or even in my home kitchen that I have outfitted with everything that makes my professional kitchen easy to work in, like giant super clingy cling film that sticks to everything, a box of full sheet sized parchment, a bakers bench with drawers full of every tool I could want, full of every pan I could need, bowls, sieves, and a stack of boxes filled with every pantry item I think to need.

My super easy strawberry buttermilk panna cotta is a breeze to me. But I have to admit, that the process might seem overwhelming to the novice. The cream is heated with sugar and lemon zest (everyone has a microplane, right?). The gelatin is soaked (everyone stockpiles sheet gelatin right?). Then the gelatin is melted into the hot cream and cooled slowly to body temperature (you have an hour to wait, right?). Meanwhile the strawberries, which have been frozen and thawed half way to damage the cell walls for better flavor, pigment, and pectin release, are pureed in a blender and sieved to remove the seeds and kept as cold as possible (you have a blender, sieve, and froze those berries in a single layer last night, right?)

Now, after all this, strain the cream into the strawberry buttermilk mixture, and pour into pretty little serving dishes (you have pretty serving dishes, and the refrigerator space to chill them, right?)

Well, I made a cake this weekend for a back yard barbecue that finally, *finally*, made me see what I was battling against when I tell people something is easy.

This cake is popular the country over with your church pot luck, back yard barbecue, and family gathering. While my family never made it, (we would have if my mom had the recipe), I have tasted this cake at friends gatherings. It's nothing a "foodie" would claim to enjoy, although I bet many of them secretly do. During a plated dessert class we discussed nostalgic desserts and 3 of the students claimed this cake as their favorite nostalgic childhood dessert.

It's called a poke cake, and it's made by baking a white cake mix, and poking holes all over it, to which you pour jell-o across. The jell-o (I used orange) soaks in, and makes a moist, sweet, and yes, yummy dessert. Cover the whole thing with whipped cream, or better yet, a frosting recipe made by mixing a box of instant vanilla pudding with one cup of milk, and a tub of cool whip.

The result was actually fairly tasty. It's not going on my menu, but I understand how it can be considered a favorite and brought to various events.

But after all was said and done, this cake was *EASY*. I had opened 4 containers, used only 3 ingredients that would be in everyones kitchen (eggs, oil, milk), and spent a maximum of 15 minutes preparing it. I used only 4 dishes, a measuring cup, a whisk, a spatula, and a bowl

While I know this cake isn't the crowining glory of american cuisine, it is the median. It is a cake that represents the word "easy" to many many home cooks. Compared to my experience in the kitchen this weekend, my easiest of recipes is a handful.

This cake helped put me in my place, and remind me that when I teach and discuss food with people not as entrenched in cuisine as I am, I need to remember where they are coming from. I need to remember you.

For further reading on my panna cotta process link here

For further reading on my puree process read here

"Easy" Strawberry Buttermilk Panna Cotta

250 g. heavy cream

200 g. sugar

Zest of 1 lemon

5 sheets gelatin

250 g. buttermilk

250 g. strawberry puree

1. Soak the gelatin leaves in ice water until soft and hydrated.
2. Mix the cream, sugar, and lemon zest in a small pot, and bring to a boil, whisking until the sugar is disolved. REmove from heat.
3. Remove the gelatin from the ice water, squeeze the excess water from it, and add it to the hot cream, stirring until disolved and evenly distributed.
4. Let this sit on the counter away from heat and come down in temperature slowly, until it is just below body temperature.
5. Meanwhile, mix the buttermilk and strawberry puree well and keep cold.
6. When the cream has come down in temperature, strain it into the cold strawberry buttermilk, and whisk to combine.
7. Pour this into pretty serving dishes, and chill overnight, or at least 8 hours.

L20

I know I haven't had a terrible amount to say lately, save a little on one of the easiest Rhubarb preparations I know, and a blurb about cherries I worked with last year. I've been BUSY!

I have multiple jobs you know.

Veil, I spend 20 hours a week split between two days preparing the desserts. Then there is Molly Moons, you could have guessed that I could never just make toppings for that lovely girl, and I'd end up churning ice cream a couple days a week.

I just love it there. It has the feel of hanging out with a friend, mixed with the ease of a high school summer job, and the exciting challenge of working with something completely new. Ice cream certainly isn't new to me. But producing ice cream in large batches is a very different animal, and I am loving it.

So despite my best attempts at writing interesting things for you, I continue to come up empty. This post is no different, I am instead pointing you to the blog I have been pouring over these past few weeks.

L20 is a blog following the opening of Laurent Gras new restaurant in Chicago. It's interesting to me because the chatter amongst chefs I know is that fine dining is dying, particularly in Seattle where the hottest new restaurants aren't temples to cuisine, rather late night pasta joints, fried fish served under a club, small plates of every kind. Even in New York, Stupak went on record about his future plans to open a cheap casual Mexican restaurant, and David Chang, it seems, is taking over the world. But here is a restaurant resurrecting the guiredon, a cart used to heighten the tableside experience. Where as other chefs are stripping the experience they offer, Laurent Gras is doing everything to add to his, like installing deck ovens to bake bread in house, and hiring a brigade of 25 cooks!

I am not saying there is a better or worse. I myself spend far more time in casual restaurants, and abhor a mediocre fine dining experience. It's just nice to see someone creating what appears to be the real deal, fine dining with every detail thought out and pushed to excellence.

All Rhubarb, All the Time

In other parts of the world, fruit is in season. In places other than Seattle, pastry chefs are working with more than Rhubarb.

But no matter how many sunny Seattle weekends drive a burning desire to work with fruit, nothing but Rhubarb, which technically isn't even a fruit, is available to me.

I know, I know. Soon I will be whining that there is so much fruit and so little time. You see, here in this great green city, our fruit seasons are compacted onto each other for 3 quick and furious months.

In two weeks strawberries will come, followed quickly by raspberries. Plums will begin the stone fruit season, and by the time I have a dish worked out for them, cherries will be piling up and the first of the peaches and nectarines will be coming in.

But until then it's all rhubarb, all the time.

This year, I have been making a *lot* of my favorite rhubarb recipe, orange rhubarb compote. Aside from being a fixture in my refrigerator and being gifted to friends, this working girl of a compote has a healthy professional career. She wakes up early dressed in soft hues of pink, to work at Veil's brunch, served with toasted Columbia City breads in the morning. Moving into evening, she slips into something sexy, and nests a quenelle of buttermilk sorbet. Across town, this lady changes into her jeans and t-shirt and spends each day covering scoops of Molly Moon's fantastic ice cream and is featured in a sundae with lemon ice cream, Chukar cherries, and vanilla whipped cream.

In a near brush with fame, this compote was to be featured in a local magazine. However, it hit the cutting room floor, making it necessary to share the recipe here with you. Soft, luxurious, and intensely deep in flavor, this compote's real attraction is the simplicity in which it is prepared. I think you too will find yourself coming back to this recipe again and again, maybe even well into the onslaught of seasonal fruit.

Orange Rhubarb Compote

2 tbsp butter

1 lb rhubarb

3/4 cup sugar

2 tbsp orange liquor

zest of one orange

1. Trim the Rhubarb of the ends, and split it lengthwise down the center. Cut across in 1 cm. intervals, leaving you with rough cubes of rhubarb.
2. In a large bowl, toss the rhubarb with the sugar and orange liquor, and orange zest, and set aside.
3. Melt the butter in a medium heavy bottomed saucepan over medium heat. When the butter has melted add the sugar coated rhubarb. Let this cook over a medium heat, undisturbed, for about 2 minutes. When the rhubarb has started to release juices, gently stir.
3. Continue cooking the compote over medium heat, stirring occasionally, until the juices are all released, then begin to thicken. Cooking time is about 10 to 15 minutes total, until the compote looks thick and the rhubarb is tender.

Notes:

* I set a timer last time I made it, just for you, and it took 13 minutes and 17 seconds until the desired texture and thickness was reached. This time will depend on the size of your rhubarb pieces, the particular heat of "medium" on your stove, etc, etc, etc. So use your intuition.
* Many of the cubes will break down from cooking, but some of the larger ones will remain as little tender lumps, offering bursts of tart rhubarb flavor in the mouth, and a pleasant texture on the tongue. If you like, you can break all the rhubarb apart with aggressive stirring, using the spoon to break the rhubarb up. You might even puree it and pass it through a sieve if you are looking for a smooth compote. But the less you stir, the more chunks you will leave intact.

SOUR CHERRIES

You may remember last summer, when I staged at WD-50. What I didn't tell you was that I rushed home for cherries. Not just any cherries, Montmorency sour cherries, picked fresh from a tree in my neighborhood, by one of my favorite people on the planet, Iris.

Iris came over with the cherries, and her parents, she's only 4 after all. And her dad brought with him two more friends, Lara, and Neil.

We spent the afternoon making treats with the cherries, a goat cheese panna cotta with sweet pickled cherries, zeppolle with a sour cherry sauce for dipping, and a clafouti with an attempt at cherry pit ice cream.

The attempt failed when I took my chilled base out to churn, and looked in my freezer for the bowl to my counter top ice cream maker. It was not frozen, and my base was not to be ice cream that day. But all was not lost, we dipped zeppolle in the cherry pit infused custard as well.

I must argue for this clafouti batter. This was the batter I learned clafouti with, blind to the fact that it is a bit nontraditional. Where as most batters are just that, batters that sink a bit below the fruit, and bake into a custardy pancake, this batter contains whipped egg whites and cream, and soufflees above the fruit a bit, light and creamy, and unforgettable. We kept it on the menu at Lampreia for as long as there was fresh fruit to sit below, which in Seattle means about 6 months out of the year.

The cherry pits ice cream, I must argue as well. With trace amounts of cyanide, eating a handful of cherry pits is not something I would advise. However, cracking them and infusing them into cream releases an amazing potent flavor, reliant on the flavor molecule benzaldahyde which is found in bitter almonds, apricot pits, peach pits, and regular cherry pits, and is responsible for what we consider, "fake" almond flavoring. If you have ever wondered why an almond in no way tastes like almond flavor, it's due to the fact that almond flavor is extracted from bitter almonds, not the kind we eat out of hand.

I didn't write about it because Matthew, Iris's dad did. He wrote, Lara photographed, and finally Gourmet published it online! So take a quick trip over to Gourmet.com, and read about our day in detail. The clafouti recipe is published, along with the pickled sour cherries. Following is the goat cheese panna cotta recipe, which is pictured covered with pickled sour cherries, and the cherry pit ice cream, which was replaced with vanilla for the day, delicious no doubt, but not quite the same.

Goat Cheese Panna Cotta

3 cups cream

8 oz goat cheese, at room temp

1 cup milk

½ cup sugar

Salt to taste

1 envelope powdered gelatin, bloomed in 3 tbsp water

1. Bring the milk and sugar to a simmer and add the bloomed gelatin. Remove from heat and stir until the gelatin is completely dissolved.
2. Warm the goat cheese slightly to soften, and mix the cream and goat cheese in a blender until the mixture is smooth and even. Taste the mixture and add salt to your liking.

Strain in the warm milk/gelatin, and spin until the mixture is even.

3. Pour the panna cotta mixture into molds, ramekins, pyrex custard cups, or pretty little teacups you may also collect from rummage sales.
4. Chill these for 6 hours.

Cherry Pit Ice Cream

3 cups cream

1 cup milk

1 cup sugar

6 egg yolks

The pits 50 to 70 cherries

1. Crack the pits open and extract the kernel inside, discarding the hard shell. I do this by folding them inside a dishtowel and hitting them with a hammer, or the back of a small heavy pot.
2. In a food processor, pulse the sugar with the kernels until the kernels are fine. Alternately, chop them with a knife, then mix with the sugar.
3. In a medium saucepan with a heavy bottom, bring the cream and milk to a boil and stir in the cherry pit sugar. Remove the cream from the heat and allow to steep for an hour, longer if you want a more intense flavor, and bring it back up to temperature before adding to the eggs. Strain this mixture through a fine mesh strainer before adding to the eggs.
4. Whisk one third of the hot cherry pit cream into the eggs, and return this mixture to the pot of cream, stirring with a heatproof rubber spatula.
5. Cook this over a medium heat stirring constantly until the mixture thickens and reaches 170 degrees and thickens.
6. Immediately chill this over an ice bath. When the ice cream base is cooled, transfer to a storage container and refrigerate over night, allowing the flavors to marry.

7. Churn in an ice cream maker according to the manufacturers directions.

BALTHAZAR, NEW YORK CITY, NEW YORK

My love for Balthazar is not a secret. I always question how much of my enjoyment of their food is connected to their warm, well worn, perfect environment. I try so hard to not let things like decor affect my enjoyment of the food, but I admit with Balthazar it's a difficult web to untangle. So, with my admittedly possibly biased viewpoint, onto breakfast.

It was a quick meal. Perfectly cooked bacon, scrambled eggs and asparagus in pastry dough, and buckwheat crepes with ham and gruyere. As usual the food matches the decor. It's very well executed and completely coherent with the French bistro identity. The ham and gruyere were a lovely combination, salt, smoke, tangy cheese, against the slightly rustic crepe texture. The scrambled eggs were seasoned a little unevenly, but in the spots where they were right, they were quite yummy.

And as nice as the atmosphere is at Balthazar, I am still convinced that if you fed me their food in my garage, I'd enjoy it just as much.

Molly Moon's Homemade Ice Cream

For everyone in the Seattle area, Molly Moon's Homemade Ice Cream shop is opening today.

I am making the toppings for sundaes and splits, including hot fudge, butterscotch, vanilla bean caramel, and a rotating seasonal fruit compote, currently a luscious orange rhubarb.

Molly has sourced everything as locally as possible, with the cream itself coming from Snoqualmie Gourmet in Maltby, berries from Carnation, Hazelnuts from Holmquist, everything being organic. IF you decide against a cone, no worries, cups and spoons are completely compostable.

As far as toppings are concerned, I recommend the orange rhubarb on a scoop of strawberry, made with Remlinger farms strawberries. Although the strawberry with a balsamic ribbon is hard to argue away, especially if you ask for an extra drizzle of the balsamic reduction over the top. I wouldn't turn down a scoop of scout mint, mint ice cream with crushed thin mint cookies, doused in hot fudge either.

The vanilla bean caramel would do nicely with the vivace coffee, or over a plain jane scoop of chocolate. And would it be gilding the lilly to ask for caramel sauce over the tres chic salted caramel ice cream?

But where to put the butterscotch?

Certainly not on the honey lavender, my absolute favorite of molly's flavors.

Definitely not on the bubble gum ice cream, studded with confetti bits of gum, the most popular with the little ones.

Not on the creamy lemon ice cream, or the local raspberry sorbet.

No way on the creamy thai iced tea ice cream, or the cardamom.

Maybe over the maple walnut, an old fashioned flavor that tempts the old woman that lives inside me.

I've got it! Nothing could be a better foil for my bu-bu-*buttery* butterscotch than the queen of all flavors, vanilla.

Come down today for the party, free scoops from 3 to 5 for the kids, and a little treat for us older kids, a series of DJ's, friends of Molly's from her former career in the music biz, including a member of the Shins!

If you can't make it today, no worries, the shop is open from noon until 11 from now on.

SUPERMAC, NEW YORK CITY, NEW YORK

I am a big big believer in focus leading to quality. (Note: not just a big believer. That's TWO bigs!) I enjoy all sorts of restaurants that focus on one item – chocolate, hot dogs, bagels, etc. But one of my favorite foods is macaroni and cheese.

It's a perfect food item in my opinion. And honestly, I grew up eating a lot of orange powder on my elbows. It didn't ruin me though. Over the years I have experimented often with finding just the right combination of the right shape of not-overcooked pasta, non-rubbery cheese, just the right amount of crunchy topping, and flavor with a capital F. In my kitchen I am still an infinite distance from my goal.

(I will claim a small victory here in that my children have been trained carefully to categorically reject the orange stuff and prefer freshly grated high quality cheese and butter on their pasta. Anyone with small kids knows that this is just a baby step, but an important one nonetheless.)

Wandering by Supermac in Manhattan today I wondered if there was a break in the clouds. True, it's not something that I was able to make myself, but I'm a big believer in relying on professionals to do their jobs — especially when it comes to food. I'm also a big fan of single purpose restaurants. I don't want to eat somewhere that makes sushi, steak, pasta, and "gourmet" ice cream.

I'd rather stop at a variety of small establishments each doing their best at one thing. My perfect world is a bunch of stalls - think of them as slightly bigger than street food carts.

Supermac has some variety on the menu but it's all fundamentally macaroni and cheese. I got a small serving of the basic. And honestly, I loved it. The topping was the special house blend of toasted and seasoned breadcrumbs.

They had a nice uneven texture to them almost like the fancy sea salt flakes you buy. The seasoning was nice, and they weren't too baked in to the top. They weren't quite resting on top either. They were somewhere in between. Most importantly there was just the right amount. You don't want to run out of crunchy stuff while you still have a bunch of noodles and cheese to eat. Should part of your experience be crunchless? I say no!

The noodles were cooked nicely. And the cheese? I got the four cheese mix. Getting the cheese right is very difficult. Not only does it need to be cream and flavorful, but it has to mix completely with the noodles. And it also needs to stay pretty liquidy. I'm not a fan of gelatinous cheese. I spied the Supermac folks using a saute pan to prepare my noodle cheese mixture. Excellent work. No pre-done stuff for them. Everything was to order.

All in all, I can't wait for Supermac to open up a branch in Seattle. Next time, I'll have to try some of the variations they serve.

ETHNIC CUISINE: AFRICA

African cuisine combines traditional fruits and vegetables, exotic game and fish from the oceans that surrounds her, and a marinade of cultures, colonies, trade routes, and history. Africa is a whole continent, from arid desert, to sub tropical wetlands, plains, and the oft- featured movie "jungle." Films have given Westerners an exotic view of Africa, from the big game hunter movies of the 1950's to recent movies showing colonization such as "Out of Africa." Woven within these movies are scenes of colonial food traditions, from the British to the Dutch, glimpses of native cuisine. Western views of Africa then, even if we have not traveled there, comprise a combination of the exotic, environmental preservation, hunting, and local cultivation.

African cuisine, formerly not well known in the West, is growing in popularity as immigrants bring the dishes of their country to small family restaurants in the West. To a traveler, it would be impossible to categorize "African food" just as it would be impossible to state the cuisine of any continent by one name. If you are intrepid, and take a safari tour from Kenya, your culinary experience will be much different from eating at the French and British influenced restaurants of Johannesburg, tasting Doro Wat of Ethiopia, Portuguese inspired spices of Angola and Mozambique, or the coconut and fish stews of Nairobi. Yet, all are part of African cuisine.

Northern Muslim Africa, along the Mediterranean from Morocco to Egypt is part of the Mediterranean culinary rim. Saharan Africa is for the most part subsistence. This article will cover sub Saharan Africa. Certain regions are distinctive for the development of indigenous cuisine, or incorporation of outside influences. These were distinctive by trade, colonization, or adaptation of imported foods, such as the New World peppers, peanuts, and corn. They are: Ethiopia, Nigeria, East and West Africa, the former Portuguese colonies of Angola and Mozambique, and South Africa. You, the adventurous traveler, are encouraged to seek out local restaurants, outside of the large tourist hotels, to savor African cuisine.

Ingredients

What are ingredients for the traveler? African American cooking, with ingredients carried from the New World to Africa and back, gives us some clues. *Mealie*, the African name for corn, is used to make the soft cornmeal mush and batters that are a characteristic of African and American southern foods today. *Fufu*, brought to America by Nigerian slaves, is a stiff cornmeal or yam mush, directly related to southern spoonbreads and cornmeal. Porridges and ground millet, sorghum, teff, barley, and cassava flour make up the fritters, batters, flatbreads, griddle cakes, and grits known not only in the American South, but is part of the homemaker's repertoire in Africa.

The prime characteristic of native African meals is the use of starch as a focus; accompanied by a stew containing meat or vegetables, or both. Starch filler foods, similar to the rice cuisines of Asia, are a hallmark. Cassava and yams are main root vegetables. Steamed greens, mixtures of hot spices with root vegetables, stew with and without meat, particularly chicken, all are African inspired. Peanuts, called groundnuts in Africa, feature heavily in many dishes from a garnish to peanut soups. Melons, particularly watermelon, are popular.

Nigeria and the coastal parts of West Africa are fond of chilies in food. Coastal recipes include fish marinated in ginger, tomatoes, and cayenne, cooked in peanut oil. French cooking influence in Senegal uses touches of lime juice, chopped vegetables including scallions, garlic, and marinades. Peanut oil, palm oil, and often coconut oils are common. The black eyed pea is a staple of West Africa. Okra, known also in the American South, is native to Africa; used in many dishes to thicken soups and stews. Tropical fruits, particularly the banana and coconut are important ingredients.

Outside of Muslim Africa, alcoholic beverages are part of the diet. South Africa is known for the production of good quality white and red wines. South Africa also produces a tangerine based liqueur called Van Der Hum. Tusker, the famous Kenyan beer, is exported for those who want to recreate a meal. Beer goes well with most African cuisine.

The most famous alcoholic drink in the interior is the Ethiopian honey wine, *Tej*, which has been made for centuries. Bees are the earliest domesticated animals. Wine made from their honey is a slightly acquired taste, similar to the mead of Old England. Ethiopia lays claim to another first, the cultivation of coffee. The Ethiopian coffee ceremony includes lighting of incense, passing around the beans for guest's approval, and roasting on the spot. From Ethiopia, coffee spread to Yemen, and on through the Arabic world to Europe.

Let's start with Ethiopia, with the most isolated of the African cuisines. Removed geographically from the rest of Africa, it is one of the purest indigenous cuisines. Its high interior plains, cool nights and long growing season provide an abundant variety of food. It is a meat based diet. Ethiopians are very particular about the freshness of their meat. It is typical at traditional Ethiopian weddings for the bride and groom to serve fresh slices of just slaughtered raw beef to guests. A popular dish remains a version of steak tartare; raw ground beef served with assorted condiments. Accompanying many dishes is the fiery Berbere, a spicy hot pepper paste. Doro Wat, a stewed chicken, is the national dish. Doro Wat is composed of meat, onions, tomato, stock, and hard cooked eggs. Teff, the smallest form of millet, is ground into flour, used in a thin fermented batter to make *Injera.* Injera batter is poured upon a griddle in a large spiral, where it blends into a large 24" circular flatbread. Cooked in minutes, the spongy sourdough like bread becomes the plate for the Wat, and replaces a spoon.

South Africa has emerged as a polyglot cuisine. European colonization, the adaptation of the native Bantu cooking, and large scale immigration of foreigners and workers have all contributed. Dutch settlers brought their forms of agriculture, and the British merchants imported the "mixed grills" that now include African game meats. French cultivated the vineyards, known worldwide today. Malay workers contributed curries, adding spice to a traditional plain English-Dutch influence. British empire Indians who came to build the railroads forever influenced cuisine with dals, lentil soups, and curries. Game, and lamb, the famous South African lobster, and a vast repertoire of fish add to a truly cosmopolitan cuisine. Still, in the bush and smaller towns with mostly native Africans, the main meals remain starch and stew based. South Africa's most unusual meat is called Biltong. It is a spicy form of jerky, wind-dried, used in traveling, snacks, and can be found not only country wide, but throughout Africa.

In the bush, one may find the most traditional African foods. The African village diet is often milk, curds and whey, (Ethiopia is justly known in the Bible as the land of milk and honey) and dishes of steamed or boiled green vegetables, peas, beans, and cereals. Starchy cassava, yams, and sweet potatoes round out a daily diet. The most unusual use is the local Baobab tree. This thick trunked tree looks somewhat in silhouette like an upside down carrot, growing wider at the base. Baobab seeds are dried, crushed and ground, and the flesh of the fruit is used in powder form to thicken sauces. In each locality there are numerous wild fruits and greens that are used in all manners of cooking. Yam feast days are common, often accompanied with eggs. West African cuisine makes croquettes of yams, fried in peanut oil. Along with the banana and plantain, the starchy vegetable form of banana, these comprise important elements of the diet. Yams are often served with eggs.

Cooking techniques of West Africa often combine fish and meat. Flaked and dried fish is browned in oil and combined with chicken, yam, onions, chili oil and water to make a highly flavored stew. Beef and mutton are not common in West Africa, used mostly as a condiment; as it is very tough.

East Africa is huge. Kenya is larger than France; Uganda is the size of the Midwest, they are huge countries with immense plains. The European influence is less, as this side of Africa was last changed by the trade ships. The diet of the East African is again starch based, with millet, sorghum, bananas and milk mostly found as curds and whey. Cornmeal is now such a basic part of African cuisine is hard to believe that it was a new World import.

Home to some of the greatest game preserves, East African cuisine is distinctive for the almost total absence of meat. Cattle, sheep and goats are regarded as more a form of currency, and status, and so are not eaten. The Masai, live almost entirely upon the milk and blood, but not the meat, of their cattle.

Settlers influenced East Africa by importing their cuisine almost in its entirety. The first settlers, were the Arabs, settling in the coastal areas. The many pilaf dishes, rice cooked in the Persian steamed and spiced manner remain. Pomegranate juice, saffron, cloves, cinnamon, all spice East African food; showing the Arabic origins. Eventually, and many centuries later, the British, and their imported workers from India conspired to forever influence the East African diet, including boiled vegetable, and curries.

The Portuguese influence upon Angola and Mozambique is pervasive and subtle. They were the first Europeans to move to Africa south of the Sahara in the 15th century. Settling so long, this relatively inconspicuous European country influenced African life more than the more direct and intrusive British, French, and Dutch. Just as in their Indian colony of Goa, the Portuguese brought the European sense of flavoring with spices, and techniques of roasting and marinating to African foods. These influences blended with local cuisines and ingredients to produce subtle and aromatic recipes. Separated across the tip of the continent, Mozambique is more fish based and Atlantic. Angola is reflective of the west side, with drier climate, and corresponding change in ingredients. Catholicism also introduced to the Portuguese African cuisine the sense of feast and fast days, meatless Fridays, changing the native African cuisine. The Portuguese brought from their Asian colonies, the orange, lemon, and lime. From Brazil, another colony, they brought the foods of the new world; chilies, peppers, corn, tomato, pineapples, banana, and the domestic pig. The Portuguese gardeners, farmers, fishermen profoundly influenced native stews.

In addition to growing cashews, Mozambique is most known for its *piripiri,* or hot pepper dishes. Using the small tremendously hot peppers of that country, sieved lemon juice is warmed, adding red freshly picked chilies, simmered exactly five minutes, then salted and pounded to a paste. This pulp is returned to heat with more lemon juice and eaten over meats, fish, and shellfish...and hot! In a way, this simple condiment of blended techniques and imported ingredients is a perfect exam example of African food sensibilities.

A quick tour...and exotic. To plan an African meal, consider a starch base, emphasize yams, cornmeal, and variety of greens. If palm and coconut oil do not appeal in heart healthy menus, use corn oil, but not olive oil. There are many African books around, and most of the ingredients are easily available. Natural food stores now commonly stock millet, teff, stone ground white corn grits, and varieties of greens. African cuisine is and remains, a melange of native ingredients simply prepared. Add to the tubers and starch the food greats of the new World, the peanut, chili, tomato, and pepper, overlaid with the spices and sauces of colonial countries, Indian and Malaysian spices, and local drinks. Hospitable, generous and filling, African dinners will be a welcome addition to a festive meal.

Terms

Baobab: tree, fruit, juice, leaves, and seeds used

Berbere: red pepper spice paste used in Ethiopia

Cassava: a tuber which is the source for manioc and tapioca

Cola nut: flat seed from a West Africa native tree, flavoring for colas. Used in Africa to lessen thirst

Efo: multipurpose name for greens, including cassava, sorrel, mustard, collards, chard, and turnip

Elubo: yam flour

Foofoo: mashed yam, or yam, corn, and plantain pudding

Groundnuts: the African name for peanut, introduced by the Portuguese from Brazil

Gombo: the West African word for Okra, American derivative of any stew using okra is called a gumbo

Garden eggs: term for a small green skinned African eggplants

Gari: starch from the cassava. Used in Ghana, in porridge breads

Joloff rice: spicy chicken and rice

Mealie and Mealie meal: maize of American Indian corn, a drier type of field corn. Stone ground white cornmeal substitutes

Millet: grain bearing grass, a smaller version is called Teff

Niter Kibbeh: Ethiopian spiced butter oil. Clarified butter to which nutmeg, cinnamon, and cardamom seeds are added with turmeric for color, browned, strained and uses as seasoning and cooking oil in Ethiopia

Okra: native to Africa, pods are gelatinous, adding a thickening agent to soups and stews. available frozen throughout the year, fresh seasonally

Palm nut oil and butter: from the palm nuts in Ghana. Almost impossible to find in the United States, highly saturated

Plantain: a starchy banana, cooked like a root vegetable

Sorghum: cane like grass with a small cereal grain (similar to millet)

Yam: all purpose term for yellow-orange tubers.

Recipes

Berbere / Ethiopia

Use a processor or electric blender. Traditionally, a mortar is used.

1 clove garlic, peeled

1 green onion white part only

1T red wine vinegar

1/2 C water

1/2 paprika

2 T ground cayenne

2 Tsp. salt

1/2 Tsp. ground black pepper

1/4 tsp. ground cardamom

1/4 tsp. ground coriander

1/8 tsp. ground fenugreek seeds

1/8 tsp. ground nutmeg

pinch each of ground cloves, cinnamon, and allspice

1 T palm, peanut, or vegetable oil

Combine the garlic, onion, vinegar and water and puree. In a small skillet, combine all dry ingredients EXCEPT oil. Stir over medium heat until mixture is warmed and aromatic but do not scorch. Remove from heat, cool, then stir in the blended mixture. Return pan to heat and cool over low heat, stir for 10 minutes. Transfer to a non metal container, pour oil over the surface to cover it. To use, saut the amount needed in oil or butter and add to sauces or stews.

Doro Wat / Ethiopia

2 T Niter Kibbeh

3 lb chicken, cut up

2 large onions

2 cloves garlic

1/2 inch fresh peeled chopped ginger

1/4 C berebere

1/4 tsp. each: ground fenugreek, ground cardamom, ground nutmeg

1 C chicken stock

2 T lime or lemon juice.

To garnish: 4 hard cooked eggs, sliced

Rinse and dry the chicken. Heat spiced butter in a heavy skillet. Brown chicken in oil. When all pieces are browned, remove chicken and add onion to drippings in skillet. 30 minutes. Add broth and lime juice, simmer 3-4 minutes until thickened. Return the chicken to the pan, cover, and simmer slowly for 30 minutes, turning the chicken in the pot from time to time. Transfer the stew to a platter, garnish with eggs, and serve with injira, or flatbread.

Coconut Bean Soup/ Tanzania

The use of coconut or bananas usually indicates a Swahili influence. (Use a 3 quart saucepan)

1/2 C chopped onions

1/2 C chopped green peppers

1 tsp. curry powder

1 tsp. salt

1/4 tsp. pepper in 3 T butter.

add:

I C fresh seeded tomato cut into chunks

Simmer for two minutes.

add:

2 1/2 C kidney beans with liquid, or black eyed peas

2 C coconut milk

3 C water

Simmer for 10 minutes then add 1/2 C cooked rice

Correct seasonings, serve garnished with 1 tsp. coconut on top of each soup bowl.

Jollof Rice / West Africa

(cook in a 10 inch skillet)

2 Lb. cooked meat: chicken, shrimp, pork in:

1/2 C oil

In a separate soup kettle:

saut in 1/4 C oil:

1/2 C each: chopped onions, green peppers

1/2 Tsp. grated ginger in

1/4 C oil until soft.

Add 1 16 oz can whole stewed tomatoes.

simmer for 5 minutes.

Add:

12 oz tomato paste

2 quarts water

1 T salt

1/2 tsp. each black pepper and thyme

1-2 tsp. crushed red pepper flakes.

Add to this mix the cooked meat and simmer 20 minutes longer.

In a 2 quart saucepan cook:

2 C white rice in

5 C chicken stock

Combine the sauce with the rice, pour the Jollof Rice in a deep platter, arranging the meat in the center.

Ndizi/ East Africa steamed bananas or Plantains

(These are usually served as a vegetable, you may sweeten them with some cinnamon, but not too much. If no banana leaves are available from

specialty fruit shops, use aluminum foil, or substitute with wet corn husks as used for tamales.)

Line a 4 quart pan with banana leaves.

Place 8 peeled whole plantains or rather green bananas, side by side in the pan.

Sprinkle with 1 tsp. salt and 1/2 C brown sugar. (optional)

Lay the banana leaves or corn husks over the fruit to form a tight seal, or cover with foil.

Pour 1 Cup of water at the side of the pan, to go under the leaves.

Cover tightly and simmer for one hour.

Remove leaves, arranging bananas on a platter, top with melted butter

6

African American Menus

African American cuisine predominant in the southern United States is influenced by African styles of preparation and cooking.

African American food, known as soul food, is closely related to the cuisines of both AFRICA and the American South. African slaves brought many of their native fruits and vegetables to the Americas, including YAMS, watermelon, okra, and several varieties of beans, all of which were soon adopted into the diets of their owners. Slaves who were taken into the plantation owner's house as cooks and household servants learned to combine their own food with their masters' food. African American cuisine also grew out of the slaves' resourcefulness in using the cast-off ingredients of the master's meals. For example, they developed methods to cook parts of the pig not eaten by their owner's family, feasting on the snout, ears, feet, tail, ribs, thighs (hocks), stomach (maw), and small intestines (which when boiled and fried are known as chitterlings, or "chitlins").

The West African diet featured starchy foods such as rice and yams, both of which became important parts of the African American diet. Although African slaves did not introduce rice into the Americas, their experience with rice cultivation in Africa helped make possible large-scale rice production in the Carolinas and the Gulf Coast states. Using both African and American cooking methods, African American slaves roasted, boiled, fried, and baked native yams and sweet potatoes. Sweet potato pie continues to be a popular Southern dessert.

Beans were a major component of the African diet and were brought to the Americas by slaves. As in Africa, these bean varieties, including black-eyed peas, lima beans, and kidney beans, were typically simmered and flavored with a piece of meat. Another popular African import, the okra plant, was usually fried or boiled and is a principal ingredient in gumbo, a spicy Cajun dish that is associated with Louisiana's Creole culture but has its roots in seventeenth-century Africa.

Chicken, fish, and goat constituted important sources of protein for West Africans. While Africans usually cooked these meats in stews or over flames, many slaves in America adopted the European practice of frying meat, which best prevented it from spoiling on road trips. Fried chicken was developed in the South during the nineteenth century and quickly became popular throughout the United States. In addition to chicken, the meats most widely consumed by African American slaves were pork, opossum, and raccoon.

In the eastern colonies the mingling of Native American, Anglo, and African cultures produced a hybrid cuisine that included, among other things, barbecue. Many of the Africans who came to colonial South Carolina arrived from the WEST INDIES, where, as linguistic evidence suggests, barbecue originated (*barbacoa*). Thus, enslaved Africans may have learned some culinary techniques, including barbecue, from West Indies. When cooking over a fire, American slaves began to baste their meats with sauce instead of serving the sauce on the side, as had been the practice in Africa. Regional differences in livestock availability caused "barbecue" to mean pork in the eastern United States and beef in the western United States.

The West African tradition of cooking all edible parts of plants and animals helped the slaves to survive in the United States. Although Europeans occasionally ate the leaves of plants, slaves often prepared the leaves of plants, especially collards, by simmering them in oil, peppers, and spices. They also creatively processed and cooked corn, the food most often made available to them by their owners. From corn, slaves made corn bread, grits (bleached and hulled corn kernels), hoecakes (cornmeal cooked on the blade of a hoe over a flame), and hush puppies (deep-fried cornmeal with onions and spices).

In spite of emancipation, urbanization, and migration to the cities of the North, African Americans have preserved their foods and cooking methods. In the twentieth century, African American foods have been produced for the mass market, and many celebrated soul food restaurants have opened, most notably Sylvia's in HARLEM, NEW YORK CITY. Today, African American cuisine is heavily influenced by Caribbean and South American cooking, including dishes such as Jamaican jerk chicken and fried plantains, and bean dishes such as Puerto Rican *habichuelas* and Brazilian *feijoada*.

AUSTRIA

Geography

Modern Austria: It is the homeland of world renowned skiers, of talented musicians, of lovers of table etiquette, and of people big on cooking, eating, and drinking well. It is also an internationally very active European republic which today, with 32,375 square miles, covers only a small fragment of the former Austrian empire.

For over 600 years, until World War I, the Austrian Empire had extended its national borders into modern Switzerland, France, Germany, Italy, former Czechoslovakia, Hungary, former Yugoslavia, Poland, and old geographical areas that were once upon a time called Bohemia and Moravia.

It is a multi-ethnic melting pot that includes over 8 million people, who are 99% German-speaking but are not Germans. It is a country of Austrians who speak Viennese with a special, softer, Germanic accent, Austrians who commonly are bilingual and who speak Austrian/German with either a Hungarian, or Serbo-Croat, or Czech, or Northern Italian-Tirolean accent. It is located in the southern part of Central Europe. Mountainous, wooded, and quaint, modern Austria borders Switzerland and Liechtenstein in the west, Germany in the northwest, the Czech Republic in the north, Hungary and former Yugoslavia in the east and southeast, and Italy in the southwest. It is today the political-administrative reflection of a federation of nine smaller states called the "Bundeslander." The nine Austrian Bundeslander are: Burgenland (with Eisenstadt as the state capital); Kaernten/Carinthia (with the city of Klagenfurt); Niederoesterreich/Lower

Austria (with St. Polten); Oberoesterreich/Upper Austria (with Linz); Salzburg (with Salzburg); Steiermark/Styria (with Graz); Tirol (with Innsbruck); Vorarlberg (with Bregenz); Wien (with the internationally known city of Vienna, which is both capital of the state and capital of the country).

Regional Cuisines

Austrian cuisine in general: It is the culinary reflection of an ethnically mixed people who, during the many centuries of the Austrian Habsburg empire's expansion and contraction, have exchanged culinary know-how with Turkish, Swiss, Alsacian, French, Spanish, Dutch, Italian, German, Bohemian-Moravian, Hungarian, Polish, Croatian, Slovenian, Slovakian, Serbian, and Jewish cuisine. Typical Austrian dishes vary today according to the Bundeslander culinary history and to each "Bundesland's" agriculture with its export/import tradition.

For example, Burgenland cuisine is influenced by its flat topography and proximity to Hungary. Its specialties are prepared with abundant locally grown fruits and free roaming chicken and geese, and include dishes like the "Buergenlandisches Erdbeerkoch" (a type of baked strawberry mush dessert) and "Buergenlandische Gaenseleber" (goose liver simmered with onions). East southern Kaernten/Carinthia and Steiermark/Styria's cuisines, with Hungarian, Yugoslavian, and Italian culinary influences, feature Mediterranean style foods, including ham, a favorite ingredient in all three surrounding countries, and mild climate herbs and vegetables. Dishes from these areas include "Steirisches Verhackert's" (diced "Speck" (Austrian cured ham) mixed with minced garlic and heavy flavored pumpkin seed oil) or "Steirisches Poulard" (roasted herb stuffed capon or chicken). Niederoesterreich/Lower Austria's way of cooking reflects historic ties with eastern, Middle Eastern, and oriental cooking, and includes "Serviettenknoedel mit Semmelkren" (baked bread loaf with saffron gravy) and "Gezogener Apfelstrudel" (an almost transparent roll of pastry dough filled with apples which has common culinary roots with oriental "baklava").

Oberoesterreich/Upper Austria and ancient Salzburg states, which border with Germany and the Czech Republic include culinary classics like the well known "Linzertorte" (a flaky cake lined with currant or raspberry jam, encased and covered by a lattice of cake dough), and Mozart's home town's specialty, "Salzburger Nockerln" (a very light dessert souffle dusted with vanilla sugar). Tirolean and Vorarlberg specialties, inspired by ingredients native of mountainous poor soil and cool wooded areas with a tradition of importing from Italy and exchanging with Switzerland, include "Tiroler Leber mit Polenta" (veal or beef liver with onions, "speck," capers, lemon juice and white wine served on corn mush), "Groestl" (sliced pan fried onions and potatoes with or without meat), or "Schlutzkrapfen" (spinach stuffed pasta pockets, served like "ravioli," without tomato sauce only topped with melted butter and Parmesan cheese).

Due to the city's historic past steeped in European history, Vienna' s cuisine is unique and international. Viennese specialties were created by, and for, people who were influenced by a monarchic system that until the early part of this century was among the most influential European political powers and which had cultural ties to Europe as well as the American New World. As Vienna's Habsburg royal family was involved in power politics as far away as Spain, its cuisine absorbed many international ingredients. Viennese cuisine includes "Wiener Schnitzel" (breaded veal cutlet which has its twin version in Milan, Italy, called "Cotoletta alla Milanese"), "Parmesanschoeberlsuppe" (clear broth with diamond shaped Parmesan cheese flavored souffle dumplings created after Vienna's political power became dominant in Northern Italy), and Fiaker Goulash (Viennese paprika beef stew very similar to chili and to Hungarian goulash), and, of course, the renowned Sacher Torte (chocolate glazed cake filled with either apricot, currant or raspberry jam).

A typical Austrian meal includes usually from 2 to 7 courses according to the importance of the meal's guest or occasion. It is usually made up of an appetizer (Vorspeise), a soup (Suppe), and a main course (Hauptspeise) with one or two either raw or cooked side dishes (Beilagen). It may also include a dessert which can be either a cake ("Kuchen" or "Torte"), any baked specialty made with flour ("Mehlspeise"), or a warm or cold after-meal sweet treat ("Nachspeise"). With a fine meal, Austrian adults favor drinking either beer, wine or "sekt" (sparkling wine). Fruit juices, soft drinks like fruit flavored waters, and wine spritzers are also favorites among the younger generation of Austrians.

Austrian Recipes

Liptauer (paprika cheese spread) – Appetizer

serves 4-6

Every classic collection of Austrian recipes includes at least one version of "Liptauer." All recipes call for three very important ingredients: a creamy type of ricotta known as "Topfen" (also called "Quark"), paprika, and chives. Liptauer is very much a question of taste; some Austrians mix into it a lot of paprika, butter, sour cream; others add chopped anchovies instead of anchovy paste, and even beer. This recipe retains the flavor of the Austrian specialty and is made with an American type of Topfen, called Quark, and has no butter.

2 cups (16 oz.) Topfen, also called Quark

1/2 small onion (about 1-2 oz.), trimmed, peeled, minced

15 medium-large sized pickled capers, drained, minced

1 medium size pickle, minced (optional)

1 bunch fresh chives, rinced, snipped finely (about 4 Tablespoons OR about 1 oz.)

1 teaspoon mild (Edelsuess type) paprika

1/8 teaspoon ground caraway seeds

1/2-1 teaspoon anchovy paste (1 large squirt)

1 teaspoon prepared mustard

1 teaspoon beer (optional)

salt (to taste)

1/8 teaspoon freshly ground white pepper

In a food processor, mince onion, capers, and pickle. Snip fresh chives with kitchen scissors finely (do not chop with a food processor). In a medium size bowl combine and mix well "Quark," paprika, caraway, minced onion caper mixture, anchovy paste, mustard, salt (optional), pepper, and finely snipped chives. When the mixture is smooth, refrigerate, let rest for at least 10 minutes before serving over rye or whole wheat bread. Serve sprinkled with more fresh snipped chives with either beer or new wine (Heuriger Wein).

Tafelspitz (Viennese boiled beef) – Main Course

serves 4-6

Cooked according to classic preparation rules, Tafelspitz (literally translated: the point of the table) is known to have been Austrian Hungarian Emperor Francis Joseph I's favorite meal. Viennese "Tafelspitz" for Austrians is not only a way to boil beef, but is a whole special culinary science prepared with a special cut of beef. It is not a pot roast. The authentic Tafelspitz requires a custom cut fresh piece of the hind part of beef (comparable to the American tri tip, also called silver tip); on the North American market a substitute can be fresh beef chuck brisket (not corned brisket).

The secrets of a juicy Tafelspitz are: heating the water to a rolling boil before the piece of meat is put in the water; the sudden sealing of the meat's juices as soon as the the meat's pores close when the Tafelspitz touches the boiling water; not too much salt, but enough to enhance the meat's flavor; a few pieces of vegetables (sometimes also sections of bones with marrow), the right cooking time, and the gentle rolling of the boiling water which will cook but not break the meat's fiber. This recipe is a simplified version of this very Austrian dish.

2 1/2 pounds fresh beef brisket

enough water for your suitable Dutch oven pot (about 5 Qt. pot capacity with about 4 Qts. of water) + salt (about 1/2 Tablespoon for every Qt. of water)

3 whole cloves garlic, slightly crushed, peeled

3 whole green (freeze dried) or white pepper corns

2 juniper berries (you may substitute with 1 bay leaf)

3 whole medium size carrots, peeled, trimmed (about 4 oz.)

1 small-medium onion, trimmed, unpeeled, halved (about 2 oz.)

3 sprigs fresh parsley OR

3 sprigs fresh lovage

In a suitable covered Dutch oven, bring water to a rolling boil over medium heat. When the water boils, add meat, garlic, pepper corns, juniper berries, and cover. Bring the water to a boil again and add carrots, onion, and parsley. Cover and let everything simmer for 60 minutes. Turn the meat over, add salt, and let everything cook, covered, for 90 additional minutes. Switch off the heat and let the meat steep for 20 minutes. Remove the meat from the broth and cut meat across the grain when you serve it. Serve Tafelspitz with "Apfelkren" and your choice of raw and cooked vegetables.

Note: Keep the broth for soups. Cut cold meat leftovers in thin strips and use like a meat salad mixed with raw sliced onions dressed with a simple oil, vinegar, salt and pepper vinaigrette.

How to make "Apfelkren" (apple horseradish sauce) for Tafelspitz: Combine and blend 1 pound Golden Delicious apples, cored, peeled, grated and cooked until very mushy with 1 Tablespoon wine vinegar, 1 Tablespoon lemon juice and 3 Tablespoons prepared horseradish. B'soffene Brataepfel (Tirolean baked "drunken" apples) – Dessert

serves 4

For this southwestern Austrian specialty absolutely do not use any of the flavored or green Peppermint Schnapps that are available on the American market. If you must, you may substitute the Austrian Schnaps with Italian "Grappa." The alcohol will evaporate during the cooking and the flavor will be superb.

4 whole Golden Delicious apples, cored, peeled

1/4 cup "Schnaps" (preferably made from apple or pear)

1/2 cup raisins

1 Tablespoon lemon juice

1/2 cup granulated sugar

1/4 teaspoon powdered cinnamon

1/2 cup white wine

enough oil to brush a pie pan (use any suitable unflavored vegetable oil)

enough aluminum foil to cover the pie pan

Place one oven rack in the middle of the oven and preheat oven to 425 degrees F. Brush the pie pan with oil. Place apples in the oil-brushed pan so that they are not touching each other. Drizzle the apples with the lemon juice to prevent apples from turning brown. Soak raisins in Schnaps.

In a small sauce pan, on medium heat, heat the wine, the cinnamon, and the sugar, stirring until everything is syrupy and the mixture boils (about 10 minutes). Divide soaked and drained raisins into four portions (keep the Schnaps juice) and stuff them into the apples.

Spoon half of the wine sugar syrup and the leftover Schnaps juice over the apples. Cover everything with aluminum foil and bake covered for about 30 minutes or until the apples are soft. 10 minutes before removing from oven pour over the apples remaining wine juice. Serve everything warm, not too hot, topped with sweetened whipped cream.

Wiener Phariseer Kaffee (Viennese rum liqueur spiked coffee)

serves 4

This recipe is an adaptation of the same Viennese coffee specialty served at Vienna's Cafe' Landtmann, located just across from the prominent "Volksoper" Theater-Opera house along the Dr. Karl Lueger Ring. There are many legends on why this coffee has its name. One that makes sense tells of a hypocritical priest who especially loved liqueur and wanted to hide it from his congregation. To brew this coffee use about 1 Tablespoon of freshly ground coffee per cup + 1/2 Tablespoon for the pot.

1/2 teaspoon unsweetened cocoa powder

3 cups freshly brewed Mocha type coffee (either Viennese Mocha, Mocha Java, or light French roast)

4 teaspoons sugar

4 Tablespoons either dark rum, Austrian red cherry liqueur, or Rum Topf juice enough sweetened whipped cream to top all coffees enough powdered cinnamon to dust the whipped cream

Place, in each of four coffee cups, 1/8 teaspoon cocoa powder, 1 teaspoon sugar, 1 Tablespoon liqueur. Fill each cup with coffee and stir. Top each coffee with a portion of whipped cream and sprinkle with powdered cinnamon.

Staples

Austrian Topfen (Quark): A type of cottage cheese used in many local specialty dishes like Liptauer. It is mild flavored, creamy, slightly acidic, white and delicious. Topfen/Quark can be also substituted with ricotta mixed with butter and sour cream.

Austrian cured ham (Speck) : Genuine Speck is a cold smoked fairly lean ham seasoned to traditional recipes, cured and matured for several months in cool Tirolean mountain air. It is often served as an appetizer with rye bread and pickles; it is a must in Tirolean dumplings called "Speck Knoedel."

Capers (Kapern) : Usually sold in glass jars pickled in salt brine and vinegar, capers are the closed buds of white flowers that grow in abundance throughout the Mediterranean regions and which are harvested while the buds are firm. They usually don't grow in Austria but are imported from nearby Italy where, in summer, they are found climbing along ancient walls like English ivy.

Mustard (Senf) : Prepared Austrian mustards come in a wide variety of flavors and degrees of spiciness. The most common mustards are the sweet types (*Suess*), the horseradish flavored types (*Kren Senf*), the spicy types (*Scharf*), the tarragon flavored types (*Estragon Senf*) and the wine flavored types (*Kremser Senf*).

Heavy cream (Schlag/Obers, also called Sahne) : Heavy cream in Austria is called either "Schlag," "Obers" or "Schlagobers," according to whether or not the cream is whipped. "Obers" is often served in Austrian homes and coffee houses as a side portion with either desserts, cakes, or flavored coffees.

Austrian coffee (Oesterreichischer Kaffee) : Coffee seems to be a staple nourishment to Austrians, who are very selective about the type of coffee they prepare and about the type of coffee beans they use for their coffees. By 1730 Austria's capital Vienna already had more than 30 public coffee houses. Today Austrians use three main ways to brew their coffee: the espresso way (of Italian origin), the filter way, and the Turkish way. Each coffee brewing method requires its special type of coffee grind and each Austrian "Hausfrau" has her special coffee roast and blend preference. Eduscho and Meinl Kaffee are among the popular Austrian brands. Mocha coffee seems to be the Austrian's all-round favorite. It is among the oldest type of coffee. Whether Austrian coffees are served simply black, with or without milk, or fancy – with sugar sprinkles, with pieces of chocolate, with cherries, or spiked with liqueurs and brandies – all have their special coffee name in the Austrian classic list of hot beverage.

Cherry liqueur (Kirschenliqueur) : It is absolutely not sherry or German distilled "Kirschwasser." It is an alcoholic sweet cherry liqueur similar to the Danish product "Cherry Heering." It is often used to flavor and color cakes.

Austrian "Schnaps" : It is not the green or colored syrupy "Schnapps" found on the North American market. It is a clear type of fruit brandy that is made from the distillation processes of various fruits. Common Austrian schnaps include: Plum schnaps ("Zwetchken-Schnaps," also called "Pflaumen-Schnaps"); Apple schnaps ("Apfel-Schnaps"); Pear schnaps ("Birnen-Schnaps"); and Apricot schnaps ("Marillen-Schnaps," also called "Aprikosen-Schnaps").

Austrian fruit bounce (Rum Topf) : It is a crock pot that in early summer is filled by Austrians with fresh seasonal fruit, sugar and sugar beet rum. The rum juice that absorbs the flavor of the fruit is usually dark reddish in color.

Sacher Torte (Sachertorte) : Yes, it is the world renowned chocolate glazed cake lined with jam. It was created in the early/middle 19th century by the Austrian baker, Herr Sacher, in honor of his benefactor, German-Austrian statesman Prince Klemens von Metternich, who played a major role in the European Congress of Vienna and in the demise of Napoleon Bonaparte. In Austria the original cake is still made, sold, and dispatched worldwide by the Sacher Hotel in downtown Vienna. The Sacher Hotel was founded in 1876 by the son of the baker who created the Sacher Torte. The Sacher Torte's recipe is said to be an Austrian national secret (see the Austrian source list below to order the authentic Viennese Sacher Torte worldwide).

Spices

Caraway (Kuemmel) : Small, brown, long and thin seeds that look like cumin or celery seeds and that, together with paprika, are vital in Austrian cuisine.

Their flavor and aroma is totally different from cumin, which sometimes is mistakenly used instead of caraway for the similarity of both names. In Austrian, cumin is called "Kreuzkuemmel."

Paprika (Edelpaprika) : Dark or bright red powdered product made from Hungarian type chile peppers. It is much milder than cayenne pepper and should not be substituted with it or with chile powder. It is available either mild or sweet (Edelsuess) or hot-spicy (Scharf).

Cinnamon (Zimt) : It is the all-purpose dessert spice favorite. It is available whole, chipped, and powdered. It is a must in Austrian mulled wine (Gluehwein), in cinnamon rolls (Zimt Schnecken), in rice pudding (Milchreis) and fruit compotes (Kompott).

Herbs

Chives (Schnittelauch)

Green, tubular, pointed, onion-flavored stems which are usually the first herb that is visible after the cold snowy Austrian winter season. Freshly chopped chives lift many simple Austrian dishes.

Sprinkled in soups, mixed with Topfen in Liptauer, chopped over salads, and used over rye bread with butter or "Schmalz" (rendered Speck fat), chives are a must in many Austrian specialties.

Parsley (Petersilie)

Native to mild climate Mediterranean regions, Austrian parsley is available fresh, with either flat or curly leaves, and dried. It is also usually included in a fresh vegetable addition for soups and stocks, called "Suppengruen" (carrot, celery, celeriac, kohlrabi, and parsley bunched together). When fresh it is rich in vitamin C, has a pleasantly mild flavor, and is best used mixed with minced garlic or onion.

Marjoram (Majoran)

It is basically the north-central European oregano with a milder flavor than the southern European oregano. Dried, it is a must in every Austrian pantry for dishes like goulash and roasted stuffed poultry.

Lovage (Liebstockel)

Available fresh and dry, celery flavored lovage looks like a miniature celery top. In Austrian cuisine, lovage is a celery substitute for stocks and in dishes which require mild celery flavored greens.

Ethnic Cuisine: Belgium

Introduction

Sandwiched between France and Holland along the North Sea, Belgium covers a strip of land almost 200 miles long and 100 miles wide. With over 10 million people, it is the second most densely populated country in the world. Its people divide into two distinct cultures — the Flemish in the Northern half, and the Walloons in the Southern half. The languages spoken include French, Flemish, and German, though in tourist centers people speak English as well. The capital, Brussels, stands in the center of the land and ranks as an expanding and expensive international city.

History

Belgium is a highly industrialized country with only 5 percent of the working population involved in agriculture. Even so, they produce 165 different kinds of cheeses and many notable food products. Through history, the country has been invaded and ruled by many other people-the Romans, Vikings, French, Spanish, Austrians, Dutch, English, and Germans-and many great and famous battles have been fought on Belgium soil. This land has become a meeting point for the Germanic cultures of northern Europe and the Latin cultures of the south, and this has influenced their cuisine.

Cooking techniques and ingredients of the invaders were acquired by the natives, who by the Middle Ages developed a cuisine of their own. Today Belgians proudly say their food is cooked with French finesse and served with German generosity.

The country is famous for its mussels and frites (French-fried potatoes), waffles, and endive. Fine chocolates are a passion and exquisite chocolatiers dot the marketplace of every city. More beer is consumed than wine by the populace. Many beers are crafted by small artisanal brewers whose family recipes and techniques go back generations. Beer laces the national dish, carbonnades flamandes, a Flemish beef stew.

Belgians love potatoes and are fond of game and meat. Charcuterie, a basket of bread, and beer often make a meal. Fish and seafood are important. Hearty soups play a big role, and the so called waterzooies are the most typical.

Medieval cookery still influences the cuisine with today's prevalence of condiments, mustards, vinegars, and dried fruits that lend a sweet-sour and sweet-salty flavor to dishes. Almonds and spices are used in abundance, and fresh herbs lace appetizers, salads, meats, and even desserts.

Few cookbooks exist, but the newly published volume, Everybody Eats Well in Belgium by Ruth Van Werebeek (Workman) covers recipes from three generations of her family.

Visiting Belgium today, one is easily captivated by the endive, mussels, and chocolates, and each has a story behind it.

Belgian endive, or chicory, has a place of honor in dining and a unique style of cultivation. This vegetable was accidently discovered by a Belgian farmer, Jan Lammers, in 1830, when he returned from war and found his chicory (used for coffee and stored in the barn) had sprouted white leaves. He was captivated by its tangy, distinctive flavor. It was another 30 years before endive, known as witloof, became a successful crop. In 1872 it was introduced in Paris, to rave reviews, so popular it was called white gold.

Today it is still cultivated as a labor-intensive crop, either in soil in gardens or sheds, or hydroponically. Visiting Belgian in October 1996, I had the pleasure of seeing both methods harvested, and what a fascinating production it is. There are two phases to its growth. First the roots, or chicory, is harvested in July or August. Then the grower forces the endive to sprout the leaves. To achieve this, on small farms the roots are buried in damp sand-filled trenches inside a cellar or heated metal corrugated covers. The roots then produce thick, pale conical buds in 20 days and are hand pulled and the leaves cut. The roots become fodder for animals.

More recently, endive is also produced by hydroculture, by growing in water, and this is done year around. Today endive production has spread to California. We were told that the red endive now available in the States was accidentally produced from a disease of the seed. In the past, it used to be thrown away. Very little of the red strain is grown in Belgium.

A restaurant famous for its fifty endive dishes is Traiteur Restaurant Veilinghof, located at Lewensesteenweg 22, 1910 Kampenhout, Belgium. This bistro means "garden of the auction" as it is situated close to the auction house for produce that is marketed world-wide.

Dining at the bistro with Rudi Coosemans, the charming young president of the Belgian Endive Marketing Board and owner of Coosemans Belgium Specialty Produce, we savored superb endive dishes-a luscious creamy potato soup and braised endive gratin, the leaves sealed in ham and a rich cheese sauce, and we learned about this delicious leaf.

"In Belgian 99 out of 100 times endive is served hot, whereas in the States more likely it is served raw," said Coosemans. There is only 1 calorie per leaf and considerable nutritional value in its mineral content. The fresher it is, the sweeter and less bitter. Belgium now exports 3,000 tons a year to the United States. The price paid for endive grown in the traditional soil method is higher than for the water method.

In Brussels one evening, we delved into another food specialty-mussels at Chez Leon. Located in the Galerie de la Reine, a shopping street and market square with 60 restaurants, this is a bustling 100-year-old fish restaurant. It has expanded over the years into a row of eight old houses and is said to average 1,500 covers a day. It offers 12 different mussel preparations ranging from mussels escargot made with parsley butter, to a huge pot of mussels steamed in broth. Gratineed mussels with tomatoes and cheese and cold marinated mussels are other specialties. The busy restaurant also offers chicken, fish, and meats. It is smart to choose the beer over the house wine. The address is Rue des Bouchers 18, tel: 02/511-14-15. No reservations are necessary. There are dozens of other restaurants alongside, each displaying a fancy array of seafood and fresh produce on tables outdoors. Even in late October, night-time patrons were enjoying dining outdoors under canopies and heat lamps at many establishments.

On an afternoon food walking tour, we learned there are 90 breweries making 400 beers in the city. There are 2,00 restaurants in Brussels and 20 brands of chocolate shops. Among them, Leonidos is considered "the fast food of Belgian chocolate." Godiva and Neuhaus are popular and top-of-the-line, and Wittamer is considered the ultimate. Belgian praline is a general term for filled chocolates. In the shops, each candy has a name. It helps to know that gianduja is a milk chocolate and hazelnut paste blended while hot. Praline also means a mixture of milk chocolate and finely ground nuts or toffee. Nougatine is the same as praline, only larger pieces of nuts or toffee are used for a slight crunch. True Belgian chocolates have no preservatives and use no artificial flavors or coloring. The best ones are made with fresh cream and last only a few days. The chocolates are beautifully packaged and sold in boutiques decorated with gold, crystal, and mirrors.

Street food in Belgium means frites or French fries. Stands serve them in a paper cone accompanied by mayonnaise, bearnaise or curry sauce. Another popular fast food is the Belgian waffle. Stands in outdoor markets bake them with crunchy bits of pearl sugar in the batter. Roasted chestnuts are an aromatic item heating in outdoor stalls in the winter months.

Dining in Belgium

Dining in Belgium ranges from modest bistros to elegant Michelin three-star restaurants. Our best meal was at one, De Karmeliet (Langestraat 19, Brugge; tel. 050/33-82-59). Located in an 18th century house in this medieval canal city, the chef serves dazzling plates, as delicious as they are decorative. In the glass-ceilinged entrance area, we were served mussels in aspic, salmon tartare, and rabbit pate with fresh grapefruit and champagne cocktails. In the high-ceilinged dining room, a codfish carpaccio was rimmed with fried leek shavings, and a supreme of pheasant was accompanied by endive, wild mushrooms, and a mashed potato round encased in a sliver of celery root.

Dessert featured poached pears and prunes in a red wine sauce paired with ice cream made with Armagnac brandy. A tray of petit fours encompassed miniature babas, cherries in fondant, chocolate-covered orange peel, and scallop-shaped cinnamon cakes. The luncheon tab per person with wine was just over $100.

Another excellent meal, a farmhouse lunch, was savored at wood plank tables outside of Damme. Chef Marc Nyssen runs De Stampe, 12 Zuiddijk, 88340 Damme, Belgium. Tel: 050/5001997. His is a working family-owned farm, since 1906. He has 80 head of cattle and has developed three guest rooms in the stucco farmhouse that dates from 1680. The dining room used to be a stable. He serves groups during the week and for Sunday dinner by reservation only. He uses all local products and bakes his own bread and tarts in a wood-fired oven.

At two trestle tables, candelabra illuminated our buffet of three local cheeses, platters of pate, a crusty meat loaf, tart cherries in a sauce, and a wonderful shredded carrot, onion, and mushroom open tart. Loaves of crusty whole-grain bread and field greens with olive oil were passed.

Blond and dark beer and Cote du Rhone wine were poured. While we dined, Marc picked the apples from the orchard that swiftly baked into an open-face streusel-topped tart. A pear tart also accompanied the spread.

Our two hotel dinners, featuring such famous Belgian dishes as waterzooi of chicken and eel in sorrel sauce, were a disappointment. By contrast, the hotel's breakfast buffets were spectacular, more sumptuous than anyone could savor with dozens of choices in smoked fish, hot and cold meats, egg dishes, fruits, juices, a cereal bar, and hot breads and rolls.

Recipes

Here are specialties from Belgium. The Belgian Endive Marketing Board shares endive dishes.

Cream of Belgian Endive Soup

Makes 4 servings

2 Belgian endives, cored

1 white onion, diced

1 garlic clove, minced

2 tablespoons butter

2 large potatoes, peeled and diced

2 cups chicken broth

1 cup milk or cream

Salt and pepper to taste

Chopped chives

Dill sprigs for garnish

Mince the endives, reserving a few small leaves for garnish. Saut the onion, garlic, and endives in the butter for 3 minutes. Add the potatoes and chicken broth and simmer for about 15 minutes, or until the potatoes are soft.

Blend until smooth. Ad the milk, salt, and pepper and blend. Serve hot or cold garnish with chopped endive leaves, chives, and dill.

Leek and Potato Soup

Makes 6 servings

1 tablespoon olive oil

1 onion, finely chopped

1 bunch leeks (white part only), sliced

2 garlic cloves, minced

3 cups home-made or canned low-salt chicken broth

2 large golden or russet potatoes or 3/4 pound sunchokes, peeled and diced

2 teaspoons chopped fresh tarragon or 1/2 teaspoon dried tarragon

Salt and freshly ground black pepper, to taste

1/4 cup dry white wine (optional)

1/4 cup heavy cream or plain low-fat yogurt

2 tablespoons finely chopped fresh flat-leaf Italian parsley

Plain low-fat yogurt or sour cream for garnish

In a large saucepot, heat the oil over medium heat and saut the onion, and leeks until soft. Add the garlic, chicken broth, potatoes or sunchokes, and tarragon and bring to a boil. Cover and simmer for 20 minutes or until the vegetables are tender. Let cool slightly, then puree in a blender or a food processor. Season with salt and pepper. Blend in the wine, if desired, and cream or yogurt. Serve hot or cold. Garnish with parsley and a dollop of yogurt or sour cream.

Braised Belgian Endive

Makes 4 servings

8 whole heads of Belgian endive, cored

2 tablespoons butter

3 tablespoons lemon juice

1/2 teaspoon salt

1 tablespoon sugar

Slowly saut the endive in butter in a shallow pan over a medium hot heat. Turn to cook both sides. Add the

other ingredients, cover the pan, and simmer on low for 25 minutes, adding a few drops of water if necessary.

Serve with meat, poultry, or game.

Steamed Mussels

Makes 3 to 4 entree servings or 12 first-course servings.

3 quarts mussels in the shell (about 4 pounds)

3 garlic cloves, minced

6 shallots or green onions, chopped

3 tablespoons olive oil

1 cup dry white wine

1/3 cup minced parsley

Freshly ground black pepper

Melted butter

Soak the mussels for 30 minutes in salted water. Scrub the mussels well under cold running water with a stiff brush. In a large soup kettle, saut the garlic and shallots in oil until soft, stirring. Add wine, parsley, and pepper, and bring to a boil. Add the mussels, cover, and simmer gently until the shells open, about 8 minutes; discard any that do not open. Spoon the mussels into soup bowls and ladle the broth over them. Pass the butter, if desired, for dipping the mussels.

Scallops and Endive with Pasta

Makes 4 servings

2 shallots, chopped

2 garlic cloves, chopped

3 tablespoons olive oil

1 pint cherry tomatoes, halved

1 pinch each of thyme, oregano, and basil

4 Belgian endive, cut up

1 1/2 pounds bay scallops

Splash of sherry

2 tablespoons butter

Basil sprigs for garnish

Hot cooked pasta, such as penne or fettuccine

Saut the shallots and garlic in oil until the shallots are translucent. Add 3 cut up endive, tomatoes, scallops, spices, sherry, and butter. Saut until the scallops are cooked through, about 5 minutes; remove from heat.

Add the reserved cut up endive and stir. Serve over cooked pasta. Garnish with basil.

Pine Nut and Chicory Salad

Makes 2 servings

About 2 cups torn chicory or frisee

1-1/2 tablespoons olive oil

1 tablespoon Balsamic vinegar

1 teaspoon Dijon mustard

Salt and pepper to taste

1 teaspoon fresh chopped tarragon or 1/4 tsp. dried tarragon

1 shallot, chopped

2 tablespoons toasted pine nuts or pistachios

Place the chicory in a medium bowl. In a 1-cup measure combine the oil, vinegar, mustard, salt and pepper, tarragon, shallot, and nuts. Microwave on High 30 seconds to 1 minute or until hot. Toss with the chicory.

Flemish Beef Stew

Makes 6 servings

2 tablespoons flour

Salt and pepper

2 pounds boneless beef chuck, cut in 1 1/2 inch pieces

2 tablespoons butter and olive oil

4 medium onions, sliced

1 garlic clove, crushed

1 bay leaf

1/4 teaspoon dried thyme

2 tablespoons chopped flat-leaf parsley

1 tablespoon brown sugar

1 bottle (12 oz.) dark beer

Beef stock

1 tablespoon cider vinegar

Combine the flour, salt, and pepper in a bag. Add the meat and shake well. Melt half the butter and oil and fry the onions until tender; do not brown. Remove the onions. Brown the meat on all sides in remaining oil and butter. Add the onions, herbs, and sugar. Pour the beer over. Add stock if needed to cover. Cook covered, over low heat for 1 1/2 hours or until the meat is tender, adding more beer or stock if necessary. Just before serving add the vinegar. Serve with hot boiled potatoes and a green salad.

Streusel-Topped Apple Tart

Makes 8 servings

9 or 10-inch pastry-lined pan

10 large Granny Smith apples, cored and sliced

1 tablespoon lemon juice

1 teaspoon cinnamon

1/4 cup sugar

Topping:

4 tablespoons butter

1/3 cup brown sugar, packed

1/2 cup all-purpose flour

Fit the pastry in the pan. Toss the apples with lemon juice, cinnamon, and sugar. Mix the topping until fine crumbs and scatter over. Bake in a preheated 425 degrees Farenheit oven for 15 minutes; reduce heat to 375 degrees and bake 30 minutes longer, covering the top with foil if it browns too much, or until apples are tender.

Serve with cream or ice cream.

BRAZIL

Geography

Brazil, the largest country in South America, borders every other South American country except Chile and Ecuador. From west to east it stretches nearly 2,700 miles from the Andean foothills eastward to the Atlantic Ocean. Its official name is the Federal Republic of Brazil, or, in Portuguese, the Repýÿblica Federativa do Brasil.

It occupies almost half the area of South America and is the world's fifth largest country. Although just slightly smaller than the United States in area, Brazil's population is about 40% less.

Most Brazilians live in the densely populated areas of eastern Brazil. Although urbanization has not produced actual declines in rural population, internal migration has caused cities to grow much faster than rural areas.

The largest cities are Sao Paulo (16 million people), Rio de Janeiro (11 million), Belo Horizante (3.8 million), Salvador (2.3 million), Recife (1.8 million), and Porto Alegre (3.1 million).

Brazil is politically subdivided into 26 states and territories plus the federal district of Brasilia.

Brazil's Eclectic Cuisine

About 1 million native Indians lived in Brazil when the first Portuguese explorers arrived early in the 16th century. Beginning in 1538, almost 5 million Africans arrived before the abolition of slavery in 1888. Portuguese immigrants were followed by Italians, Germans, Syrians, and Lebanese. Asians arrived during the 1930's.

This population mixture has created a national cooking style marked by profound differences. "The cuisine did not evolve, however, by absorbing these influences, eliminating their identity in the process" explains Joan and David Peterson, authors of Eating Smart In Brazil (Ginko Press, 1995). "The distinct contribution of each is still apparent in many Brazilian dishes today. Interestingly, the national cuisine of Brazil is more a collection of unique regional ones."

If one were to divide the country into regions by cuisine there would be five:

North (Acre, Amazonas, Amapÿÿ, Rond)

Collectively, the region is known as Amazÿÿ tributaries flowing into the Amazon River. Culturally, the Amazon basin is heavily populated by native Indians or people of mixed Indian and Portuguese ancestry who live on a diet of fish, root vegetables such as manioc, yams, and peanuts, plus palm or tropical fruits.

The cuisine of this region is heavily Indian influenced. One popular dish is Caruru do Parÿÿ, tomato, cilantro, and dend.

Northeast (Alagoas, Bahia, Cearÿÿ, Maranh)

Geographically the region comprises a dry, semi-arid region used for cattle growing inland from the fertile costal plain, an economically important sugar cane and cacao growing area. The spectacular beaches make the coast Brazil's fastest growing tourist region.

Within the State of Bahia the predominate cuisine is Afro-Bahian, which evolved from plantation cooks improvising on African, Indian, and traditional Portuguese dishes using locally available ingredients.

In the remainder of the coastal plains there is less African influence on the food, but seafood, shellfish, and tropical fruits are menu staples.

Inland, in the drought stricken, arid cattle growing and farm lands, foods typically include ingredients like dried meat, rice, beans, goat, manioc and corn meal.

Central-West (Federal District of Brasilia plus Goýjas, Mato Grosso, and Mato Grosso do Sul)

A region comprising dry open savannahs or prairies with wooded terrain in the north. The famous Pantanal, one of the finest game and fishing regions on earth, is also located within this region.

Fish from the important rivers and beef and pork from the vast ranches of the region dominate the menu, along with the bounty harvested from the agricultural crops of soybean, rice, corn, and manioc.

Southeast (Sao Paulo)

The industrial heart of Brazil is home to the several distinctive styles of cooking.

In Minas the regional dishes include a lot of corn, pork, beans, and local soft ripened cheeses. Around Rio and Sao Paulo a simmered bean and meat dish of Bahian origin, feijoada completa, is popular especially in restaurants as a Wednesday and Saturday luncheon.

Also consumed frequently is arroz-feijao, or rice and beans. Traditionally, black beans are prepared in Rio, red or blonde beans in Sao Paulo, and either black or red in Minas Gerais.

In Sao Paulo, the influence of European and North African immigrants is noticed in the region's cuisine. The majority arrived from Italy, along with many from Portugal and Spain, plus other Europeans and Arab countries.

South (Paranýý, and Santa Catarina)

To the national cuisine the gaucho, or cowboy, contributed dishes made with sun or salt dried meats and churrasco, a meal of wood fire grilled fresh meats.

The immigrant homesteaders, many from Germany and middle Europe plus a few from Italy, were accustomed to a wheat based diet. They were agricultural people who worked the land and introduced wine, leafy vegetables, and dairy products. When potatoes were not available they improvised and discovered the native sweet manioc could be cooked and served in the same way potatoes were served in their homeland.

Staple Ingredients

Beans (feijao)

Beans appear on the table daily in many forms and colors. Some consider the black bean (feijao preto) to be the preferred national bean. It is not uncommon, however, to find dried red beans, blonde beans, brown beans, and pink beans plus black-eyed peas, chick peas, and others in the markets.

Coconut

An important ingredient throughout the country, it is used in soups, cocktails, poultry, fish, and shellfish recipes, as well as desserts and sweets. Various forms are utilized: unripe green coconuts.

Dendýý Oil (azeite de dendýý)

A heavy tropical oil extracted from the African palm growing in Northern Brazil. One of the basic ingredients in Bahian or Afro-Brazilian cuisine, it adds a wonderful flavor and bright orange color to foods. There is no equivalent substitution, but it is available in markets specializing in Brazilian imports.

Dried, Salted Codfish (bacalhau)

Introduced by the Portuguese, it finds its way into appetizers, soups, main courses, and savory puddings. To freshen, one common method is to soak large pieces with the skin and bone removed in cold water for three to four hours, changing the water every hour.

Dried Shrimp (camarao seco)

In various sizes, dried shrimp are utilized in many dishes from the northern regions of the country. Usually obtainable in North America at oriental or Latin food stores. Before use they are covered with cold water and soaked overnight (do not keep refreshing with fresh water). The water is discarded before the shrimp are used. The residual salt is usually enough that more is not added to a recipe.

Lemon (limýÿo)

In Brazil the fruit is green, small and quite tart, more like our lime as is specified in most recipes here.

Rice, Brazilian Style (arroz brasileiro or arroz simples)

Long grained rice briefly sauteed in garlic and oil before the addition of boiling water. In addition to garlic, some Brazilian cooks add small amounts of onion, diced tomato, or sliced black olive for additional flavor. Properly done, each grain is fluffy and separate from others.

Hint on making Brazilian-style rice: Heat vegetable oil in a saucepan and saute a clove of garlic. When browned add salt. Add the rice and saute 2 to 3 minutes – until it looks translucent. Do not allow the grains to brown. Add hot water (about 2 to 2-1/2 cups per cup of rice). Cook, partially covered, over medium-high heat until most of the water is absorbed. Uncover, lower the heat and continue cooking until fluffy.

Toasted Manioc Meal (farofa or farinha de mandioca)

Manioc flour lightly sauteed in butter until it resembles buttered bread crumbs. Other ingredients are frequently added (see recipe).

Recipes

The recipes have been selected to illustrate typical foods from throughout Brazil that will appeal to North Americans. All can be easily recreated in home kitchens from ingredients available in any supermarket. One or two special ingredients might be found in Latin or oriental markets.

It does not include the foods that have been frequently described in the press and cookbooks – dishes such as feijoada (the Brazilian national dish of black beans and meats), vatapa (a spicy, Bahian seafood dish), Couve ýÿ Mineira (sauteed kale from Minas Gerais), Bolinhos de Arroz (fried rice balls), Brigadeiros (a candy), or desserts like torta de banana.

Appetizers

Sopa de Palmito (Cream of Palm Heart Soup)

Serves 4

1 can Hearts of Palm

4 tablespoons Butter

4 tablespoons Flour

2 cups Chicken Stock

1 cup Milk

1 cup Heavy cream

White pepper, to taste

Drain and rinse the palm hearts. Place in a food processor and puree.

Melt butter in a saute pan. Add flour and cook over low heat, stirring constantly, into a blonde roux.

Slowly add warm chicken stock, stirring with a wire whip so it is lump free. Blend in the palm hearts. Add the milk and cream just before serving. Bring to serving temperature, but do not allow to boil. Add a little pepper to accent the taste.

Pasteis Fritos (Fried Turnovers)

Pastry shops frequently use the same fillings (chicken, beef, seafood, vegetables, or cheeses) to make small tartlettes (empadas) which also are served as appetizers. Makes two or more dozen depending on diameter.

Pasteis generally are filled with mixtures of meat, chicken or cheese. They are best served warm immediately after frying.

Pasteis dough:

2/3 cup Butter (or part vegetable shortening)

2 cups Flour, all purpose

1 teaspoon Salt

1 Egg yolk, beaten

3/4 cup Water, cold

Combine the flour and salt in a bowl. Add the rest of the ingredients and most of the water. Mix well with the finger tips, adding a few more drops of water if the dough sees dry. Cover with plastic film and let rest an hour.

In the same family are Risoles, a turnover shaped appetizer made with a cooked dough that is egg or water washed then coated with manioc meal before frying. Risoles are usually filled with cheese, shrimp or hearts of palm mixtures. One advantage is they can be held warm for a longer time than a Pasteis.

Risoles dough:

2 tablespoons Butter

2 cups Milk

1 teaspoon Salt

2 cups Flour, all purpose

Combine the butter, milk, and salt in a medium saucepan. Bring to a boil, remove from the heat, and add the flour. Stir until well combined. Cool completely then knead until smooth. Cover with plastic film and let rest an hour.

Recheio de Carne (meat filling)

1/2 pound Ground beef

1 tablespoon Olive oil

1/2 cup onion, minced

2 tablespoons Fresh parsley, chopped fine

2 tablespoons Tomato sauce

to taste Salt, pepper, pepper sauce

1 egg, hard cooked, chopped

12 Olives, pitted

Cook and cool the meat filling. On a lightly floured surface, roll out dough until very thin. Cut 4-inch circles, remove scrap (which may be combined with fresh dough for re-rolling). Brush the circles lightly with water. Place about 1-1/2 teaspoon of filling in the center of each circle. Fold in half and pinch to seal. Preheat oil to 365 degrees Farenheit in a deep fryer or high sided pan. Fry until golden, about two minutes. Drain on absorbent paper and serve warm. They will hold in a 250 degrees Farenheit oven for up to 30 minutes.

Bolinhos de Bacalhau (Codfish balls)

A wonderfully tasty appetizer (salgado). Great with a cocktail or glass of cold beer.

1 pound Dried codfish

1 tablespoon Butter

2 teaspoon Chives, chopped

2 teaspoons Parsley, chopped

1/2 cup Onion, diced fine

1 cup Milk

2 cups Potatoes, cooked and mashed

3 tablespoons Flour

1/2 teaspoon Paprika

3 large Eggs, slightly beaten

Soak codfish overnight. Drain, cover with fresh water and simmer for 25 to 30 minutes. Remove bones and skin then chop fine. Heat butter in a saute pan.

Add chives, parsley, onion, and fish. When the onion is translucent remove from the heat and add remaining ingredients. Combine well. Check seasonings. Let the mixture cool and firm up for about 10 minutes.

Shape into small balls or cakes. Drop into hot oil, frying until golden. Drain on absorbent paper and serve warm.

Pao de Queijo (Cheese bread)

A famous bread from the state of Minas Gerais served at most steak houses in southern Brazil. Unusual in that the recipe calls for manioc starch (available in some Latin groceries) rather than wheat flour. Leavening is from steam during baking, similar to the way eclairs are leavened. These rolls do not hold well and are best consumed while warm, directly from the oven. In Brazil these rolls would be made with Queijo de Minas, a mild, white cheese similar to Muenster in texture - but quite different in taste. They are addictive.

16 ounces Manioc starch (polvilho)

1/2 cup Sunflower seed oil

3/4 cup lowfat milk

3 eggs, large

1/3 cup Parmesan cheese, grated

1-3/4 cups Mild cheddar, grated

Bring milk and oil to a boil in a small saucepan. Add to the manioc. Mix and allow to cool a little. Incorporate the eggs, one at a time. Add the cheese and blend well.

Divide into pieces the size of a walnut or small plum. Place a little oil on the hands and round dough into balls. Arrange on a baking sheet. Bake at 375 degrees Farenheit until done, about 10 to 12 minutes. Serve warm.

Main Dishes

Caruru do Par (Shrimp and Okra entree)

Serves 6

From the northern state of Parýÿ, a dish with African origins made with dried shrimp, okra, and dendýÿ oil. Other versions from the states of Bahia and Maranh o are prepared with a combination of fresh and dried shrimp and sometimes peanuts.

2-1/4 pound Dried Shrimp, skin on

1 pound Fresh, small okra, cut in 1-inch slices

1/4 cup Olive Oil

1 large Onion, diced

3 medium Tomatoes, de-seeded and cut in medium dice

6 sprigs Parsley

6 leaves Cilantro

2 cloves Garlic

2 tablespoons Manioc (farinha de mandioca fina), lightly toasted

Soak shrimp overnight in cold water. Drain and discard the soaking water. Peel the shrimp and place in a sauce pan. Add 3 cups of water and bring to a boil. Strain the shrimp water into another sauce pan. Reserve the shrimp. Cook the okra in the shrimp water until tender, but still crisp.

Heat olive oil in a saute pan. Saute shrimp with the onion, tomato, parsley, cilantro and garlic. Add these ingredients to the shrimp water and okra.

Dissolve the manioc meal in 1/2 cup of water. Add and cook over low heat until the manioc swells up. Add the dendýÿ oil. Serve at once accompanied by white rice and farofa.

Moqueca de Camarao (Shrimp Stew, Bahian style)

Serves 6

These savory stews are made with a variety of proteins including shrimp, dried shrimp, or, when economy is important, fish. They always include two of the three ingredients referred to as the "Holy Trinity of Bahian cuisine" – coconut milk, dendýÿ oil. The third, malagueta pepper, is placed on the table for adding as desired.

30 Shrimp, 21-25 count headless

3 tablespoons Fresh lime juice

1/2 teaspoon Salt

3/4 cup Thin coconut milk (see recipe)

1/3 cup Olive oil

2 large Onions, halved and thin sliced

1 large Garlic clove, crushed and minced

1 medium Green pepper, seeded and sliced

3 medium Tomatoes, seeded and sliced

2 tablespoon Tomato paste

3 stalks Green onion, sliced thin up to the green

1-1/2 teaspoon Fresh parsley, minced

1/3 cup Dendýÿ oil

Peel and devein the shrimp. Place in a small bowl and sprinkle with lime juice and salt. Marinate while preparing the other ingredients. Heat olive oil in a saute pan. Add onion, garlic and peppers. Saute until the onions are almost translucent then add tomatoes, tomato paste, scallions, and parsley. Cook until soft then add the shrimp and lime juice. Continue cooking until the shrimp are done (2 to 3 minutes).

Add the coconut milk and dendÿÿ oil. Return to almost a boil for a minute. Adjust seasonings. Serve over white rice or rice cooked in coconut milk.

Frigideira (Seafood fritatta)

A savory dish traditionally baked in an earthenware platter. The top layer of a Frigideira is always a layer of beaten eggs. In southern Brazil these dishes are called fritada.

3/4 cup Coconut milk (see recipe)

1 pound Seafood - crabmeat, shrimp, fish or a combination

2 tablespoon Lime juice

1 teaspoon Salt

1 large Onion, chopped

2 Tomatoes, seeded and chopped

2 sprigs Fresh coriander, minced

1 clove Garlic, minced

2 tablespoons Olive oil

Salt and pepper to taste

4 eggs, well beaten

Prepare the coconut milk. Season seafood with lime juice and salt. Marinate briefly before gently sauteing until cooked. Chop about half the seafood in a food processor. Reserve the remaining.

Heat oil in a saute pan. Add onion, tomato, coriander, garlic, and chopped seafood. Saute until the onions are translucent. Add coconut milk and adjust seasonings. Cover, continue cooking on low heat for 10 minutes.

Beat the eggs. Combine about 2/3 of the egg with the cooked mixture and reserved seafood. Pour into an oven proof baking dish (glass pie pans work well if a Frigideira casserole is not available). Top with the remaining beaten egg.

Place into a 375 degree oven and bake about 15 minutes, until set.

Serve hot accompanied with farofa.

Strogonoff de Camarao (Shrimp Stroganoff)

Serves 4

A favorite in fine restaurants around Sao Paulo. Also appears on menus with chicken or beef although shrimp is much more elegant.

1 pound Shrimp, peeled and deveined

1 Lime

1/2 large Onion, chopped

1 tablespoon Vegetable or olive oil

1/2 cup Catsup

2 cups Heavy cream

1/4 cup Cognac

1 can Hearts of Palm, drained & cut in 1/2-inch slices

Squeeze lime juice over the shrimp and marinate while preparing other ingredients.

Heat oil in a saute pan. Add shrimp and rapidly cook. Remove and reserve.

Add onion and cook over medium heat until translucent. Add the cream and bring to a boil. Reduce by about one-quarter to thicken slightly. Add the catsup and cognac.

Return the shrimp to the pan. Add hearts of palm and bring to serving temperature. Adjust seasoning with salt and white pepper. Serve, accompanied by Brazilian white rice (arroz simples).

Lombo com Farofa (Roast Loin of Pork accompanied by toasted manioc)

Serves 8

6 pounds Boneless pork loin

2 Limes

Salt to taste

1 large onion, cut in thin slices

1/4 cup Soybean oil

2 tablespoons Parsley

2 tablespoons Green onions or scallions, sliced

2 tablespoons Margarine

1 quart milk, warm

Farofa:

2 cups Manioc flour

1 tablespoon Margarine

1 tablespoon Soybean oil

1 medium Onion, grated

2 Tomatoes, peeled, seeded and chopped

2 tablespoons Parsley, chopped

2 tablespoons Green onions, chopped

1 Hard boiled egg, chopped

1/4 cup Raisins

1/4 cup Dried prunes, chopped

1/4 cup Walnuts

The day before roasting, cut some shallow slashes in the top of the loin and season with salt and lime juice. Top meat with onion, oil, and scallions. Cover with plastic film and refrigerate.

The next day, rub the margarine on the loin and brown-off on all sides in a hot pan. Add warm milk, cover and continue cooking until soft.

Transfer the meat to a roast pan. Strain juices from the overnight marination and pour over the loin. Place in a pre-heated 325 degree oven to roast until done.

To prepare farofa, place manioc flour in a bowl, add a little water and stir until evenly moistened. In a saute pan, heat the margarine and oil. Add onion and tomato, sauteing until the onion is translucent. Add manioc and combine well. Remove from heat and stir in the remaining ingredients.

Slice the pork, reassemble and arrange on a platter with the farofa alongside the meat.

Bife – Parmigiana (Beef steak Parmigiana)

Serves 6

My wife, Marcia, prepares and fries steaks in the same manner and then serves it without the toppings or sauce. When prepared in this simpler, and even more popular style, is called Bife ýÿ Milanesa.

6 pieces Round steak or sirloin, 1/4" thick slices

to taste Salt & pepper

1 small Onion, cut in thin slices

2 large Eggs

Flour

Olive oil

6 slices Mozzarella cheese

6 slices Boiled ham

1-1/2 cups Crushed tomato

1/2 cup Beef stock

to taste Fresh oregano

Flatten the steaks slightly, season with salt, pepper and onion. Set aside to allow seasonings to penetrate a little. Beat the eggs, add a little salt. Dip the beef in flour then egg then again in flour.

Heat about an inch of oil to 365 degree in a large saute pan. Fry steaks until evenly browned and crisp on both sides. Remove from the pan and arrange in an oven proof serving dish. Top each steak with a slice of ham then cheese.

In a small saucepan bring the tomato to a boil, add beef stock and oregano then simmer for a few minutes. Pour over steaks, place the pan in the oven and heat for about 8 minutes, until hot and the cheese is melted. Serve with thin cut french fries.

Frango ao Vinho (Breast of chicken in red wine sauce)

Serves 6

3 slices Bacon

6 pieces Chicken breast, skinless and boneless

to taste Salt & pepper

1 cup Flour

2 tablespoons Olive oil

1-1/2 cups Small pearl onions, peeled

1 cup Dry red wine

1/2 cup Chicken stock

to taste Thyme, dry

Fry bacon until crisp, drain on absorbent paper, break into pieces and reserve.

Season breasts with salt and pepper. Dip in flour. Heat olive oil in the saute pan. Add breasts and brown well on both sides. Remove from the pan and keep warm.

In the same pan add onions, wine, stock and thyme. Cook until the onion is soft and the sauce thickens. Adjust seasonings. Return the meat to the pan and continue cooking until done.

At service, place some sauce on the plate under the breast. Garnish the onions and bacon.

Accompaniments

Farofa (accompaniment to many meat and seafood dishes)

For an elegant variation see the Lombo com farofa recipe.

2 cups Manioc flour

2 tablespoons Butter

pinch Salt

Melt butter in a heavy saute pan. Add the manioc and slowly cook over low heat until a light golden brown. It will resemble buttered bread crumbs.

Add a pinch of salt. Serve as an accompaniment from a ceramic bowl (farinheira).

Farofa is frequently prepared with one or more added ingredients such as raisins, onion, olives, sausage (lingýÿiýÿa), hard cooked egg, parsley, etc.

In Bahia, the manioc is sauteed in dendýÿ oil giving it a yellow color, hence the name farofa amarela.

Aipim frita (Yuca or manioc fries)

Serves 6

1 pound Fresh manioc (aipim, mandioca doce, or macaxeira)

salt, to taste

Slice fresh manioc into 3-inch pieces. Peel and place in a saucepan. Cover with water, bring to a boil and simmer until tender (20 to 30 minutes). Drain well, cool and cut into 3/4-inch wedges. Discard the woody center core.

Heat oil in a deep fat fryer to 360 degrees. Fry the wedges until golden brown. Drain on absorbent paper and salt to taste.

Coconut Milk (an ingredient in many other recipes)

One coconut yields about 1 pound of fresh meat, enough to make about 3/4 cup of thick milk plus about 3 cups of thin milk.

To make milk, pierce the three small eyes in the end of the shell, drain and reserve the water.

Crack the shell, peel off the outer rind and grate the white meat. Place it in a double boiler and warm gently. When hot add 1/2 cup of warm water. Press this thick milk thru a fine sieve or cheesecloth.

To make thin milk combine the grated residue, drained coconut water, and enough additional warm water to make about three cups. Extract the thin milk as above.

Desserts

Creme de Abacate (Avocado Cream)

Serves 4

Brazil is possibly the only cuisine that sweetens avocado and serves it as a dessert, rather than salted as in guacamole or salads.

2 medium Avocados

2 tablespoon Lime juice

4 tablespoon Granulated sugar

1/4 cup Ice water

Peel and slice the avocado, discarding the seed. Place fruit, lime juice and sugar in a food processor or blender. Puree at high speed until completely smooth. Add a little water if the puree is very stiff (some prefer white wine). It should be absolutely smooth and creamy. If lumpy, force through a wire strainer. Serve in a clear glass.

Merengue de Morango (Strawberry meringue)

In Brazil tortes are generally not iced with butter cream, but more traditionally with fresh whipped cream, glazes, meringue and marshmallow.

In Sao Paulo, at the leading upscale shopping centers, the company Amor aos Pedaýÿos prepares a delightful fresh strawberry creation that is typical of Brazilian style pastry.

Deceptively simple to make, it almost must be assembled at the last minute to minimize the migration of moisture into the crisp meringue layers. These 10-inch diameter, about 3/4-inch high, layers can be baked ahead using any standard meringue recipe.

Just be sure to keep the meringue from browning and to bake very, very dry – in other words, keep the heat down to dry then out rather than "bake" them.

The torte is assembled by layering the meringue rounds with fresh strawberries and fresh whipped cream.

Brazilian whipped cream is flavored with vanilla, but has much less sugar than normal. This allows the wonderful flavor of the cream to come through.

Some of the strawberries are cut into pieces and combined with a little sugar to make a slightly sweetened fresh filling. The top is garnished with halves of fresh, vine ripened berries.

By leaving the sides exposed and allowing the whipped cream filling and meringue layers to show, the torte presents a genuine home-made appearance.

Biscoitos de Maizena (Cornstarch cookies)

Yield: about 3 dozen

A light, airy cookie made with cornstarch rather than flour. Sold in cellophane bags in nearly every supermarket and pastry shop in the country.

2 cups Cornstarch

1/4 teaspoon Salt

1 cup Granulated sugar

1 large Egg

1/4 teaspoon Vanilla

3/4 cup Butter

Combine the cornstarch, salt and sugar. Add egg and vanilla. Blend completely. Add the butter and mix well.

Let rest 15 minutes then form into 1-inch balls. Place on a greased or paper lined baking sheet. Bake at 375 degrees for 5 to 7 minutes.

8

Cuisines of Britain and China

INTRODUCTION

Great Britain, an island country in northwestern Europe, is really four countries – England, Northern Ireland, Scotland, and Wales. It goes by the familiar names of Britain and the United Kingdom, as well. It ranks 73rd in size among the countries of the world and has about one percent of the population.

Though this country contains few natural resources, it has played a prominent role world-wide. It started the Industrial Revolution and founded the largest, most powerful empire in the world – and then declined. By 1900 its empire covered one-fourth of the world's land, containing one-fourth of the people. Though still a leader, it is no longer the world power it once was.

British cookery has been much maligned and has improved ramatically in the restaurants and country inns in the past decade.

Traditional British cuisine is substantial, yet simple and wholesome. The Brits have long believed in four meals a day. Their fare has been influenced by the traditions and tastes from different parts of the ritish empire: teas from Ceylon and chutney, kedgeree, and ulligatawny soup from India. The British nanny has also played a role with her nursery favorites, such as Bread and Butter Pudding, Spotted Dick, and Treacle Tart. Roast beef with Yorkshire Pudding and Plum Pudding are important contributions to international cuisine. Other popular dishes include Cornish Pasties and Beefsteak and Kidney Pie. The English developed a line of spicy sauces including ketchup, mint sauce, Worcestershire sauce and deviled sauce.

Today there is an emphasis on fine, fresh ingredients in the better restaurants and their markets offer countless worldly items. Salmon, Dover sole, prawns, game, and lamb are choice items. Wild fowl and game are specialties.

Among English cakes and pastries, many are tied to the various holidays of the year. Hot Cross Buns are eaten on Good Friday, Simnel Cake is for Mothering Sunday, Plum Pudding for Christmas, and Twelfth Night Cake for Epiphany. Local delicacies include Bath Buns, Chelsea Buns, Eccles Cakes, and Banbury Cakes. Cheeses are choice regional specialties, including Stilton, farm-house cheddars and Cheshire Cheese.

The Scottish have their own national dishes, based upon wild products and food, locally produced in this northern region. They include oats, barley, fowl, game, mutton, salmon, herring, and haddock. Oat cakes, shortbread, black buns, bannocks, finnan haddies and haggis are specialties.

Ethnic restaurants – French, Italian, Indian, Greek, Thai and many others – are very popular in the British Isles.

CHINA

Chinese food, having been served to generations of Americans, has a strong hold on our culinary imagination. For many, the delightfully salty, flavorsome dishes served in the spartan restaurants with names like " Dragon Garden" and "Five Happiness" are their first taste of a foreign cuisine. Most American towns have a Chinese restaurant. When we were children and bored with Mom's cooking, the arrival of the little white cartons of takeout Chinese promised a taste of the exotic and uncommon. Dishes such as chop suey, General Tso's chicken, and mu shu pork are deeply familiar to most of us. And the inevitable fortune cookie, it might be argued, is something of a cultural icon.

And yet, true Chinese cuisine, as it is found in China, is worlds away from these tastydishes. As the hamburger seems to represent American cooking for foreigners, so do these restaurant dishes signify Chinese food for many Americans. Happily, travelers to China (and food enthusiasts at home, thanks to the surge of well researched Chinese cookbooks) are discovering that China is nothing less than a universe of food. This country, with a culinary history of thousands of years, employs a staggering variety of ingredients and methods of preparation in its cuisine, none of which make it to U.S. restaurant tables. This article will discuss the components of true Chinese cuisine, and give a breakdown of the four major regional styles.

General Remarks on Chinese Food

Climate and Agriculture

In order to feed its 1.3 billion people, China must produce a tremendous amount of food. It is one of the most densely cultivated countries on earth. Agriculture varies from region to region given climate and landscape factors, although today there is plenty of trade between north and south. China's enormous northern half, stretching from Beijing to Xinjiang in Chinese Central Asia, is comprised of grasslands, mountains, and deserts. The climate is harsh; cold and dry in winter and hot and dusty in summer. Mostly hardy crops are grown and eaten in these areas—corn, sorghum, wheat, cabbages and root vegetables. Traditionally wheat and corn are the staple grains, yet today some rice is consumed in the North as well. The bottom half of the country, basically the provinces surrounding and south of the Yangtze River, is green and lush, with rivers, lakes, and a higher rainfall. Rice is the staple crop of these areas, with some wheat and mixed grains grown as well. China, particularly south China, is a produce-rich country—among other things, north China grows peaches, apples, and melons, while south China produces enormous amounts of produce such as taro root, eggplants, tomatoes, and leafy greens, and tropical fruits—longans, litchis, mangoes, bananas, and coconuts.

A Typical Meal: 'Fan' and 'Cai'

Anyone who's eaten Chinese food knows that steamed white rice always accompanies the meal. But what is perhaps less well known is just how integral rice and grain based foods are in Chinese culture. The Mandarin word *fan* means both 'rice' and 'food.' In China, a good deal of casual talk centers around the expression, "*ni chi fan le ma?*" literally meaning, "Have you eaten rice (food) yet?" Regardless of region, a typical Chinese meal consists of a grain base—the *fan*—such as rice, noodles, or buns, with meat and vegetable dishes, referred to as *cai*, adding flavor and variety to, but not overriding the integrity of, the *fan*. The possibilities for *cai* are enormous. China's abundant variety of meats and vegetables are stir-fried, stewed, steamed, baked, roasted, oil and water-blanched, deep-fried...every kind of cooking method is well represented. Throughout China, pork is the most widespread and best-loved meat. In the north and west, pork and mutton are eaten in abundance, while south and east China have a profusion of fish and shellfish, as well as poultry, pork, and soy products.

Seasonings in Chinese cooking are too numerous to count. A few commonly used seasonings are soy sauce, fermented bean paste, black rice vinegar, rice wine, sesame oil, chili oil, ginger, red chili pastes, and garlic.

Regardless of region, the food of China's poorest is similar everywhere. These meals will usually consist of simple grain foods eaten with salty pickles to add flavor. Meat is used relatively sparingly, as it is expensive. However, Chinese peasant food is often quite tasty, and a trip to a country village is well worth the simpler fare.

Drinks and Desserts

In China, mealtime drinks range from delicate teas to blinding moonshine-style liquors. By far the most well known Chinese drink is tea, of which there are numerous types. These teas range in flavor, from sweet to bitter, earthy to smoky. Highly favored are green teas, the choicest being "Dragon Well" tea from Hangzhou province. Oolong teas, in which the leaves are allowed to partially ferment, are slightly bitter and metallic tasting. There are also black teas (the Chinese call them red teas.) These teas are dark and strong tasting, the leaves often double fermented. Tea is drunk with breakfast, lunch, and dinner, with snacks or whenever one feels like it.

As with tea, alcoholic drinks have a longstanding tradition in China. Chinese women generally do not drink, leaving the country's alcohol consumption to the men. In China, wine *(jiu)* is made from fermented rice and other grains, with varying degrees of alcoholic strength. Grape wine is not commonly drunk, although today there are vineyards in China producing western style Cabernet

Sauvignons, Merlots and the like. Many Chinese rice wines, such as wines from Shaoxing in southeastern China, have a nutty, sherry-like quality. Spirits are grain-based, often made with sorghum and herbs. Many of them are extremely strong and have an unforgettably strange, sweet fragrance. Extremely popular (especially in the north) is a strong smelling sorghum liquor called *bai jiu*. This is close to moonshine in strength and appearance. Many Chinese men drink *bai jiu* in copious quantities, and will usually offer it to interested foreigners. Be warned – the cheaper kinds are little better than bathtub liquor!

Traditionally, the Chinese have not had much of a taste for western-style desserts. Chinese versions of western desserts such as cookies, cakes, and ice cream tend to be much less sugary tasting than their western counterparts. Pastries are made with rice flour and a number of fillings, such as bean paste, candied egg yolk, lotus seed, or mashed pumpkin. The Moon Festival in early autumn brings *yue bing*, moon cakes, round pastries with various sweet fillings which are given as gifts. Often Chinese meals simply end with fresh fruit.

The Four Major Cuisines

Divisions between Chinese culinary regions have blurred somewhat in modern times, given trading and migration between regions over the years. But today, as in the past, Chinese food is classified into four schools, based in the north, south, east, and west of the country. Each cuisine boasts of famous dishes as well as lesser-known specialties of the city, town, and countryside. The amazing number of available foodstuffs, and a variety of preparations, provides presents travelers in China with a happy problem: one hardly knows what to try next.

The North

I have asked many Chinese friends in Beijing which region of China has the poorest food. "The north!" is always the answer, accompanied by a rueful smile. General opinion deems northern Chinese cooking the 'poorest' of the four schools, because of the lack of variety in ingredients and preparation relative to other regions. Nonetheless, the traveler will find plenty of delicious dishes available. Northern cuisine favors straightforward tastes, with garlic, scallions, leeks and chilies some primary flavor notes. Mutton and pork are the meats of choice (mutton being particularly used in the Muslim northwest.) Poultry is only used by the wealthy or on special occasions (chickens are commonly kept by poorer folk, but used for their eggs.) Seafood is rare. Northern cuisine uses salt and oil liberally and doesn't shy away from animal fat (especially pork fat.) These last two seasonings have the advantage of adding calories to the diet in the north's bitterly cold winters. Often northern Chinese will preserve vegetables for the winter, such as cabbages, carrots and radishes (Korean *kim chi* style pickles are common.) Cabbages and mustard greens are made into side dishes.

Rice, while common in cities and restaurants, is secondary to wheat products such as pancakes, steamed buns, noodles, and dumplings. The north is famous for these grain-based foods, many of which are eaten as snacks. Travelers in north China (particularly to Beijing) will become familiar with *jiaozi,* delicious meat or vegetable filled dumplings dipped in a black vinegar sauce. For breakfast there are *mantou* or *baozi,* steamed buns eaten with *zhou,* rice porridge. Noodles abound, stir-fried or in soups. The Chinese liking for noodles would seem to rival that of the Italians. A wealth of pasta shapes, thicknesses, and textures are available in markets, freshly made or dried, and in restaurants.

Beijing, the nation's capital, is a gastronome's delight, with many national and international cuisines available. The area has always had, and continues to have, its own particular cuisine. From about 1000 A.D. onwards, the imperial presence in Beijing demanded suitably elaborate foods, with thousands of dishes prepared for state dinners and private banquets. Bear's paws, camel's humps, and bird's nests were just a few of the exotica gracing the emperor's tables. The Beijing cuisine of today is called *lao Beijing cai,* ('old Beijing food') and, being classic northern food, is nowhere near as exotic as the imperial cuisine of old. Roasted mutton and chicken are common in *lao Beijing* restaurants, as well as salty vegetable dishes.

Certainly one of the most elegant and famous Chinese dishes, both in China and abroad, comes from Beijing— Peking duck. Classic Beijing duck meals are three courses, with almost every part of the duck used. First, a meticulously raised duck is glazed and roasted. The first course is crispy duck skin, wrapped in thin pancakes with scallions and dipped in a black bean sauce. In the second course, the duck meat is stir-fried; in the third, the bones are used to make soup.

The East

Eastern Chinese cuisine, found in the cities of Shanghai and Hangzhou as well as the surrounding provinces, is primarily a cuisine of sweetness. This school uses sugar, wines, and vinegars to provide sweet tastes and create subtlety of flavor. Like the north, eastern cooks favor oily dishes, although these are more subtle than in those in the north. Seafood is abundant, as the Yangtze River drains into the ocean near Shanghai. The lakes and river tributaries provide abundant fish and shellfish to this region. Pork and poultry are used as well. Soups and soupy dishes are very popular. Shanghai is known for its unusual 'soup inject,' dishes, which are meatballs, dumplings, or buns filled with a gelatin and stock mixture and cooked until the inside is soup. Because of the French and British presence there in the 19 th and 20 th centuries, Shanghai cooking incorporates some European influence. There are Shanghai-style *zakuski* (Russian cold appetizers) in fancy restaurants, and French-style cakes and pastries in the sidewalk cafés.

The West

The food of China's west, including the provinces of Sichuan, Hunan and Yunnan, is nothing less than vibrant. It combines a cornucopia of eastern spices with a natural abundance of ingredients. Meats are primarily pork, beef, and poultry, while vegetables and fruits are tenfold. Bean dishes, such as tofu, are also common. This is a sophisticated and highly spiced cuisine, often extremely spicy hot. Red chili appears in many dishes, often to extremes rivaling that of Mexican or Thai preparations.

Of this school, the cooking of Sichuan (Szechuan) is the most famous, although Hunanese food, which is quite similar, is also popular. (Mao Zedong was from Hunan and preferred the dishes of his home province above all others.) While many Chinese-American 'Szechuan' restaurants serve some version of Sichuan food, it is generally a pale imitation of the real thing. Common Sichuanese spices include cassia bark, cumin, cinnamon, various peppercorns, star anise, and dried tangerine peel, among others. As in the region as a whole, red chili peppers are extremely common in Sichuanese food. It is by no means always spicy, however. One classic Sichuan dish is *ma po dou fu*, soft tofu cubes in a 'numbing-spicy" ground pork and chili sauce. The unusual 'numbing' flavor, called *ma la* in Chinese, comes from the Sichuan red peppercorn which, when eaten, makes the tongue and mouth numb and tingly. The Chinese believe *ma la* dishes are good for the health in cold, wet weather.

The South

The food of the south is widely regarded as the country's best. Southern Chinese cuisine centers on Guangdong province and its capital, Guangzhou (once called Canton), and Hong Kong. A famous proverb illustrates the fame of Guangdong food: "Live in Hangzhou, marry in Suzhou, dine in Guangzhou, and die in Luzhou." (These cities are said to have the best view, the prettiest women, the best food, and the best coffin wood, respectively).

This subtropical region is rich in resources, and Guangdong chefs have abundant produce, seafood, and meats at their disposal. Guangdong cuisine incorporates ingredients from all over China and is known for its sometime use of 'exotic' animals.

As another culinary proverb states, in Guangdong cuisine, "anything that walks, swims, crawls, or flies with its back to Heaven is edible." To be sure, travelers to this region will notice a perhaps-shocking array of animals for sale in the marketplace—dogs, cats, snakes, and turtles are some of the more commonplace. However, these foods are not eaten that often, and there are plenty of 'ordinary' dishes available—let it only be said that this region of China is ideal for the gastronomic adventurer!

Above all else, classical Guangdong cooking emphasizes absolute freshness of ingredients and correct technique. Ingredients are usually prepared with a light touch, just enough cooking and seasoning to bring out the natural flavors of the foods. Guangdong cuisine uses a wide range of cooking techniques, but steaming and stir frying are especially common. The cuisine is famous for its seafood, especially steamed fish and shellfish prepared in various ways. Pork and duck are glazed with mixtures of sugar, wine, and soy and roasted to a beautiful golden-red.

These Guangdong-style roasted ducks are often seen hanging in Chinatown shop windows the world over. Dishes are almost always served with freshly cooked rice, since Guangdong is part of a rice growing region.

Travelers to China, and food enthusiasts interested in authentic Chinese cuisine, have discovered an amazing amount of unusual ingredients, flavors and preparations in Chinese food. It may soon be that diners in Chinese-American restaurants will sit down to a dish of twice-cooked pork belly, Beijing-style mustard cabbage, or duck and taro stew. Here's hoping.

Recipe

Ma po dou fu (Sichuan)

(The following recipe is adapted from "The Chinese Kitchen" by Eileen Yin-Fei Lo. For a more intensive Sichuan "numbing spicy" taste, substitute whole Sichuan peppercorns in the dish.)

For the sauce:

1 tablespoon dry sherry or Shaoxing rice wine

2 ½ teaspoons Chinese rice wine vinegar, or distilled vinegar

1 tablespoon sugar

¼ teaspoon salt

2 teaspoons soy sauce

2 ½ teaspoons dark soy sauce

¼ cup ketchup

2 ½ tablespoons cornstarch

1 tablespoon sesame oil

pinch Sichuan peppercorn powder

1 1/3 cups chicken stock or broth

(For the rest of the dish)

¼ cup peanut oil

2 teaspoons peeled, minced fresh ginger

5 small dried Chinese chilies, chopped (or use fresh red Thai chilies if Chinese are unavailable.)

1 ½ teaspoons minced garlic

½ pound lean ground pork

1 ½ tablespoons chili sauce

6 cakes fresh medium-firm tofu, cut into ¼ inch cubes

1/3 cup sliced scallions

1 tablespoon sesame oil

Mix together the sauce ingredients and set aside.

Heat a wok or large pot over high heat for 30 seconds and add peanut oil. Coat the wok with the oil. When the oil is barely smoking, add the ginger, Thai chilies, and garlic and cook, stirring, for 1 minute. Add the ground pork and cook for 1 minute, or until the pork is no longer pink. Stir in the chili sauce until well-combined then add the tofu and cook, mixing together, for 3 minutes or until it begins to boil. Make a well in the center of the tofu-pork mixture, stir the sauce ingredients, and pour them in. Stir and cook for 1 minute or until the sauce begins to bubble and thicken. Turn off the heat, garnish with chopped scallions, and serve with hot cooked rice.

Glossary

- *Baozi*—a steamed bun with a pork and vegetable filling
- *Cai*—Mandarin, 'dish,' (type of cuisine, i.e. ' Shanghai cai') or 'vegetable'
- *Cha*--tea
- Cassia bark—a type of bark with a cinnamon-like odor, used in western Chinese cooking
- *Dou fu*—(tofu) soybean curd
- *Fan*— 'rice' or 'food '
- *Jiaozi*—boiled dumplings with meat and vegetable fillings
- *Jiu*—wine
- Litchi—(lychee), a small, round sweet fruit with a brown peel and white flesh grown in south China

- Longan – a litchi-like fruit
- *Mantou* – steamed bun
- *Ma la* – 'numbing-*spicy*,' used to describe a certain combination of flavors in Sichuan food
- *Mien* – noodles
- *Rou* – 'meat' *Jirou* – chicken, *Zhurou* – pork
- Sichuan peppercorn – a tiny reddish peppercorn with a flower-like appearance and a 'numbing' taste, used in Sichuan cooking
- Taro root – the starchy, potato-like root of the taro plant, used in soups and stews
- *Yue bing* – moon cake, small round cakes with various sweet fillings, eaten during the Moon Festival
- *Zhou* – rice porridge

9

France and its Cuisines

Introduction

French cooking is considered by many to be the standard against which all other cuisines are measured (it is also referred to as *haute cuisine*). This standard was introduced into the French courts by

Catherine de Medici in the 1500s, and later perfected by Auguste Escoffier (1846-1935), who is considered the Father of French Cooking.

Nouvelle Cuisine, which became popular in the 1970s, was in reaction to the rich cooking of classic French cuisine. This new cuisine has a healthful cooking philosophy: crisply cooked vegetables, and fruit based sauces as opposed to flour and cream sauces. From classic French cooking to Nouvelle Cuisine, and the many French regional cooking styles, there is something to satisfy just about every palate.

Dining at French restaurants is easy, once you know the rules of the road, or menu as the case may be. According to Steve Ettlinger, author of *The Restaurant Lover's Companion*, "French meals consist of small portions of food served in a definite sequence of courses...Many restaurants offer a prix-fixe menu, consisting of a series of courses from a set menu at a set price."

Regional Styles

Books on Provencal style cooking abound, however, there are not many cookbooks on the other French regional styles. Peter Franey's book, listed in the French Cookbooks section, has recipes for all the various regions. Regional French cooking styles are reflected in the character of the land and its surroundings. The rich raw materials of the fertile land in Burgundy are apparent in this region's robust cooking style. Beef Bourguignon is one of the popular dishes from this region. The Provence region is bordered by the Mediterranean Sea, and Provencal specialties naturally revolve around the fresh seafood of the area. Adjacent to Switzerland and Germany, the Alsace region exhibits influences of their neighbors in its cooking style, as in the dish choucroute (sauerkraut, pork and potatoes). Parisian cooking has many influences, however, when dining in Paris, you will always have a wide choice of restaurants. Below is a list of some of the French regional cooking styles:

Alsacienne

typically involving sauerkraut and pork

Basquaise

typically with ham and tomatoes

Bourguignonne

typically with red wine, bacon and onions

Normande

creamy seafood sauce

Provencal

typically with olive oil, garlic and tomatoes

Sauces

Most French sauces are wine based. Wine is used in combination with cream or spices and/or stock. Below is a partial listing of French sauces:

Bearnaise

egg and butter based with white wine

Bechamel

flour, milk and butter based with onion

Bordelaise

red wine based with shallots

Hollandaise

butter and yolk based with lemon juice

Rouille

pepper, tomato, olive oil and garlic

Recipes

Brioche Braid

makes 1 loaf

1 package active dry yeast

3/4 cup warm water

2 tablespoons sugar

1 teaspoon salt

3 cups unbleached flour

3 eggs

1/2 cup soft butter

1 cup diced Fontina, Gruyere or Jarlsberg cheese (optional)

Sprinkle the yeast into warm water in a large mixing bowl. Let stand until puffy. Add sugar, salt, and one cup of flour; beat well. Add three eggs, one at a time. Beat until smooth. Beat in the butter and gradually add enough remaining flour to make a soft dough. Turn out on a floured board. Knead until smooth and satiny. Place in a greased bowl. Butter the top of dough lightly. Cover with a towel. Let rise in a warm place until doubled in size. Mix in the cheese if used and turn out on a floured board. Knead lightly. Divide into three pieces and shape into long ropes; braid the strands and tuck ends under. Place on a greased baking sheet and cover and let rise in a warm place until doubled in size. Preheat the oven to 350 degrees F. Bake in the oven for 30 to 35 minutes or until golden brown, and the loaf sounds hollow when thumped.

Quiche Lorraine

makes 8 servings

4 eggs

1 pint light cream or milk

1/2 teaspoon salt

1/8 teaspoon nutmeg

1 cup ham, cut in julienne pieces

1 1/2 cups shredded Gruyere cheese

1 tablespoon butter

9-inch prebaked pastry shell

Beat the eggs lightly and blend in the cream, salt, and nutmeg. Mix the ham and cheese and place in the baked pastry shell. Pour in the custard and dot with butter. Bake in a preheated 375 degrees F oven for 35 minutes or until slightly puffed and browned. Let cool five minutes, then cut in wedges.

Baked Potatoes Anna

makes 6 servings

6 large baking potatoes

1/2 cup butter

Salt and freshly ground pepper

Peel the potatoes and slice crosswise 1/8 inch thick. Generously butter a 10-inch round baking dish and melt remaining butter in a small saucepan. Overlap the sliced potatoes in the dish, forming circles, and sprinkle with salt and pepper. Repeat layers until all the potatoes are layered. Pour over the melted butter. Bake in a preheated 425 degrees F oven for 50 minutes to one hour or until the top is crusty and the potatoes are tender. Invert on a serving dish. Cut in wedges.

Sirloin in Mustard Cream

makes 4 servings

1/4 cup unsalted butter

1 1/2 pound sirloin steak or 4 boneless fillets

Salt and pepper

1 tablespoon Dijon mustard

1/4 cup dry Vermouth

1/2 cup whipping cream

1 tablespoon minced chives

Heat a large frying pan, add 1 tablespoon of the butter, and when it stops foaming add the meat. Saute on both sides until browned and cooked to desired state. Season with salt and pepper. Remove to a platter and keep warm.

Mix together the mustard, Vermouth, and cream and stir into the pan juices.

Boil, scraping up the drippings. Add the remaining butter to the pan and heat, stirring until blended. Remove from heat. Slice the whole steak on the diagonal, or leave the fillets whole, spoon over the sauce, and sprinkle with chives.

Shallot Salad with Cheeses

makes 8 servings

2 heads butter lettuce or 2 quarts choice greens

1/4 cup each safflower oil and olive oil

3 tablespoons red wine vinegar

Salt and pepper

1 tablespoon Dijon mustard

3 tablespoons chopped shallots

Chevre or Brie

Tear the greens into bite-size pieces. In a bowl, whisk together the oils, vinegar, salt, pepper, mustard, and shallots. Place greens in a bowl and pour over dressing, and mix well. Serve with a plate of cheese.

Chocolate Mousse

makes 8 servings

6 ounces bittersweet chocolate

5 eggs, separated

1 teaspoon vanilla extract

1/8 teaspoon salt

1/8 teaspoon cream of tartar

1/2 cup sugar

1 cup whipping cream

Place the chocolate in a microwavable bowl and microwave on medium for two minutes or until melted; let cool. Beat the egg yolks and stir them into the chocolate. Add the vanilla.

Beat the egg whites until foamy, add the salt and cream of tartar, and beat until soft peaks form. Gradually add the sugar and continue beating until stiff. Whip the cream until stiff. Fold the egg white meringue and the whipped cream into the chocolate mixture. Spoon into glasses and chill. If desired, cover and freeze; let thaw 10 minutes before serving.

Lemon Cheese Tart

makes 8 servings

butter tart shell

1 cup all-purpose flour

1/2 cup unsalted butter

2 tablespoons powdered sugar

With an electric mixer or a food processor fitted with the steel blade, mix flour, butter and powdered sugar together and until particles are crumbly. Pat into the bottom and sides of an 11-inch flan pan with scalloped sides and removable bottom. Place in the freezer for 10 minutes to firm up. Bake in a 425 degrees F oven for 8 to 10 minutes or until lightly browned.

filling:

8 ounces natural cream cheese or one cup Yogurt Cheese

3/4 cup sugar

3 eggs

2 teaspoons grated lemon peel

1/2 cup lemon juice

Mint sprigs

First prepare Butter Tart Shell. Using an electric mixer, beat the cheese until creamy and beat in the sugar, eggs, lemon peel and juice. Pour into the baked tart shell and bake in a preheated 350 degrees F oven for 20 minutes or until set. Let cool and chill. Garnish with mint. Cut in wedges.

Glossary

This glossary contains French food terminology for cooking basic French dishes.

Aioli: made with garlic, olive oil and eggs

Confit: meat preserved in its own fat

Florentine: with spinach

Gratine: with toasted cheese or crumb topping

Cooking Terms

Brule: burned

Fume: smoked

Fish, Meat & Poultry

Abats: organ meats

Canard: duck

Coq au vin: chicken stewed in wine sauce

Coquille Saint-Jacques: sea scallop

Cuisses de Grenouille: frog's legs

Jambon: ham; also refers to thigh or shoulder of meat, usually pork

Tartare: chopped raw meat with egg, onion, parsley and capers

Tornedos: beef filet (center cut)

Desserts

Creme brule : custard with carmelized sugar topping

Glace : ice cream

GERMANY

Germany is a nation that until a few years ago was divided in two parts, West and East Germany. Reunited since 1990, it is now, with its capital-designate, Berlin, one of the largest, most populated and productive European countries, covering about 137,828 square miles with an estimated population of 81,912,000 people.

Germany is a federation of sixteen smaller states: Baden-Wuertenberg (with Stuttgart as the capital); Bayern/Bavaria (with the city of Muenchen/Munich); Brandenburg (with Potsdam); Bremen (with Bremen); Hamburg (with Hamburg); Hessen (with Wiesbaden); Mecklenburg-Vorpommern (with Schwerin); Niedersachsen/Lower Saxonia (with Hannover); Nordrhein-Westphalen (with Duesseldorf); Rheinland-Pfalz (with Mainz); Saarland (with Saarbruecken); Sachsen (with Dresden); Sachsen-Anhalt (with Magdeburg); Schleswig-Holstein (with Kiel); Thueringen (with Erfurt); and Berlin (with the internationally known city of Berlin, which is both capital of the state and capital designate of the country). Germany is located in the heart of Europe and borders Denmark, Poland, the Czech Republic, Austria, Switzerland, France, Luxembourg, Belgium and the Netherlands.

Germany is not only BMW, Volkswagen, Mercedes-Benz, Braun kitchen appliances, and Kaiser cake pans. It is a land of northern flat and green lowlands, northeastern wide lakes and woodlands, northwestern and eastern rich coal fields, western long and winding rivers flanked by steep sided valleys lined with vineyards, and a southern region famous for its castles, and for events like "Oktoberfest" (Festival of October).

Germany is, more importantly, Germans, with their "Gemuetlichkeit" (friendly joviality), their hearty cuisine that has adapted to healthy trends and tastes of recent immigrants, their dairy products and sausage industry, and their cheering spirit, which in time has given impetus to an industry of beers, wines, and distilled spirits, like Hacker-Pschorr and Lowenbrau beers, Asbach Uralt brandies, Joseph Freiderich's wines, and Fuerst Metternich Sekt.

Regional Cuisines

Typical German cuisine varies according to each German state's culinary tradition, to its regional agriculture, and to the new tastes of new Germans who have settled in the reunited Germany. Nordrhein Westfalen, Rheinland-Pfalz, Saarland and Baden-Wuertenburg's traditional specialties, for example, include ingredients typified in the agriculture around the Black Forest and the Rhein river, and by a wine tradition influenced by the proximity to Belgium, France and Switzerland. They include dishes like the "Badener Schneckensuepple" (a snail chowder flavored with herbs), "Schwarzwalder Kirschtorte" (Black Forest cake), and "Rheinischer Sauerbraten" (beef roast stewed with wine).

Bayern/Bavaria and Hessen's cuisine, with their abundance of beer, meats, and dairy products, feature specialties like "Spannferkel" (spit roasted baby pig), "Handkaes" (a smelly type of cheese mixture made with sour cream) and "Schwaebische Kasespaetzle" (small drop-shaped flour dumplings topped with cheese and butter).

Thueringen, Bremen, and the Saxonian states (Niedersachsen/ Lower Saxonia-Sachsen-Sachsen Anhalt), include "Dresdner Stollen" (a holiday fruit cake shaped like a wrapped infant and covered with confectioner's sugar), "Blechkuchen" (a simple flat layer of cake dough covered with seasonal fruit), and "Welfenspeise" (vanilla flavored dessert made with wine).

Schleswig Holstein, Hamburg, Mecklenburg-Vorpommern, Brandenburg and Berlin, with their access to the North and Baltic Seas, their availability of spices, and their exchange of culinary know-how with Scandinavian and Eastern countries, include "Rote Gruetze" (fruit soup), "Sauerfleisch" (meat in aspic made with fish gelatin), "Bulletten" (meat balls), "Helgolander Krabbensalat" (Helgoland shrimp salad), and "Soeier" (pickled eggs).

Principal crops grown now throughout the German states and used in its regional way of cooking include hops (Germany is the second largest producer in the world), sugar beets, barley, wheat, potatoes, oats, and rye. Cabbage and carrots are the most important vegetable crops, and apples, pears, currants, strawberries, and raspberries are the most important fruit crops.

A typical German meal today may include from two to seven courses. It is commonly made up by an appetizer (Vorspeise), a soup (Suppe), a main course (Hauptspeise) with one or two either raw or cooked side dishes (Beilagen). After-meal treats are called "Nachspeise." With a fine meal, Germans drink either beer, wine or "Sekt" (champagnoise type sparkling wine). With their meals, young and old Germans also like to drink soft drinks that have interesting names like "Radler" (literally translated, "bike rider" – a light beer mixed with lemonade or apple juice) or "Limo" (sweetened sparkling water combined with lemonade).

Throughout the day, Germans love to drink drip coffee brewed in large automatic coffee makers with either paper or metallic filters, and then serve majestic "Torte" or "Kuchen" (cake). No good German "Hausfrau" would want to be so rude to not serve coffee and cake to her welcomed guests! German coffee is usually lighter in caffeine content compared to Austrian and Italian coffees. When it is very light it is also called "Bluemchenkaffee" (small flower coffee). The tradition of this last term originates from wartime, when real coffee was substituted with the roasted roots of chicory, which has a small blue flower.

German Recipes

Wurstsalat (Sausage salad)

serves 4

Everybody in Germany likes to prepare Wurstsalat once in a while. It is very easy to make and is one of those German specialties that best reflects the German food industry. It is either made with fine grain sausages like Knackwurst or Frankfurter. German summer afternoons spent at home working in the garden often end with a meal of wurstsalat. Wurstsalat is also an everpresent item in almost all the menus of German inns and restaurants.

4 precooked cold knackwurst, peeled, and sliced thin (about 3/4 of a pound)

1 small onion (about 2 oz.), trimmed, peeled, sliced thin

salt (to taste)

freshly ground black pepper (to taste)

3 Tablespoons wine vinegar

4 Tablespoon vegetable oil

In a salad bowl combine sliced knackwurst and sliced onion. In a small bowl whisk together vinegar, oil, salt and pepper. Pour dressing over knackwurst, toss and serve with a good rye bread.

Klaus's Heringsalat (Klaus's herring salad)

serves 4

Heringsalat in Germany is very much a matter of personal taste. Basic ingredients are apples, herrings, and raw onions. Some Germans like to mix horseradish into their herring salad, others add chopped capers. Some include chopped pickled cucumbers and others add mayonnaise instead of Quark (a sour cream type cottage cheese). This recipe is the adaptation of a German family recipe that was brought to North America from Darmstadt.

Contents of one 8 oz. jar of pickled herring, drained, diced in bite size pieces (keep herring juice for dressing!)

1 medium size Golden Delicious apple (no more than 8 oz.), cored, peeled, diced

1 small onion (about 2 oz.) trimmed, peeled, chopped finely

1 sweet sour pickled cucumber, chopped finely

1 hard boiled egg, shelled, chopped

2 either red or yellow Yukon Gold type potatoes (about 1/2 pound), steamed with their jackets on, peeled, sliced

1 small leafless red beet (about 1/2 pound), steamed, trimmed, peeled, OR the contents of one 8 oz can of beets, drained and diced

1 Tablespoon mustard

1-2 Tablespoons Quark

1 Tablespoon fresh dill (about 1 young stem) minced salt (about 1/4 teaspoon, or to taste) freshly ground white pepper (about 1/8 teaspoon, or to taste)

In a medium size bowl combine herring pieces, apple, onion, pickled cucumber, hard boiled egg, red beet and potatoes. In a separate bowl blend mustard, quark, salt, pepper, 2-3 Tablespoons herring juice and fresh dill to make a dressing. Pour dressing over salad and toss. Serve with rye bread.

Schweinsmedallions mit Sommermajoran (Boneless pork cutlets with fresh marjoram)

serves 4

This easy-to-make recipe is an adaptation of a Rhine country dish, updated for a reduced cholesterol diet. It is a beautifully color-contrasting meal if you serve it together with red stewed cabbage.

1 1/2 pounds boneless pork loin cutlets (cut no thicker than 1/3 of an inch)

1/4 cup golden raisins, soaked in white wine

1 large Golden Delicious apple, cored, peeled, quartered, sliced

1 large onion, trimmed, peeled, sliced

3 Tablespoons vegetable oil

1/3 cup mustard

leaves of 10 full grown stems of fresh marjoram (about 1 oz. or 1 cup of loosely packed leaves), rinsed, chopped salt (to taste)

freshly ground white pepper (to taste)

On a cutting board, season cutlets on both sides with salt and pepper to taste (both optional). Evenly spread the mustard on only one side of the meat. In a large, covered non-stick pan, over medium heat, heat the oil and saute onions until lightly golden and limp (about 5-10 minutes). Drain raisins (keep juice). To the translucent onions, add apple slices and raisins. Cook for an additional 5 minutes. Add cutlets, placing them first on the side without the mustard and making space for them by pushing the onions aside. Brown cutlets for about 5-10 minutes on each side. Drizzle the cutlets with raisin wine juice and sprinkle them with the marjoram. Reduce the heat to medium low, cover the pan, and cook the cutlets until they are done. No pink should be visible when you serve the meat. The internal temperature should be at 160-165 degrees F.

Gedunstetes Rotkraut or Gedunsteter Rotkohl (Stewed red cabbage)

serves 4

Cabbage (which on the German produce market is available either red or green) and Sauerkraut are absolutely star ingredients in typical German cuisine. Red cabbage has a somewhat sweeter taste than the green variety. It makes an interesting color contrast with a main course that is pale in color, such as herbed pork cutlets.

1 small whole (about 1 1/2 pound) red cabbage, trimmed, cored, rinsed and sliced

1 small onion (about 2 oz.) trimmed, peeled, sliced or chopped

3 Tablespoons vegetable oil

salt (to taste)

freshly ground white pepper (to taste)

1/3 cup broth

2/3 cup white wine

In a covered medium-size non-stick stir fry pan, heat the oil over medium heat and saute the onions until golden brown and translucent. Add the cabbage, season with salt and pepper to taste (both optional). Stir cabbage to coat everything with oil. Reduce the heat to medium, add broth and let simmer covered until cabbage has absorbed the liquid and has softened (about 10 minutes). Occasionally stir to prevent the cabbage from sticking or burning. Add wine, stir, cover again, and cook for an additional 10 minutes. If necessary, add more wine and stir occasionally until the cabbage has reached your desired doneness (the cabbage should have lost all its crunchiness).

Note: You may follow the same procedure with green cabbage and with sauerkraut. If you use sauerkraut, rinse it in abundant water and drain it before using it as instructed above.

Erdbeer Bowle (Strawberry wine punch)

serves 4

Bowle is a classic German party wine punch. During the month of May throughout Germany, bowle is served flavored with fresh woodruff (Waldmeister), a sweet scented herb with white flowers, which grows especially well in wooded and shady areas away from hot climates and sunshine. Later, during strawberry season, bowle is made with strawberries which grow abundantly everywhere. As German summer season progresses, bowle is prepared with other fruits like sweet imported peaches, chunks of juicy watermelon, pieces of bright orange cantaloupe, or plump raspberries.

1/2 pint fresh strawberries, stemless, rinsed, cut in half or in quarters (the cutting will not be necessary if you use wild

strawberries) 1 Tablespoon granulated sugar

1/2 bottle German Riesling, well chilled

1 Tablespoon brandy (preferably Alsbach Uralt)

1/2 bottle German Sekt, well chilled

Place the strawberries in a large covered glass jar (a sun tea jar will be fine), sprinkle them with sugar and drizzle them with the brandy. Set them aside to marinate for two hours to allow the sugar to draw out the juice from the berries. Add white wine, stir, and set aside for two additional hours. When ready to serve, pour in serving punch bowl. Add Sekt and serve chilled in wide champagne type glasses, making sure to distribute strawberries with the wine.

Staples

Pork meat (Schweinefleisch) and Sausage (Wurst)

Pork meat is the most popular source of meat in German cuisine. Cured pork meats and sausages from Germany are renowned all over the world. They come packed in cans, glass jars, or vacuum packed. There are about 1,500 kinds of sausages on the German sausage market. Germans also like to prepare dishes with veal (Kalb), beef (Rind), chicken (Huhn) and venison (Wild).

Herring (Hering)

Herring are, especially in the northern part of Germany, a staple favorite. The small silvery fish are fished in the North and Baltic Seas; they are eaten raw, pickled, smoked and canned.

German Cottage Cheese (Quark)

Quark is an all-round favorite ingredient in German cuisine. It ccounts for half of the total cheese consumption in Germany. It is very similar to cream cheese but has a mild yogurt flavor, is softer and creamier.

Wines, Sparkling Wines, Brandies (Wein, Sekt, Weinbrand)

Wines, champagnoise-type sparkling wines, (called "Sekt" in erman), and brandies are usually first quality in Germany where stringent production, labeling, and denomination laws regulate the making and distribution of these alcoholic beverages. Riesling, for example, is a legal denomination of a fairly light and fruity wine made from the white Riesling grape variety, the name "Sekt" always indicates a sparkling wine; and "Weinbrand" is the legal German term for brandy distilled from grape products. German wineries are usually grouped in member cooperatives that represent growers who are periodically checked for product quality. With the wine cooperatives system, German wineries can combine traditional wine making skills with the latest technologies in wine making and wine marketing. Famous

German wines are produced throughout the wine growing regions of Ahr, Mittelrhein, Mosel-Saar Ruwer, Rheingau, Nahe, Rheinhessen, Pfalz, Franken, Hessische Bergstrasse, Wuerttemberg, Baden, Saale-Unstrut and Sachsen.

Spices

Caraway (Kuemmel)

Small seeds, usually sold dry, that look almost like celery seeds or cumin seeds, which are vital in German cuisine. They are a must in rye bread, in cabbage and in sauerkraut specialties. Their flavor and aroma is totally different from cumin, but they are often mistaken because of the similarity in their name. Cumin in German is "Kreuzkuemmel."

Juniper (Wacholder)

Dark blue juniper berries grow on stout prickly bushes and are easily found in higher wooded areas in Germany. They have a clean flavor that is first slightly bitter, and later almost sweet. Juniper berries often substitute bay leaf in the typical German "bouquet garni." They are also used in marinades of venison to cut the game flavor of the meat, in sauerkraut specialties, and to make a white transparent distilled spirit called "Steinhaeger."

Black and white pepper (*Schwarzer* und *Weisser Pfeffer*)

Black and white pepper corns are native to Asia and are an imported product in Germany. They are the small berries of a plant called Piper Nigrum. Both black and white pepper corns come from the same basic plant, and are used abundantly in all German dishes. Black kernels have been picked still red when the pepper berry is not yet fully

mature while white kernels are simply the mature pepper product removed of its outer coating. The difference is in appearance and in flavor. Black peppercorns have a stronger flavor; white peppercorns have a milder aroma.

Herbs

Dill (Dille)

It is frequently mistaken for fennel and anise because of its feathery green appearance when fresh. It has a pungent and unique flavor. It is often added to potato salads, to pickled cucumbers, and to seafood dishes like northern shrimp cocktails. Dried dill herb is used during winter months in soups. Dill seeds are frequently used to flavor German bread specialties.

Marjoram (Majoran)

This green-stemmed plant with round, almost hairy leaves is similar in flavor to oregano but tastes milder. It has a slightly bitter savory flavor and is added frequently to meat dishes and herb butters (*Krauterbutter*).

Parsley (Petersilie)

Native to Mediterranean regions, it is available fresh, with curly and flat leaves, and dried everywhere in Germany. It is rich in vitamin C, has a pleasant mild flavor, and goes very well with minced garlic and onion mixtures. It is a must in German herb butters.

GREECE

Greece, a republic 50,962 square miles in area, is located in the southern Balkan Peninsula of southeastern Europe. The population of the country numbers around 10 million and the capital and largest city is Athens. The basic monetary unity is the drachma.

Ancient Greece is considered the cradle of Western civilization, starting about 2500 years ago. In those days Greece controlled much of the land bordering the Mediterranean and Black Seas. In Athens and elsewhere in Greece, magnificent ruins stand as monuments to the nation's glorious past.

The Greeks came under control of invaders for more than 2,000 years. They lost their independence to the Macedonians in 338 B.C. and did not regain it until A.D. 1829, from the Ottoman Turks. Since then, Greece has had many serious political problems. Yet their arts, philosophy, and science became foundations of

Western thought and culture. About a fifth of Greece consists of islands and no part of Greece is more than 85 miles from the sea.

Greece and its sun-kissed isles offer a tantalizing cuisine that is fresh and fragrant, served with warmth and vitality. The Greeks' zest for the good life and love of simple, well-seasoned foods is reflected at the table. Theirs is an unpretentious cuisine that makes the most of their surroundings.

It is a cuisine entrenched in history and punctuated by the cultures of its neighbors for centuries: Turkey, the Middle East, and the Balkans.

This land of blue skies and sparkling seas offers a variety of fresh ingredients close at hand. Olive trees flourish, providing a flavor-packed oil to bathe other foods. Vineyards thread the rolling hills, and the grape crush and ferment produces excellent wines, some resin-flavored. Fragrant lemon trees produce the golden fruit whose tang pervades Greek gastronomy.

The seas are blessed with a variety of fish and shellfish and harbor-side tavernas serve them grilled, baked, and fried and often whole, with the head still on.

Lamb is the principal meat served and a holiday festivity calls for ceremoniously spit-roasting a whole carcass out of doors. For everyday meals, lamb is braised and stewed in casseroles with assorted vegetables and skewered and broiled. Pork, beef, and game are marinated, grilled, and baked. Chicken is broiled or braised. Good meat and vegetable combinations are endless, often embellished with the golden lemon sauce, *avgolemono*, or a cinnamon-spiced tomato sauce.

Moussaka, layered with eggplant or zucchini and a garlic-scented meat sauce, and bearing a custard topping, is the ubiquitous casserole dish. Pilaffs are laced with spices and nuts. Fila pitas, composed of the wafer-thin pastry, and layered with chicken and mushrooms, spinach and feta, or lamb and leeks, are a delight. An abundance of fresh vegetables inspires imaginative cooked and marinated vegetable dishes and salads, often strewn with mountain-grown herbs: garlic, oregano, mint, basil, and dill. Fresh feta, Romano, and Kasseri, in particular, are used lavishly to accompany homemade whole-grain bread or salad or to grate and top vegetables or pasta. Undoubtedly *baklava* is the most famous pastry, a multi-layered affair ribboned with nuts and oozing with honey syrup.

A visit to a Greek pastry shop reveals the versatility of fila dough in dozens of different fila pastries, many of Turkish derivation.The honeyed fila pastries and buttery nut cookies compose a separate late afternoon meal accompanied by thick Greek coffee. Fresh fruit – generally figs, orange, apples, and melon – usually conclude the late evening dinner.

Feasts and festivals are integral to Hellenic life. Name days, saints' days, weddings, and holidays are the occasion for merriment, a bounteous table and spirited folk dancing.

Common Greek Cooking Terms and Ingredients

General Terms

Arni: lamb

Avgolemono: An egg and lemon mixtures used as a sauce or a soup base.

Baklava: the most famous Greek dessert, made of layers of fila pastry, chopped nuts, and a honey-flavored syrup

Bourekakia: fila puffs made with various fillings

Dolmades: grapevine leaves stuffed with rice or meat

Feta: the classic white goat cheese of Greece

Fila, filo, or phyllo: the paper-thin pastry dough essential for appetizers, entrees, and desserts.

Gouvetsi: the Greek word for casserole, or baked in the oven

Garides: shrimp

Kafes: coffee

Kalamaria: squid

Kalamata: probably the most famous Greek olive

Kasseri: creamy farm cheese with a bitey flavor

Kefalotiri: a hard, salty cheese, good for grating

Kourabiedes: butter cookies topped with powdered sugar

Mezethes: small savory appetizers

Moussaka: a layered casserole usualy made with eggplant and chopped meat, and topped with a custard sauce

Orzo: tiny melon seed-shaped pasta

Ouzo: a colorless alcoholic drink flavored with anise.

Pastitsio: a layered casserole of macaroni and chopped meat topped with a custard sauce

Pilafi: rice boiled in broth and flavored with onion and spices

Psari: fish

Retsina: white or rose wine flavored with pine resin

Rigani: oregano, an indispensable herb used in countless dishes

Skordalia: garlic sauce

Souvlakia: skewered food

Spanakopeta: spinach fila pastries

Tahini: crushed sesame seed paste

Tarama: fish roe from gtray mullet

Taramosalata: fish roe spread

Tiropita: fila stuffed with Greek cheese

Tsatziki: cucumber yogurt dip

Definitions for the following Greek cooking terms are from Steve Ettlinger's book *The Restaurant Lover's Companion.*

Tyria (Greek Cheeses)

Haloumi: A semisoft cheese, not very salty; usually made from sheep's milk

Kefalograviera: a mild Gruy?re-type cheese; made from either sheep's or cow's milk

Manouri: a soft unsalted cheese; made from sheep's or goat's milk whey; served with fruit

Mizithra: soft and hard varieties; made from sheep's or goat's milk whey

Greek Olives

Amfissa: black and round with a nutty-sweet taste; from the central mainland of Greece

Green: large and crunchy with a mild flavor; from various Ionian islands

Cracked green: made by cracking unripe green olives, placing them in water for several weeks to remove their bitterness, then storing them in brine

Black: small, wrinkled, dry-cured olives with a very strong flavor; from the island of Thassos

Glykismata (Desserts)

Karidopeta: Single-layer, dark, moist nut cake (made with coarsely chopped walnuts or almonds) topped with a light honey/sugar syrup

Pasta Flora: a lattice-topped tart filled with apricot pur?e

Ravani: Golden yellow cake made with farina or semolina and topped with a light sugar/honey or orange-flavored syrup

Fenikia or Melomakarouna: Oblong, honey-dipped cookies covered with chopped nuts

Diples: Thin strips of dough tied, folded, or twisted into bows or loops and deep-fried, then dipped in a honey syrup and topped with chopped nuts

Rizogalo: creamy rice pudding with a sprinkling of cinnamon on top

Loukoumades: made-to-order deep-fried honey balls topped with honey; served warm

Galatoboureko: A custard-filled dessert made with phyllo topped with a light honey/sugar syrup

Kadaife: Shredded dough filled with chopped nuts and cinnamon and topped with a honey/sugar syrup

Koulourakia: Crisp, golden-colored, subtly sweet cookies shaped by hand; sometimes covered with sesame seeds

Charming taverna featuring Hellenic cuisine with a California emphasis in an upscale atmosphere. Open Monday through Saturday for lunch and dinner; closed Sunday.

Greek Food Products

Purveyors of farmstead foods from Greece and the heart of the Mediterranean. Products include eight naturally cured olive varieties: Kalamata, Amfissa, Elitses, Atalanti, Ionian Green, Cracked Green, Thasos, Nafplion; olive specialties include marinated party olives, country olive mix, and Kalamata olive paste. Other products include roasted sweet peppers, dolmas, eggplant appetizer and meze, extra-virgin olive oil, red wine vinegars, pickled peppers, olive oil dressings, sauces, spreads, and salad bases.

Greek Recipes

(These recipes are published in *Greek Cooking* by Lou Seibert Pappas; Galahad Books; 1995.)

Sesame Spread / *Hummus Tahini*

makes about 2 cups

1 can (15 oz.) garbanzo beans, drained

1/3 cup lemon juice

1/4 cup tahini paste

3 tablespoons chopped green onion

2 tablespoons chopped flat-leaf parsley

1/4 teaspoon ground cumin

2 garlic cloves, peeled

Salt and freshly ground black pepper to taste

Parsley sprigs or cilantro for garnish

Lavosh (cracker bread) or pita bread, quartered

Place the beans in a blender or food processor with the lemon juice, tahini, onion, parsley, cumin, and garlic. Add salt and pepper and blend again. Turn into a bowl, cover and chill. When ready to serve garnish with a wreath of parsley or cilantro. Spread on lavosh or pita bread.

Spinach and Feta Salad / Spanako me Feta Salata

makes 8 servings

2 pounds fresh spinach

1/2 cup olive oil

2 tablespoons white wine vinegar

2 tablespoons lemon juice

1/4 teaspoon ground cinnamon

1/4 teaspoon dry mustard

Salt and freshly ground pepper to taste

1 cucumber, sliced

1 cup cherry tomatoes, halved

1/4 pound feta cheese, crumbled

2 green onions, chopped

Remove stems from spinach. Wash and drain leaves, cut into 1-inch wide strips, and place in a salad bowl. Shake together the oil, vinegar, lemon juice, cinnamon, mustard, salt, and pepper; pour half the dressing over the spinach and mix well. Thinly slice cucumbers and arrange in a ring across the top with the cherry tomatoes. Sprinkle with cheese and onions. Pour remaining dressing over the salad.

Lamb on Skewers / Arni Souvlakia

makes 8 servings

3 pounds boneless leg of lamb, cut into 1-1/2 inch cubes

1/3 cup lemon juice

3 tablespoons olive oil

Salt and freshly ground pepper to taste

1 tablespoon fresh oregano or 1 teaspoon dried oregano

3 garlic cloves, minced

1 small onion, grated

2 red peppers, cut in 1-1/2 inch pieces

1 large white sweet onion, cut into eighths

Place the meat in a bowl. Mix together the lemon juice, oil, salt, pepper, oregano, garlic, and grated onion, and pour over the meat. Cover and chill several hours or preferably overnight, turning several times. Thread the meat on skewers, alternating on each one about 4 to 5 lamb cubes, 2 pieces of pepper, and 1 piece of onion. Barbecue over medium-hot coals, basting often with marinade and turning to brown on all sides, allowing about 15 minutes for medium-rare meat.

Rice Pilaf with Mushrooms / Pilafi me Manitaria

makes 6 servings

1 medium-sized onion, finely chopped

1/4 cup butter

2 garlic cloves, minced

3 tablespoons chopped Italian-style flat-leaf parsley

2 teaspoons fresh thyme or 1/2 teaspoon dried thyme

1 cup long-grain white rice

1 1/2 cups chicken broth

1/2 cup dry white wine

1 pound mushrooms

2 tablespoons lemon juice

1/2 cup freshly grated Parmesan cheese

Using a heavy saucepan, saut? the onion in 2 tablespoons of the butter. Add half the garlic, the parsley, thyme, and rice and saute 1 minute, stirring. Bring both the broth and wine to a boil, pour over the rice, cover, and simmer 20 minutes. Meanwhile, wash and trim mushrooms; leave whole if small or slice if large. Melt the remaining butter with garlic in a large frying pan. Add the mushrooms and lemon juice and saute quicky 2 to 3 minutes, just until hot through and glazed. Add to the cooked rice, fluff with a fork, and sprinkle with cheese..

Rum Nut Cake Diamonds

makes 3 dozen

Rum Syrup: Combine in a saucepan

1 cup sugar,

2 teaspoons grated orange peel

1/3 cup water

Bring to a boil and boil until clear. Remove from heat and stir in 1/4 cup rum.

6 eggs, separated

1/8 teaspoon each salt and cream of tartar

1 cup sugar

1/2 teaspoon almond extract

1/2 cup fine bread crumbs

1 teaspoon baking powder

1 teaspoon grated orange peel

2-1/2 cups ground almonds

Preheat the oven to 350?F. First prepare the rum syrup and let cool. Beat the egg whites until foamy; add the salt and cream of tartar and beat until soft peaks form. Gradually add 1/2 cup of the sugar, eating until the meringue stands in peaks; set aside. With the same beater, beat the egg yolks until pale yellow and gradually beat in the remaining 1/2 cup sugar, beating until thick and lemon colored. Beat in the extract. Mix the crumbs with the baking powder and grated peel and beat into the yolks. Mix in half the nuts. Fold in the egg white meringue and remaining nuts. Turn into a buttered, floured 9 by 13-inch baking pan. Bake in the oven for 30 minutes, or until the top springs back when touched. Let cool 5 minutes. While hot, pour over the cool syrup. Let cool and cut into diamonds.

Dining in Greece

On a recent cruise of the Crystal Harmony with members of the Newspaper Food Editors and Writers Association, we dined in Athens and Rhodes at select restaurants. Ouzeries are a popular new style of restaurant, featuring an assortment of meze. Certain fish restaurants are stellar. On earlier trips I have enjoyed the simple taverna fare at the island beaches. Canopied lunch stands serve Greek salad, pita sandwiches, rice-stuffed tomatoes and peppers, and grilled souvlakia.

To Cafenio (The Cafe)

26 Loukianou

Athens

Located in the fashionable Kolonaki section, this ouzerie offers regional specialties from throughout Greece. A luncheon menu features 16 meze. They include:

fava

fava bean pur?e

kolokithokeftedes

zucchini fritters

lachanodolmades

cabbage leaves stuffed with beef and rice and served with avgolemono sauce

melitzanosalata

eggplant pur?e

tyropita

cheese pie

spanakopita

spinach pie

patatosalata

potato salad

melizana papoutsaka

eggplant stuffed with ground beef with tomato sauce and cheese

gardumba

lamb intestines rolled into a sausage

saganaka

fried Kasseri cheese

kolokithia yemista

zucchini stuffed with ground beef and rice and served with avgolemono sauce

splena

spleen

marides

fried white bait

souzoukakai

beef meatballs baked in the oven

keftaidakia

fried beef meatball

house salad

artichoke zucchini, green beans, mushrooms, and onion dressed with dill vinaigrette.

Zefiros (The Wind)

48 Alex Koumoundourou

Microlimano

This is an excellent fish restaurant located in the little yacht harbor next to the port of Piraeus.This is one of 15 to 20 psarotavernas or fish restaurants in this area.The owner, Thanassi Panagiotou, insists on top quality fresh fish.

A superb menu there consisted of grilled octopus dressed with oregano vinaigrette, fried white bait, fried crayfish, Greek salad, boiled wild greens dressed with olive oil and lemon, grilled sea bream served with olive oil and lemon sauce, melon, grapes, and baklava. Ouzo, beer, and a dry white wine accompanied.

Alexis Restaurant

18 Socrates Street

in the Old Town of Rhodes

An outdoor and indoor taverna, this restaurant features a comprehensive display of fish and seafood and an excellent selection of Greek wines from small boutiques.

Dining there, Yannis Katsimprakis, the chef, served grilled octopus dressed with olive oil, vinegar, and oregano; tiny fried shrimp, mussels steamed in white wine with onion and herbs; sea urchins, large clams on the half shell, little clams on the half shell, oysters, arugula salad, tzatziki: a dip of yogurt and cucumber; grilled prawns; grilled white fish, and spinach sauteed with tomato and garlic.

GUATEMALA

Guatemala is a magical destination. The heart of the Maya world — it offers stunning scenery, intriguing archeological sites, ancient colonial cities, art, culture, a varied global cuisine, and a wealth of handicrafts for shoppers. Magnificent volcanic peaks, picturesque lakes, lush agricultural lands, scrubby desert, and rain forest thread the countryside. Besides its physical beauty, it is the incredible diversity of the land and its people that makes this country such a captivating holiday destination.

Perched at the top of the Central American Isthmus below the Yucatan Peninsula, Guatemala cover 42,000 square miles, an area comparable to Ohio and home to 9 million people. It borders Mexico to the North, El Salvador and Honduras to the South, the Pacific Ocean to the West and the Caribbean Sea and Belize to the East.

Two-thirds of the country is mountainous, with the main mountain chains in the southwest forming a string of volcanoes, many exceeding 11,000 feet.

Rainforest, bush, and swamps in the North yields timber and chewing gum. The fertile plains of the Pacific and Caribbean are used for cattle, sugar cane, cotton and fruit plantations. The economy is primarily agricultural with coffee, cotton, sugar, bananas, and beef leading exports. Corn and beans, the staple diet, are cultivated at all altitudes. Tourism is a primary money maker.

The multi-faceted populace is intriguing. More than half of the population is Indian with a strong indigenous culture, though they have adopted some European customs forced on their ancestors more than five centuries ago. All of Guatemala's Indians are Maya, but at least 22 different ethnicity's, differentiated by language, exist within that group. The other half are divided among Ladinos, the descendents of Europeans and Indians, a handful of African immigrants, and the European minority, predominantly Hispanic, which maintain a colonial lease on power. This creates a colorful human tapestry where the people are the product of the merger of sophisticated pre-Colombian cultures with Spanish colonialism and the consumerist influences of modern America.

It is in the central highlands, west of Guatemala City that Indian culture dominates. This area offers wildly beautiful scenery alongside the many Indian villages with their endless array of fiestas and markets, all worth a visit. This is a prime destination locale for the tourist.

Antigua, the old colonial capital, devastated by earthquakes but still offering superb architecture and the remains of huge churches, is an idyllic base. There are many international flights to Guatemala City and Antigua lies 45 minutes away by shuttle or private van.

From here, day trips are easily accessible to Lake Atitlan and the vast market in the town of Chichicastenango. Tikal, the most impressive of the Mayan sites, rivaling any in Latin America, is reached on one or two-day tours; most visitors prefer an overnight stay as a flight is necessary from Antigua and the weather can delay departure.

Holy Week is a prime time for a visit since Antigua offers the most elaborate and impressive pageant of processions in Central and South America, rivaling those in Seville, Spain.

This past Easter season I delighted in a stay in a private home with a group of friends. We rented two spacious private homes a few blocks apart in the heart of this charming city of 50,000 inhabitants. Each house came with a cook and a maid, and had exquisite artifacts and decor, sumptuous bedrooms, and a serene interior courtyard garden with tinkling water fountains, all enclosed within the four walls of the spacious stucco homes. We could just step out the door of our securely locked abode to view the ongoing festivities and parades.

The local processions commence Palm Sunday and are carried out on Good Friday, culminating in a candlelit Saturday night display under the full moon, and a finale on Easter Sunday. Townspeople stay up all night adorning the streets with carpets of designs in flower petals, colored sawdust and sand, pine needles and greenery.

On Good Friday a procession re-enacts the progress of Christ to the Cross. Garbed in purple robes, 80 men carry a three-ton platform bearing the figures through the streets in an eight-hour or longer walk, stopping at 20 stations for replacements for the load. Women and children follow with smaller floats. Once the design is trampled upon, it is swept up and another different one is carefully laid down by design.

Thousands of people from here and abroad gathered this year, lining the cobblestone roads, to observe the pageantry and pay tribute to this century-old tradition. Security was intensified with three different police squads manning every corner with rifles and hat and ready smiles.

Our days were filled with local sight-seeing, side trips, and market soirees. It was just two blocks to the Plaza Mayor, the main square bustling with pink and white cotton candy hawkers, shoeshine boys, and vendors with trinkets and handicraft galore. Around every corner on this square are shops and cozy cafes featuring a range of worldly specialties.

The town market lies a block away. Here stallkeepers young and old displayed woven bags, purses, necklaces, hats, rugs, blankets, carvings and t-shirts, and bargaining with the customer was an essential reward of the sale. Young women, some with babies slung on their backs in a "tzute" (a rectangular cloth) prod the tourists, saying "I've spent enough time with you, now you must buy from me."

The many old ruined churches are worth perusing as is the Casa Popenoe, a superbly restored colonial mansion showing the domestic life in earlier times. The house, set around a gorgeous courtyard, was originally built in 1634 and is open from 2 p.m. to 4 p.m. Monday through Saturday. During Easter Week it was closed, due to the great number of visitors.

We took a day trip to Guatemala City by hired van to visit the Museo Ixchel, a textile museum with extensive displays representing 120 communities located in the country's highland region. The museum also features two pictorial collections, one of water colors, and another of oil paintings, on permanent display. The present contemporary building opened in November 1993 on the site of the Universidad Francisco Marroquin campus. The museum is open Monday through Friday from 8 a.m. to 4:50 p.m. and Saturday from 9 a.m. to 12:50 p.m. Tickets are 25 quetzals, or $2.50 per person for adults. The monetary unit, a quetzal, is named for the endangered sacred bird. During our stay, 6 quetzals translated to about $1.

Enroute home, we stopped at a typical local roadside eatery for carnitas, tacos, chiles rellenos, guacamole and good Gallo beer, savoring a bountiful midday repast for $5 apiece.

Another day, a drive to Lake Atitlan offered breath-taking scenery, marred only by a hazy sky due to a three-month drought an burning in the fields. At the market in Chichicastenango, bargains included a carved Saint Rafael holding a sword and fish ($45), and a wooden "flying" cherub tooting a horn ($25). Small 6-inch woven zippered bags were $2 and baggy pants $6.

Lunch at the nearby Mayan Hotel was a prix fixe menu of red pepper soup, a special plate of rice, grilled chicken, chorizos, beef strips, and guacamole, and strawberry ice cream for $7.

A short drive away from Antigua is the weaving town of San Antonio Aguas Calientes where Carolina's Weaving shop is famous for jackets, bags, belts and other weavings. Enroute we stopped to photograph the oldest church in South America, Our Lady of the Conception, built in 1534 and once buried in a volcanic eruption.

Just around the corner from our home in Antigua was a textile store and retail museum of traditional Maya dress called Nim P'ot at 5a Avenida N. #29. Its name means "ceremonial huipil" in the language of Santiago Atitlan, and the shop offers the world's largest retail collection of contemporary and antique Maya dress. A modern Maya woman may spend months weaving her huipil, or blouse, which is her statement of identity as an individual within her community. Her peers read the subtly encoded messages of design, workmanship, and materials at a glance. The extensive collection of huipils, belts, skirts, and hair ornaments, each detailed as to place origin, makes this an intriguing sojourn.

Another fine shop in town is Casa de Artes at 4a. Avenida Sur #11, open Monday through Saturday from 9a.m. to 1 p.m. and 2:30 p.m. to 6:30 p.m. It offers arts and crafts of fine quality, specializing in Indian weavings, jewelry, and folk art in a museum-like atmosphere. Accommodations in Antigua offer a range of possibilities. At the high end is the lovely Casa Santo Domingo, a luxury hotel and restaurant in a converted Colonial convent. Doubles run $150 and singles $115 per night. The Address is 3a Calle Oriente #28. The Hotel Posada de Don Rodrigo, 5 Ave. Norte #17, is a well-established hotel with rooms set around courtyards, a restaurant, and daily marimba music. Prices: $68 for a double and $60 for a single.

For a delightful stay in a 400-year-old home consider the Casa de los Cantaros, a palatial mansion called a "bed and breakfast." It offers lovely semi-suites and other bedrooms around a courtyard and communal living room and dining areas. Prices range from $60 to $00 for a daily stay, less for weekly rates. Contact the charming English-speaking owner and manager, Ana Maria Pellecer, 5a. Avenida Sur #5, 03001 Antigua. Telephone: (502) 832-0674; Fax: (502) 832-0609.

Most of the country has a temperate climate of 69 on average. The elevation of 5,000 feet keeps Antigua pleasant year-round. The rainy season is May through November, but conversations with local residents suggest that any season is a fine time for a visit.

Once regarded as the cultural and religious center of the country, today Antigua is a haven of tranquility,and a quiet break from the energy of the capital. Another prime attraction is its dozens of language schools, some of the best and cheapest in all of Latin America. The tourist office, open daily from 8 a.m. to noon and 2 p.m. to 6 p.m., is on the south side of the plaza with plenty of literature for excursions and words of caution for safety.

Guatemalan fare is a blend of the Spanish, Indian and European, with such French specialties as mushroom quiche and profiteroles with ice cream and chocolate sauce, alongside such native dishes as Chiles Rellenos and Chicken Pepian, the bird cooked in a pumpkin and sesame seed spicy sauce. Other typical restaurant dishes include shrimp ceviche, red snapper with cashews, and mushrooms with garlic. Flan is a justly famous dessert and hot bananas may come with a chile-spiked chocolate sauce.

Our daily breakfasts featured a sumptuous platter of ultra-sweet pineapple rings, cantaloupe crescents, pink papaya spears and peeled bananas, plus pancakes or eggs any style and toast and marmalade. For lunch, a homemade vegetable soup of carrots, broccoli, spinach, corn, or green beans served as a prelude to a salad platter of sliced tomatoes and red onion rings, sprouts and avocado wedges, with a chicken or ham sandwich alongside. Vegetables starred at dinner – sugar snaps, long beans, artichokes, and patty pan squash – with rice and pork chops, chicken with mushrooms, grilled snapper, prawns in tomato sauce, or leg of lamb. Fried plantains, flan and watermelon with liqueur were sweets. The two houses joined for dining occasionally, and our kindly house waiter dressed up to serve to table wearing a colorful native costume of bolero jacket, short embroidered pants and turban hat.

Recipes

Spanish Tortilla

makes 4 servings

3 large white potatoes or Yukon Gold potatoes, thinly sliced

1/4 cup olive oil

1 onion, chopped

Salt and pepper, to taste

4 eggs

1 small red pepper, seeded and sliced

Minced flat-leaf parsley

Leave the skin on the potato, if you prefer. Heat 2 tablespoons of the oil in a 9 or 10 inch skillet and saut the potatoes and onion, stirring, until golden brown. Season with salt and pepper. Beat the eggs and gently mix the potatoes with the eggs. In another frying pan, heat the remaining oil and pour in the potato and egg mixture. Cook over medium heat without stirring until set. With a plate, flip over and cook on the other side until browned. Garnish with pepper slices and parsley.

Paella Marinera

makes 6-8 servings

3 tablespoons olive oil

1 medium onion, chopped

1 red pepper, seeded and chopped

1 green pepper, seeded and chopped

10 garlic cloves, minced

1/2 pound mild or spicy Spanish sausage, diced

2 cups rice

3 cups hot seafood broth or water

Pinch saffron

1 pound raw medium-sized shrimp, peeled and deveined

1/2 pound clams in their shells

1/2 pound mussels in their shells

Salt to taste

1 cup artichoke hears, parboiled

1/2 cup green olives

In a paella pan or heavy bottomed large pot, heat the oil and saut the onion, peppers, and garlic until soft. Add the sausage and saut a few minutes. Add the rice, broth and saffron. Bring to a boil, cover and simmer 10 minutes. Add the seafood and simmer until cooked through and the rice is tender, about 10 minutes longer. Add salt to taste and garnish with artichokes and olives and heat through.

Flan (Caramel Custard)

makes 8 servings

1 cup sugar

3-1/2 cups milk

6 eggs

2 egg yolks

1 teaspoon vanilla extract

1/4 teaspoon almond extract

1/3 cup toasted chopped almonds or berries for garnish (optional)

Heat 1/2 cup of the sugar in a heavy saucepan until it melts and turns amber, shaking the pan. Immediately pour into a 1-1/2 quart ring mold and tilt to coat all sides. Pour milk into the pan and heat until scalding. Beat eggs and yolks until light and beat in the remaining 1/2 cup sugar. Stir in the milk, vanilla and almond extract. Pour into the mold and place in pan of hot water. Bake in a 350 F oven for 50 minutes or until set. Let cool and chill. With a knife, loosen the edges and unmold onto a platter. Sprinkle with nuts or accompany with berries, if you wish.

History notes on Antigua: The territory of Guatemala was explored by Pedro de Alvarado on Hernan Cortes' orders and finally conquered after months of fighting the defiant Maya. As part of the colonial expansion movement, Alvarado founded the city of Santiago de los Caballeros de Guatemala at Iximche in 1524. This was the first European community on Guatemalan soil, and the old trades of Europe and the natural talent of the Maya made for a perfect partnership, as their creativity gave birth to the Guatemalan colonial style.

Alvarado was killed in an expedition and his young wife, Dona Beatriz, took over, yet her reign was short-lived. She was killed in a flood and a wash of rain and mud. In 1527 the capital moved to Ciudad Vieja, a valley a few kilometers from Antigua. Later it moved to Antigua. After the 1717 earthquake the city reached its peak with 70,000 inhabitants and 32 churches, 15 convents and monasteries, and 10 chapels. Antigua was again destroyed by the severe earthquake of 1773.

10

Indian Cuisines

INTRODUCTION

What's for dinner tonight? Cumin, coriander and cardamom; mustard, mango powder, ginger; asafetida, fenugreek and chilies. And then there's turmeric, tamarind and saffron, curry leaf, coconut milk and kewara water, almonds, cashews and pistachios – and those are just the seasonings!

Only one place on the map incorporates this riot of sensory stimulation in its meals: India. In fact, the intensive use of spices – whole, ground, roasted and stewed – marks the unifying characteristic of an otherwise highly diverse cuisine. Characterizing Indian food is a bit like describing European cuisine – all of it at once.

Indian food presents a range of flavors, intense and subtle, as vast as the country itself. Regional influences range from climate and elevation to history and religion. They define cuisines that differ widely – no surprise in a country of 884 million people occupying an area of 1,226,595 square miles.

In addition to the pronounced use of spices, common culinary threads unifying local cuisines include the prominence of flatbreads and a far greater use of dairy products than anywhere else in Asia. Breads are made with wheat, rice and ground legumes depending on the part of the country while dairy products include milk, cream, yogurt, buttermilk, sour cream and cheese.

Beyond that, the differences take over. Northern Indians tend to use their spices ground while Southerners start out with them whole and grind them to a paste with cooked onions and other ingredients. The South is the land of rice while Northerners rely on wheat and other grains – except for Kashmir, high in the Himalayas, which produces some of the best rice in the world. Cooks of the tropical South make heavy use of coconut milk, an ingredient rarely seen in the North. Areas with access to waterways rely more heavily on seafood. Thus Bengal is a region of fish-lovers, preferably the fresh water variety.

Those parts of India with the longest history of Mughal rule exhibit strong Persian influences in their food, using fresh and dried fruit, cashews, pistachios and almonds in their meat dishes as well as a great many dairy products. The cuisine of royalty, Mughlai dishes may use as many as 12 spices in a single dish including the most expensive of them – saffron, cardamom, cinnamon and cloves. Meanwhile, the food of Goa on the Southwestern coast betrays that province's long history as a Portuguese colony. Goans eat pork and duck, meats rarely seen outside the area, and use vinegar as a souring agent, a Portuguese legacy.

Undoubtedly the strongest influence defining Indian food is religion. Centuries of Hindu practice and the profound belief in reincarnation have resulted in the most delicious vegetarian cuisine to be found in the world. For protein, vegetarians rely on a wide range of legumes, both whole and split. Mixed with grain, boosted by vegetables and dairy products, and spiced to the max, they provide a wholesome, varied diet.

But nothing is simple in India. Brahmins and members of the merchant caste may observe strict vegetarian rules, but members of other castes eat meat. Styles of vegetarian cooking differ from region to region. Non-Hindu minorities produce their own cuisines and have had a major impact on how others eat. And then there's Kashmir where Brahmins eat meat – but avoid garlic and onions.

Hinduism, however, determines what kinds of meat people eat. Beef is strictly forbidden because Hindus realized from ancient times the life-giving role cows played in society – from producing dairy products to pulling plows to providing fertilizer for the fields. Today it is illegal to slaughter a cow anywhere in the country except in heavily Christianized Goa. The meats of choice are therefore goat, mutton and chicken.

The Muslim minority in India – currently 11 percent – has impacted cuisine and eating practices nationwide. Ancient Vedic concerns with purity made for an austere lifestyle when it came to food. Socializing over a meal was almost impossible if one had to worry about contamination from a host's kitchen or the caste of his cook.

Muslims, who conquered a large portion of India in the 12th century, had minimal religious restrictions – principally prohibitions against alcohol and pork. What's more, Islam encouraged zakat, or the sharing of food with others. Hospitality played a critical role in Mughal courtly society and, as Persians, the Muslim rulers brought with them a marvelous cuisine to share.

Mughal influence is most strongly felt today in the culinary centers of Delhi and Lucknow in the North and Hyderabad in the South. But while the kebabs, pilafs, kormas and yogurt dishes may spring from similar roots, interpretations reflect local cooking styles. The foods of Delhi and Lucknow remain slightly closer to the Persian models – with the addition of cumin, coriander, turmeric, cardamom, cinnamon and ground chilies typical of the North. Meanwhile mustard seeds, curry leaves, hot chilies, tamarind and coconut milk infuse the dishes of Hyderabad.

Indian restaurant food barely skims the surface of Indian cuisine. Hindu Punjabis forced back across the border from Pakistan at the time of the partition started the first restaurants in 1945. Their beehive-shaped tandoori ovens which heat up to 1000 degrees cook meat, fish and bread lightning-fast and remain their greatest claim to glory. A mix of Punjabi and Mughal cuisine has become standard restaurant fare both in India and abroad.

Sampling the breadth of Indian cuisine thus remains a challenge inside the country and out. Serious research is necessary to locate those few restaurants dedicated to serving pan-Indian cuisine.

The alternative, of course, is to cook it yourself. Many good cookbooks can help you along and the techniques are not that difficult. Grind your spices in a coffee grinder and puree seasoning pastes in a blender or food processor. Meanwhile, what is this stuff called "curry" we've been eating all these years? Not Indian, I'm afraid. Colonial rulers have never been known for their linguistic accuracy and no one knows for sure where the British got this one. "Kari" is a South Indian word for sauce and "tarkari" is a North Indian dish – which may or may not be relevant. Clearly the sahibs and memsahibs fell in love with the flavors of India. When they returned to the homeland, they had their cooks grind up a mix of spices to sprinkle on their staid British staples. The world now knows this as "curry powder" and whatever is cooked with it is "curry."

As if the same stodgy old combination in dish after dish could begin to reflect the wonders of India!

Recipes

These recipes are from Lachu Moorjani whose restaurant, Ajanta, was named the best Indian restaurant in the San Francisco Bay Area by the 1997 Zagat Guide. If you happen to be passing through, look it up at 1888 Solano Avenue, Berkeley. Lachu deliberately provides a pan-Indian menu and rotates dishes every month. Drop in at lunchtime, but for dinners it's best to make a reservation.

Serve the lamb, chicken, shrimp and dal dishes with saffron rice.

Lamb Korma

Serves 6

As you can see from the rich array of ingredients in this dish – yogurt, cream and slivered almonds – this is a Mughlai dish,

truly fit for a king.

3 tablespoons canola oil

1 teaspoon cumin seeds

1 piece ginger, peeled and finely chopped

2 medium onions, peeled, quartered lengthwise and sliced thin

1 1/2 pounds boneless cubed lamb, excess fat removed

2 teaspoons ground coriander

1 1/2 teaspoons of a mix of cayenne and paprika – determine according to your taste for heat

1 teaspoon ground turmeric

1 teaspoon ground black pepper

1 teaspoon salt

1/4 cup slivered almonds

1 cup plain yogurt

3 ounces heavy cream

1 teaspoon garam masala (see below)

Heat oil in a 6-quart pot. When hot, add cumin seeds. When seeds pop, add ginger. Fry for about 15 seconds. Add onions and saut at medium high heat, stirring frequently, until they become dark golden brown.

Raise heat to high. When pot is very hot, add lamb and saut until nicely browned. Add coriander, paprika/cayenne, turmeric, black pepper and salt. Stir fry two or three minutes. Turn heat off, add and mix yogurt, turn heat back on (this prevents curdling).

Bring mixture to a boil (add one quarter to one-half cup water if there is not enough liquid), reduce heat, cover partially and simmer at low heat for about 45 minutes, or until lamb becomes tender. At this time, you will notice a thin film of oil on the surface. Add garam masala and cream, mix, cover, turn off heat and leave on the stove for about five minutes. Sprinkle with slivered almonds before serving.

Garam Masala

Lachu insists you make your own garam masala.

Equal quantities of whole cloves, hulled cardamom and broken cinnamon stick

Toast whole spices for about 10 seconds per teaspoon in the microwave. Grind in a coffee grinder and mix.

Chicken Baffat

Serves 6

The technique of frying spices together and pureeing them into a paste is classic South Indian. Of course, the coconut milk is a further hint as to this recipe's origins.

1/4 cup canola oil

3 dried red chilies, broken into pieces

3 teaspoons coriander seeds

1 1/2 teaspoon cumin seeds

1 1/2 inch piece ginger, peeled and chopped

9 medium garlic cloves, peeled and chopped

3 medium onions, peeled, quartered lengthwise and sliced very thinly

2 1/4 pounds deboned, skinned chicken, preferably dark meat, cut into 1 to 2 inch pieces

1 1/2 teaspoon turmeric

2 1/4 teaspoons cayenne mixed with paprika, proportion to suit your taste for heat

Salt to taste (approximately 1 1/2 teaspoon)

1/3 to 2/3 can coconut milk

3 medium potatoes, cut into 3/4 inch cubes

A few curry leaves

Ball of tamarind pulp the size of a large lemon, dissolved in warm water and strained

In a small saucepan, heat 1 tablespoon oil. When hot, add chilies, coriander and cumin seeds. Fry for 10 to 15 seconds. Add ginger and garlic and fry for about 30 seconds. Transfer mixture to a blender and puree to a thick paste, adding water if necessary.

In a large pot, heat 3 tablespoons oil. When hot, add onions and saut? at medium to high heat until slightly brown, about eight to ten minutes. Raise heat to high, wait for 1 to 2 minutes until pot is very hot, add chicken and stir-fry until chicken is browned.

Reduce heat to medium, add all spices and salt. Stir for three to four minutes and add coconut milk. Bring mixture to a boil (add up to 1/3 cup water if there is not enough liquid). Reduce heat, add potatoes, cover and simmer slowly for 20 to 25 minutes or until chicken is tender. Add curry leaves and tamarind during last five minutes.

Raj Jhinga (Prawns Cooked in a Mustard-Flavored Sauce)

Serves 6

Mustard seed is the classic spice of Bengali food. This recipe uses it in two different forms and at different stages in the cooking. This one of many ways Indians coax multiple flavors from a single spice by varying the way it is processed.

5 tablespoons canola oil

2 teaspoons mustard seeds

2 teaspoons nigella seeds

8 to 10 garlic cloves, peeled and chopped

2 medium onions, peeled, cut into quarters lengthwise and thinly sliced

3 tomatoes, chopped

2 teaspoons turmeric

3 teaspoons cayenne mixed with paprika, proportion to suit your taste for heat

2 teaspoons ground cumin

2 teaspoons cracked mustard seeds (use blender or coffee grinder to crack them)

2 teaspoons salt

5 ounces ground almonds

2 pounds prawns, peeled and deveined

Heat 3 tablespoons oil in a 6 to 8 quart saucepan. When hot, add mustard and nigella seeds. When mustard seeds pop, add garlic and saut for about 30 seconds. Add onions. Saut at high heat until soft, about 12 to 15 minutes. Add tomatoes and stir fry for 6 to 8 minutes at medium high heat.

Add turmeric, paprika, cumin, cracked mustard seeds and salt. Saut at high heat for 3 to 4 minutes. Add ground almonds, reduce heat and cook for about 8 to 10 minutes, until oil separates from mixture.

In a separate saucepan, heat 2 tablespoons oil. When hot to the point of smoking, add prawns and saut, stirring constantly until pink, one to two minutes. Add to sauce and cook for another one to two minutes.

Urid Ki Dal

Serves 4 to 6

Dals are small legumes which have been peeled and split and thus cook much more quickly than larger beans. Dals differ from one another in color, flavor and texture with urid the creamiest among them. This dish is typical of North Indian vegetarian cooking. Eat it with the green bean recipe that follows and saffron rice.

1 cup urid dal, picked over and rinsed 2 or 3 times

5 to 6 cups water

1 teaspoon salt or to taste

1 teaspoon turmeric

2 tablespoons canola oil

1 teaspoon cumin seeds

1 large tomato, chopped

1 lemon-sized ball of tamarind concentrate dissolved in water and strained

1/3 cup chopped fresh cilantro

1 green chili pepper, chopped (optional)

In a large 6- to 8-quart pot, heat water and dal together. Bring to a boil, reduce heat and simmer, removing scum. Add salt and turmeric. Cook covered for about 45 minutes checking to make sure that dal is cooked and adding more water if needed. If there is too much water, uncover and boil down. The final product should be thick, almost like a paste.

In a small pot, heat oil. When very hot, add cumin seeds. Fry all seeds until they pop, about 20 seconds. Add to dal. Add remaining ingredients to dal. Mix and cook for about 5 more minutes.

Green Beans with Potatoes

Serves 6

While you may use this hearty vegetable dish with any of the above recipes, it is particularly appropriate with the dal.

4 tablespoons canola oil

9 to 12 garlic cloves, chopped

1 1/2 pounds green beans cut into 2-inch lengths

2 medium potatoes, peeled, halved and cut into 1/4-inch thick slices

1 1/2 teaspoon turmeric

3 teaspoons ground coriander

1 1/2 teaspoons cayenne mixed with paprika, proportion to suit your taste for heat

1 1/2 teaspoons mango powder (optional)

1 1/2 teaspoons salt

Heat oil. Saut chopped garlic for about 30 seconds. Add beans and potatoes. Saut for 4 to 5 minutes.

Add remaining ingredients. Mix and cook at medium high heat for 12 to 15 minutes until done. Stir frequently (once every 2 to 3 minutes) and do not cover pot.

Zaffrani Chaval (Saffron Rice)

Serves 6

This is the standard rice Lachu serves at Ajanta. *It would serve nicely as a side dish to non-Indian dishes as well.*

1 1/2 tablespoons canola oil

1 1/2 teaspoons black cumin seeds

2 1/4 cups Basmati rice

4 1/2 cups water

1 1/2 teaspoon salt

Generous pinch of saffron dissolved in 2 tablespoons warm water

Heat oil and fry black cumin seeds for 10 seconds.

Add rice and Saut for a few minutes until rice starts to change color and become opaque. Add water and salt. Bring to a boil, turn down heat and cover. Simmer until all liquid is absorbed (15 to 20 minutes) and rice is cooked.

Pour saffron water into middle 2-inch circle of rice. Leave covered for a few minutes for water to be absorbed. Fluff up rice with a fork and mix. Rice should be a marbled mix of white and yellow grains.

INDONESIA

Chart a country's cuisine and you can chart its history.

Nowhere is this more true than in Indonesia, the fifth largest country in the world, an archipelago consisting of 18,000 islands, spanning one-eighth of the globe and occupied by 250 ethnic groups. Here tremendous ethnic diversity coupled with wave upon wave of cultural influence adds up to a world of pleasure for the culinary adventurer.

History

Indonesia's indigenous techniques and ingredients merge with influences from India, the Middle East, China and Europe. And then there are the New World products brought by Spanish and Portuguese traders long before the Dutch colonized the islands.

Aficionados can only skim the surface unless we travel Indonesia itself. Most restaurants abroad and English-language cookbooks focus on the foods of Java and Sumatra with tastes of tourist-haven Bali. But the cuisines on these islands alone provide us with plenty of opportunity to keep our taste buds happy and our tongues tingling.

Rice is Indonesia's main staple except in Maluku (the Moluccas) and Irian Jaya (Indonesian New Guinea) where sago palm flour, sweet potatoes and cassava reign supreme. As in the rest of Southeast Asia, other dishes are eaten in extremely small quantities. Meat, fish and vegetables are condiments designed to flavor the staple. Sauces such as fiery sambals lend added character. Westerners, accustomed to eating much larger portions of meat and fish, find much of Indonesian food scorchingly hot.

Natural resources include rich volcanic soils and endless coastlines as the islands arc through both the Pacific and Indian Oceans. Although some coastal areas are fished out, fresh water possibilities include lakes, rivers, ponds and flooded rice paddies. Not surprisingly, fish and crustaceans, fresh and dried, play a major role in the Indonesian diet. Flavorings indigenous to the islands establish strong family ties between Indonesian food and that of its Southeast Asian neighbors. Coconut milk, or santen, plays a critical role here as well as in Thailand, Cambodia, Burma, Malaysia, Singapore and parts of Vietnam, Laos and the Philippines. Indonesia shares the flavors of galangal, kaffir lime leaf and pandan with Thailand. Lemon grass and dried shrimp appear in the Philippines and Thailand both. Shrimp paste permeates the flavors of all three and Vietnam as well. Meanwhile delicious fruits and vegetables are common to the entire region.

But Indonesia's culinary ties are closest to those Southeast Asian countries strongly influenced by India. In fact, if there are ancient Buddhist or Hindu sites to be found on a country's soil, you can almost bet its cuisine will include ingredients such as cumin, coriander, ginger, and/or caraway. And you will find curries – highly spiced sauces often diluted with coconut milk and served with bite-sized bits of meat, fish and vegetables to enliven the blandness of rice.

Arab traders ultimately converted Java from Hinduism to Islam and exercised their culinary influence as well. Kebabs, marinated meat cubes threaded on skewers, were reinterpreted to become satay. Dill and fennel entered the repertoire of spices. Today Indonesia is the largest Muslim country in the world. Not surprisingly, goat and lamb are important meats, while pork is forbidden. It is eaten only in Hindu Bali and within the Chinese community.

Chinese merchants and traders meanwhile added their own indispensable contributions to the cookpot. Indonesian food would be unrecognizable without the wok, stir-frying, the soybean and noodles which thread their way throughout the cuisine in countless ways. Among their many vegetables, the Chinese brought mustard greens, mung beans, daikon radish and Chinese cabbage.

The Dutch, attracted by the nutmeg and cloves of Maluku, waged wars over the Spice Islands and ultimately colonized the entire archipelago. Colonization caused much suffering, but added the finishing touch when it came to flavors. Chili peppers from Mexico added their unmistakable sting. Peanuts from the Americas provided sauces for satay and gado-gado. Cassava from the Caribbean and sweet potatoes from South America furnished Maluku and Irian Jaya with their staples.

In this exotic world, Dutch colonizers sought the flavors of home. They imported cabbage, cauliflower, carrots, string beans, potatoes and corn, adding to the already vast array of vegetables. They also created an entertainment institution designed to present scores of different dishes at a single sitting. Rijsttafels might contain up to a hundred different dishes. Servants stood behind the chair of each guest ready to provide soothing morsels when necessary to cool a burning palate.

But a cuisine is more than the sum of its parts. Indonesian cooks adopted new tools, techniques and ingredients and indigenized them – some of the nearly beyond recognition. Ingenious home cooks used new techniques and forged ingredients unique to Indonesia.

Today soybeans provide not just nutritious beans for cooking on their own, soy sauce, tofu and sprouts, but tempeh, toasted soybean cakes fashionable in Western health food circles. Chinese soy sauce plays a role similar to fish sauce in Thailand, Vietnam and the Philippines. But Indonesians enrich it by the addition of sugar, star anise, salam leaf and galangal to become kecap manis or sweet soy sauce, a key ingredient and a dynamite addition to any cook's pantry. (Pronounce that "ketchup." It's the Indonesian origin of the English word.)

Not surprisingly, Indonesia has created a mix of flavors which exerts its own influence abroad. Satay has crept up the Malay Peninsula to become one of Bangkok's favorite street foods. Indonesian food plays a major role in the melange of cuisines found in Singapore. After years of colonial intimacy, the Dutch are avid fans and some of the best Indonesian restaurants abroad can be found in the Netherlands.

History can be dry as dust or it can be fresh and tasty. Eating our way through Indonesia allows us to appreciate the significance of this country as a cultural crossroads where the great art, religions, political powers and economic forces meet and interact – and lets us ache for just another bite.

Mail Order Supplies

In cities like New York, Los Angeles, Seattle, Vancouver and the San Francisco Bay area, you should have no trouble finding ingredients for cooking Indonesian food in your local Asian markets.

Certain ingredients unique to Indonesian cuisine such as kemiri, a thickening agent, and salam leaf may be marketed under English names as candlenut and Indian bay leaf. Pandan leaf is occasionally used in Thai cooking and may be found in stores catering to Thai customers.

But you surfers living in cities with small Asian populations can now sit back and order ingredients with a click of the mouse. Yup, Indonesian ingredients on-line. Check out www.lm.com/~bachris for a website run by Syamsul and Beverley Bachri, owners of Bachri's, an Indonesian restaurant in Pittsburgh. You'll find just about everything you need for a home-cooked Indonesian meal and then some.

Cookbooks

Relatively few cookbook authors devote themselves exclusively to Indonesian food and the results are mixed. However, the South-East Asian cookbooks available all have extensive sections on Indonesia, which increases your range of choice.

Because of extensive chopping and grinding, Indonesian cooking is labor-intensive and designed to be done by more than one set of hands. Contemporary cookbook authors fall into two camps. The purists favor grinding by mortar and pestle to retain the old textures and seek out original ingredients while abroad. The modernists update the equipment, using food processors and spice grinders, and substitute more accessible local ingredients Choose what's best for you.

Recipes

Satay Ayam (Chicken Satay)

Serves approximately six people, 10 to 12 as part of a rijsttafel

Satay, quick-grilled over a roadside fire, is popular street food today in Malaysia, Singapore, Thailand and Cambodia, but its home is Indonesia.

Tuti Taylor-Weber of Oakland, California's Dutch East Indies Restaurant provides us with her version.

2 lbs. boneless, skinless chicken breast or thigh meat

1 clove garlic, crushed

1 tsp. ground ginger

2 tsp. dark soy sauce

2 tsp. tamarind juice (see ingredients list)

Cut chicken into cubes of approximately 3/4" on a side. Mix together remaining ingredients and marinate chicken for two hours. Soak bamboo skewers in water for approximately 20 minutes.

Thread chicken onto skewers, four or five to a skewer, and grill over glowing coals or under preheated grill four minutes to a side or until chicken is brown on all sides.

Serve satay with peanut sauce and a fiery sambal to satisfy your need for heat.

Satay Sauce

8 Tb. crunchy peanut butter

1 1/2 cups water

3 tsp. garlic salt

3 tsp. dark brown sugar

Tamarind juice to taste

Coconut milk (see ingredients list) or additional water

Put peanut butter and water in a saucepan and stir over gentle heat until mixed.

Remove from heat and add all other ingredients except coconut milk or additional water. Use coconut milk or water to make sauce thick yet pouring consistency. Check seasonings and add more salt and tamarind juice if needed.

Rendang

Serves eight to ten people, 12 to 15 is part of a rijsttafel

Sumatrans and Javanese have very different interpretations of this favorite beef dish. Sumatrans like it hot and dry, while Javanese like it sweeter with more gravy. While, a Javanese herself, Tuti leans toward

the style of Padang in Sumatra, considered by most the source of the best food in the country. Out of sympathy for her guests, she cuts back on the hot pepper. But if you'd like to sample true Padang-style eating, load up on the sambal.

1 medium onion chopped

5 cloves garlic, chopped

1 Tb. fresh ginger, chopped

5 fresh red hot chillies chopped or 2 Tb. crushed dry chili

2 cups coconut milk

1 1/2 tsp. salt

1 tsp. ground turmeric

2 tsp. ground coriander

2 tsp. galanga powder (see ingredients list)

4 tsp. paprika

6 kemiri (see ingredients list)

6 kaffir lime leaves (see ingredients list)

1 stalk of fresh lemon grass or 1 Tb. lemon grass powder (see ingredients list)

1/2 cup tamarind juice

1/2 cup water

3 lbs. round or chuck steak cut into strips approximately 1 1/2 wide and 2 1/2 long

Mix all ingredients but meat in a blender or food processor. Add to a large saucepan, add meat and bring quickly to a boil.

Reduce heat to moderate, stirring occasionally until sauce reduces by one-half. Turn heat to low and continue cooking until gravy is almost dry stirring frequently to ensure mixture does not stick to the pan.

Allow meat to fry in remaining oil until it is dark brown. Cooking time approximately two hours. Serve with white rice.

Kari Ikan (Fish Curry)

Serves 4 people, more for a rijsttafel

No sampling of Indonesian dishes would be complete without seafood or a curry. Syamsul and Beverley Bachri, owners of *Bachri's in Pittsburgh, Pennsylvania provide us with the perfect marriage, a fish curry, and a simple one at that.*

1 Tb. oil

1 onion, sliced

1 tsp. grated fresh ginger

8 kemiri ground

1 tsp. curry powder

2 tsp. kecap manis (sweet soy sauce)

2 tsp. lemon juice

1 cup water

4 fish fillets

2 scallions, chopped

Heat oil in a wok, add sliced onion, and stir-fry until tender. Add ginger, kemiri, and curry powder, and stir-fry over low heat for 3 minutes.

Add kecap manis, lemon juice, and water, and bring to a boil. Reduce heat and simmer for about 3 minutes.

Add fish fillets in a single layer in the wok. Cover and simmer for 5 minutes on each side or until the fish is done. Place on a platter, sprinkle with chopped scallions, and serve with sambal and sliced cucumber salad along with white rice.

Semur Daging (Slices Of Beef In Soya Sauce)

Serves 3 or 4, more for a rijstaffel

On my first night in Jakarta, my hostess prepared semur. No doubt she felt it would be easy on my wimpy western palate, but I found its sweetness strange and exotic. Of course a palate trained in the Midwest during the fifties and sixties would have found anything exotic! Now that I have toughened up, I know to serve a dish like this with plenty of sambal for a balance between sweet and hot. This is Syamsul and Beverley Bachri's version.

1 lb. beef roast, thinly sliced

2 shallots, sliced

1 clove garlic, finely chopped

2 Tb. kecap manis (sweet soy sauce)

2 Tb. butter

2 hard-boiled eggs, halved

2 potatos, thinly sliced

2 tomatos, peeled and chopped

4 scallions, chopped

Salt and pepper to taste

Pinch of nutmeg

Thinly sliced fried onion

Fry shallots and garlic in butter until lightly browned. Add meat and potato slices, and saute briefly. Add the tomato, soy sauce, salt, pepper, and nutmeg. Mix well. Cover and cook for 5 minutes. Add eggs and cook for 5 minutes more. Add scallions just prior to serving and garnish with fried onions. Serve with white rice.

Sambal

And at last, the food that gives Indonesian cuisine its spark. There are sambals of all sorts to accompany different kinds of dishes. Some are used as an ingredient in dishes like sambal goreng ikan (fish fried in sambal). The heat can come from fresh red chillies for from bottled chilli paste. This is Syamsul and Beverley's basic recipe. Modify it to suit your needs.

2 large tomatoes

2 large Spanish onions

1 tsp. terasi (see ingredients list)

Several cloves of garlic

1/2 cup sambal oelek (raw chili paste) (see ingredients list)

1/4 cup oil

Salt and pepper to taste

Blend together in a food processor thc tomatoes, onions, terasi, garlic and sambal oelek until slightly chunky. Do not overblend.

Place mixture in a pot, preferable with a non stick surface with the oil, salt and pepper and lightly boil until no water surfaces. The sambal is done when the consistency is constant and it no longer seperates.

(For Sambal Manis - Sweet Sambal — a very common variation on the theme, add 1/4 cup of Kecap Manis when the sambal is almost done.)

Staple Ingredients

Tamarind juice is made from block tamarind concentrate sold in Asian stores, some supermarkets and by mail order. To make tamarind juice, break off a piece of the block and soak in warm water for 10 to 15 minutes. Squeeze and loosen the remainder of the flesh from the seeds and strain. Use a ratio of approximately 1:4 tamarind concentrate to water.

Coconut milk can be found canned at Asian groceries, many supermarkets and by mail order. Mae Ploy from Thailand is the richest brand available.

Galanga (also known as laos) powder, the ground root of a rhizome related to ginger, can be found in Asian groceries, some supermarkets and by mail order.

Kemiri or candlenut is ground and used as a thickening agent in Indonesian food. It can be found at Asian groceries and by mail order. Macadamia nut will provide approximately the same texture, but not the same flavor. Don't eat kemiri raw! They contain a mildly toxic substance which is destroyed by cooking.

Kaffir lime leaves can be found frozen and dried at Asian food stores. The frozen ones are more flavorful.

Lemon grass/lemon grass powder are both found in Asian groceries. Fresh lemon grass, also found in farmer's markets in cities with large Asian populations, is far superior to the powder and easy to grow in mild climates. Try rooting some stalks in water and planting them outdoors.

Terasi or shrimp paste can be found in Asian groceries and by mail order. In a pinch, substitute Thai or Vietnamese shrimp paste or even Filipino bagoong, all of which may be more available.

Sambal Oelek or raw chili paste is available in Asian markets and by mail order. Like many of these ingredients, you can get them from Syamsul and Beverley by ordering on-line.

ITALY

Introduction

Italy overpowered me the moment I stepped off the plane. The ancient architecture juxtaposed with modern Italian life, the endless vistas that entice artists and traveler alike, the foreigners of Italian life, the scents that wafted through the streets from the earth, the homes and the restaurants, the devastating beauty of this artistically and culturally rich and colorful country captured my heart forever in Italy's enduring embrace. My mind reached out to all the sensations, devouring them as quickly as they came. To this day I can be swiftly transported to the banks of the River Arno in Pisa if my senses are triggered by a familiar scent.

When I first set eyes on Italy, I was a nineteen year old college student ready (or so I thought) to pursue Italian art history and language at L'Universita de Pisa. I had studied Italy: its art and architecture, its history, language and culture in the States during my first years of undergraduate school. I soon realized my academic studies hadn't quite prepared me for the real thing. From the blur of the Italian customs officials and the shouts of Italian endearments and welcome, I was catapulted into the gregarious, intimidating and, sometimes, oppressive life of Italy. I learned to love her with an undying passion.

Italy Today

It is surprising for many to learn that Italy ranks seventh as a world industrial power. Well known enterprises such as Fiat, Olivetti and Baretta are located in Italy. Annual industrial trade shows are held each year in Milan and in Bari. Unfortunately, economic development has taken its toll on urban areas in the form of over building and pollution, particularly in the north.

Italy's Geography

There are approximately 210,000 square kilometers/130,000 square miles of Italy excluding the islands surrounding the country.

This is about the size of Great Britain or the state of California. Roughly 55 million people live between its shores, with most concentrations found in urban areas. Its terrain is a combination of several mountainous regions, which comprise 70% of the country, coastal plains and an abundance of rural open spaces. Yet, despite this seemingly inhospitable terrain, almost 70% of the land is agricultural. The Dolomites and the Great Alps border northern Italy. The Maritime Alps are situated in the northwest. The Appenines are the largest range and run down most of the length of Italy, hence they are known as the backbone of the country. The Italian Alps boast towering peaks such as the Matterhorn and Mont Blanc, whereas the tallest mountain situated completely within Italy's borders is located in the Appenines. It is called *Il Gran Sasso d'Italia* (Big Rock of Italy). To this day it still remains a challenge to cross the Appenines between the Tyrrhenian and Adriatic Seas using the present roadway system.

The largest islands of Italy are Sicily and Sardinia with smaller islands of Elba (Napoleon's isle of exile), Ischia, Capri and the cluster north of Sicily called Lipari, all located off the western coast. Italy is surrounded by seas on both sides: the Ligurian, Tyrrhenian, and Mediterranean on its western shores and the Adriatic on the east.

Because of it's vast length, with a coastline covering almost 1600 kilometers/992 miles, Italy has a variety of climates: from the cooler, wetter northern areas to the beautiful Mediterranean weather of the Mezzogiorno, the bright, sunbathed region of southern Italy.

A Bit of History

With its colorful history, Italy has had many forms of government. According to my grandfather, who was born and raised in Calabria and lived to the robust age of 103, one could live a lifetime and experience more than a few dozen regimes of governmental rule. Maybe in his lifetime. It is a well known fact that Italy has experienced many political upheavals throughout its history, especially in the post-war years of the twentieth century. During this period, each of Italy's governments lasted, on the average, under twelve months.

Italy is divided into twenty regions, each being autonomous yet connected to the central government of Rome. This autonomy can be seen in the differences of local policies and taxes, and cultural and historical diversities. The early colonization of Italy by Greeks and Etruscans, then invasions by countries surrounding Italy helped to incorporate pieces of each culture into a rich tapestry of provincial centers and regional pride.

Italy's Regions

The North

Northern Italy is composed of eight regions and is considered the most prosperous, likely due to its heavy industrial trade (a strong car manufacturing center in Turin, a finance and fashion capitol in Milan) and its tourism (which boasts excellent Alpine skiing in Valle d'Aosta and year-round balmy weather on the Italian Riviera in Liguria). Tall Lombardian poplars and cypresses are a common part of the landscape. The weather, which is dominated by the capricious climate of the Alps, offers seasonal changes and can get quite chilly and sometimes snowy in many of the northern regions. The exception is Liguria. Protected by the same mountains that wreak havoc on all other weather patterns of northern Italy, this area offers very mild, balmy winters.

Located in the northwest corner of Italy are Valle d'Aosta and Piedmont, known for their excellent ski areas. The cuisine of this region is a dynamic blend of Italian mountain specialties and strong Gallic flavors influenced by its proximity to France. It is common to see white truffles (*trifola d'Alba*) and butter in Piedmontese recipes. Southern Piedmont, near Asti and Alba, produce Italy's greatest wines. Polenta is another regional specialty. Once a year Piedmont celebrates with a festival in honor of this wonderful grain they call *Il Polentone.*

South of these two regions is Liguria, which borders the French Cote d'Azur. Liguria has its own version of a wealthy tourist haven called the Italian Riviera, boasting palm tree lined streets. hills of olive trees, a profusion of flowers and harbors filled with yachts. Genoa is Italy's greatest seaport. Because of this, Ligurians are known for their seafood dishes and their Pesto Genovese, a sauce made of a paste of fresh garlic, extra virgin olive oil, fresh

Italian basil leaves, pine nuts and Parmigiano Reggiano cheese. Liguria is associated with its abundance of produce and citrus fruits but is best known for the carnations it grows and the world famous honey it produces.

Heading east we intersect with the region of Lombardy. The industrial capital of Italy, Milan, reigns powerfully in this area. It is also known for its culinary contributions to the world such as *Minestrone alla Milanese* and *Risotto alla Milanese*. Polenta has also been eaten here since the days of the Roman soldiers. The Brianza district is best known for its choice beef cattle and dairy herds, the former seen as some of the best meats produced in Italy and the latter contribute to the making of Gorgonzola and Bel Paese cheeses. Milan is a great cultural center with La Scala Opera Theater, the Duomo of Milan and Leonardo da Vinci's famous fresco, "The Last Supper." Also known for its spectacular lake region which is approximately a one and a half hour drive north of Milan, this area is favored by the rich and the romantic. The six long, slender lakes, offer stunning villas and beautifully sculpted gardens.

The land mass of Trentino-Alto Adige is made up of the Dolomite peaks in the north and east and rolling hills covered with vineyards and orchards in the south. Throughout the landscape are approximately 350 old castles. The area is steeped in its original roots and traditions inherited from the Austro-Hungarian. This influence is also seen in both their blue- eyed features and their foods such as soups flavored with caraway seeds, speck (a smoke-cured prosciutto), strudels and the use of sauerkraut and vinegar in their cooking.

The influences of Yugoslavia on its eastern border and Austria on its northern border are seen in the food and languages spoken in Fruili-Venetia Giulia. Historically, the cuisine of this region was affected by many cultures, so it is difficult to pinpoint one specific ingredient or dish that reflects any one culture. Paprika, poppy seeds, cinnamon, cumin and horseradish are used as flavorings and rice and polenta supplant pasta. Sausage- making is a specialty of this area as is Goulash, a beef stew made with red wine, tomatoes, paprika and spices. Trieste, a traveler's haven, is known for its seafood dishes.

Veneto is a region of simple but charming towns including its crowning jewel, Venice. This is a city built completely on water and requires travel either by foot, by water taxis or the more romantic gondolas. Brimming with history and art, Venice offers something for everyone from its Gothic Doges Palace on the Piazza San Marco and its opera house, to the Murano glass and Venetian Burano lace produced on islands north of the Venetian harbor. The cuisine of this region offers simple, almost country food, that is well prepared. The more well known dishes are *Risi e Bisi,* a porridge-like soup made with fresh peas, rice and Parmesan cheese; Pasta e Fagioli, a stew-like concoction made of tomatoes, tiny pasta and beans; plus a myriad of seafood dishes that reflect Veneto's proximity to the Adriatic.

The cold, wet winters and the hot, muggy summers make Emilia-Romagna the most successful agricultural region in Italy. Ravenna, Parma, Modena, Bologna and Rimini are all linked by the ancient Roman road, the Via Emilia, which connects the Adriatic to the heart of northern Italy. This region is known for it's gastronomical contributions. Four ingredients permeate much of the cooking of this region: tomatoes, chicken livers, cured pork and *soffrito,* a saut of celery, onion and carrot.

Central Italy

This area is typical of Italy's countryside. With its rolling hills, tall cypress trees, ancient roads, worn and crumbling farmhouses and villas, and miles of olive groves and well-manicured vineyards, it is understandable that one would think this to be representative of all of Italy. The cuisine of this area reflects a simpler, more rustic approach to cooking that relies heavily on the produce and livestock common to the area. Lamb, beef, kid and game are widely seen on the table in the form of a stew, spit-roasted or grilled. Pasta and vegetables, particularly mushrooms and truffles, are often served alongside.

Tuscan food is simple and abundant with local produce, mellow cheeses and grilled meats. Their delicious, chewy breads are baked without salt. I found this to be a strange taste but, once I got used to the flavor of the bread flour, I became a convert. Tuscans are also known for their appreciation of beans as seen in the staple of the Tuscan table: white beans cooked with sage and olive oil. Beef Steak Florentine, many versions of roasted or wine-braised game such as boar, deer and rabbit and thick and hearty soups cover the table of a typical Tuscan meal. This is the home of Chianti wine.

Umbria is a region known for its wheat fields and black truffles. Food is simply prepared and satisfying. Porchetta, or suckling pig, is a specialty of Umbria and is prepared with herbs and spit-roasted. Game and beef play an important part of an Umbrian meal.

Because of its predominantly rugged terrain, The Marches holds less attractions to a novice traveler than its neighbor, Umbria. One city that stands to be admired is the hill town of Urbino. This city has retained most of its ancient appearance and it set amid the mountainous region that makes up a great portion of The Marches. The food is considered more peasant-like and is known for such dishes as its version of *Porchetta* (which stuffs pig with peppers, rosemary and garlic) and their rich version of lasagna called *Vincisgrassi* which incorporates cinnamon-scented chicken gizzards and saut%d chicken livers sandwiched between layers of pasta and a creamy b#hamel sauce seasoned with freshly grated nutmeg. Certainly not a dish for the cholesterol-conscious! Fortunately for those of us that need to eat a bit lighter, there exists a coastal plain that affords a variety of filling yet less fattening seafood. The best known dish is brodetto or seafood soup which incorporates all types of fish overflowing in a saffron-infused broth.

From the picturesque views of Rome at the top of pastoral Palestine Hill, where ancient Rome was purported to have started, to the Renaissance heart of the city housed behind the walls of the tiny city-state of the Vatican, Rome is a traveler's delight. Food is again the typical rustic fare of Central Italy with *Abbacchio* (a suckling lamb seasoned with fresh rosemary), *Spaghetti alla Carbonara* (a bacon, egg and cheese sauced pasta), *Saltimbocca* (marsala braised tin slices of veal topped with ham), and *Suppli al Telefono* (addictive deep fried rice balls filled with mozzarella).

Pasta in Abruzzo is made using a *chitarra*, a rectangular device strung with thin metal wires like a guitar, hence the equipment's name. Sheets of pasta are rolled over this to form strips. Each town is known for its own specialties and lamb, hearty soups, a wide variety of herbs and even chilies are seen on the dining tables of this region. It is also known for its food festivals which honor saints or simply celebrate. Their non-stop eating and drinking event is called the Panarda which serves people course after course of food.

Southern Italy

Travelers to this area of Italy, known as the Mezzogiorno to the natives, are generally unprepared for the stark beauty of this mainly agricultural land. The land is sun-drenched and so it always appears shining in the midday sun. With a semi-tropical climate in many parts, this portion of the country abounds with blooming flowers and scents of citrus fruits. The portion of land that is dominated by mountains experiences cold and sometimes severe, snowy winters.

The regions of the south, Campania, Basilicata, Apulia, Calabria and its two islands, Sicily and Sardinia, can greet the novice traveler with untold mysteries and illusions of corruption that leave a person fearful and intimidated at the thought of touring the south. Part of this may be explained by the area's underdevelopment as compared to their wealthier relatives in the north. Trains are infrequent and often irregular, and southern Italians are more intense, more expressive, more explosive and more gregarious than their polite, reserved northern counterparts. The presence of the Mafia in the life of a southern Italian, particularly in Sicily, may also explain some of a traveler's apprehension. This is a misunderstood deterrent for many people who are too timid to venture beyond Naples. Organized crime is a part of life in southern Italy and has been a part of their culture for centuries. One must keep a clear head about this. There are many charming cities and rural towns and southern Italy is full of significant historical sites and works of art.

Food in these regions is a study in contrasts. Pasta, for instance, is usually purchased in its dry state, quite the contrast to people in the north who usually make a homemade pasta and cook it fresh. *Ziti*, short tubes of pasta eaten in Naples, and *orecchiette*, round indented small pastas meaning "little ears", are eaten in Apulia. The coastal regions rely heavily upon seafood to supplement their diet of vegetables, fruits and grains whereas the inland areas are more prone to eating meats. Of course there is always an exception to this rule. Pizzas served hot from the wood burning oven and topped with an assortment of vegetables, seafood, meats and cheeses are in stark contrast to foccacia, the flatbread of the north. Olive oil, especially extra virgin, is used in lieu of butter. The cuisines of the south are earthier and more peasant-like and bolder in their flavors and combinations of foods, reflecting the outgoing personalities of the people of this land.

In Campania, Naples is the most famous and beautiful of all its cities. Neopolitan and Campanian specialities include octopus prepared in a variety of ways, spaghetti dishes using a tomato-based fish sauce (particularly clams or squid), and dishes using the indigenous buffalo milk mozzarella, including pizza. I can't forget my favorite, *Pasta Puttanesca,* a fiery tomato sauced spaghetti flavored with lots of garlic and capers, Gaeta olives and anchovies. An authentic puttanesca is pure heaven if you enjoy food with lots of gusto! One more dish not to overlook is the well known *Parmigiana di Melanzane,* or Eggplant Parmesan.

Sicily has a subtropical climate along all of its coast and a harsher, colder climate inland near rugged Mount Etna. Because of this balmy weather, Sicily grows and exports oranges and lemons. Here, you'll get an opportunity to see examples left from the invasions of the Greeks, the Arabs and the Normans. Expect to eat lots of seafood and rich, filling pasta dishes that are often highly seasoned with strong black or green Sicilian olives or the staple of the south, the eggplant. Sweet desserts are a part of every day life. The most well known of these is the Sicilian *Cassata* (a layered, frozen cake) and *cannoli* (a crisp pastry tube filled with sweetened ricotta cheese, candies and sometimes chocolate).

Foods of Italy

It is surprising how many people who believe they are familiar with Italian cooking are unaware of the regional differences that exist. Pasta is the first course in a meal for most Italians with the exception of the far north. Here risotto or polenta is the norm. For the most part, meat does not play a regular part of many Italian diets with vegetables, grains and legumes taking center stage in most homes. Olive oil is often seen in its dark green state (from its first pressing) in the south. You will see a more refined, golden oil in the north.

As far as suggesting the best olive oil to use, I must first stress your choice depends upon the use of the oil and your own personal tastes. Many people prefer a fruity, golden oil and for them I would recommend using a product from Lucca. I used to live in Pisa which is near Lucca and consequently we would have Luccan olive oil on the table all the time. It has a delicious fruity, bright green aroma and the taste would often have a pleasant sharpness or bite to it. My oil of choice, though, comes from the rich, dark green olives of Sicily. I grew up with this and find the earthy, heavier, aromatic liquid almost makes me swoon with anticipation. So powerful is the flavor, I find I use much less than when I use the more refined, golden oils.

Although focaccia originates from Genoa, you will see a softer, thicker version in Apulia which is made of potatoes. This is chewy and delicious, especially lightly brushed with that dark green, southern Italian olive oil.

Basically, Italian cuisine is a combination of vegetables, grains, fruits, fish, cheeses and a scattering of meats, fowl and game usually seasoned or cooked with olive oil (with the exception of the far north). The reliance upon what the country can produce has shaped a diet popular for centuries, particularly with the poorer Italian people, and is called *la cucina povera.* Now we are seeing a resurgence of this "poor people's food" and the Mediterranean diet is being touted as the model around which we should restructure our eating habits.

Italian Eating Customs

As the old adage goes, "When in Rome, do as the Romans do," and when I ate in Italy, I tried to behave like a native. I liked to think that I belonged there, that I didn't stand out like the touristi because I insisted in eating only at the smaller, family-run trattorias. There you can get the best of the region's cooking while blending with the natives as you bask in the flavors and culture of their life.

One way to accomplish this is to familiarize yourself with Italian eating customs.

Italians eat only two main meals a day. They generally skip what we and Britons consider breakfast and opt for a cup of cappuccino. Lots of milk in coffee is definitely a morning ritual for Italians.

I'd like to offer some advice for savoring an Italian meal. First, don't be tempted to nibble on that gelato or cannoli during the day if you are planning to enjoy the experience of a full Italian lunch or dinner. This is a memorable occasion for your palate and realize that eating is done with great pleasure and gusto.

Second, if you do decide to dine Italian style, don't rush through your courses: learn the art of slowly savoring your meal over a bottle or two of wine and good conversation.

Italians take great pleasure in serving people the food they lovingly prepare, especially foreigners who are learning about their country. If you charge through a meal as if you have a plane to catch you are insulting the restaurant chef and staff and are considered gauche. You will very likely be dealt with accordingly. So, relax and enjoy one of life's greatest pleasures and one of Italy's many great accomplishments!

One more word of advice: Italians usually eat their dinner later than Americans do. Plan on getting to your restaurant (at the earliest) by 7pm. I made the embarrassing mistake of walking into a trattoria solo at 5 pm because I was hungry.

I found the restaurant was enjoying its family meal with the staff before beginning the evening's work. Of course they were gracious and charming and hopped up from their dinner table and prepared me my meal but I couldn't help feeling guilty as I ate knowing that I cut short one of the favorite parts of their day.

The Festivals of Italy

With a culture so steeped in religion, history, the arts, food and even superstition, it should not come as much of a surprise that Italians have found an opportunity to celebrate at least one (if not several) festivals each month of the year. This is fortunate as a traveler can experience Italy's culture and history. This list is certainly not complete and dates may be slightly altered from season to season.

January : Epiphany celebrations all through Italy in early January (5-6).

February/March : Shrovetide carnivals, similar to our Mardi Gras, are pre-Lenten celebrations, they tend to be especially boisterous in Venice.

March/April : Holy week and Easter celebrations throughout Italy, particularly beautiful in Rome where the Pope leads a procession on Good Friday.

April/May : Jazz festival in Milan.

May : Palio Balestra (medieval crossbow contest on horseback) using antique weapons held in Gubbio.

June : Historical regatta of the four Ancient Maritime Republics involving boat race between rival sea towns of Pisa, Venice, Amalfi and Genoa. Spoleto's world famous arts festival is held in June.

July : The Umbria Jazz festival is held every July in Perugia and is one of the most popular festivals in Italy.

July/August : The medieval Palio festival where ancient clothed riders race bareback around the town's square in Sienna (held both months).

September : Jousting performed by Saracen, dressed in ancient suits of armor held in Arezzo. Italian Grand Prix held in Monza.

October : Truffle hunts, market and fair held in Alba. Feast of St. Francis held in Assisi.

November : Sigillo festival: A wine and chestnut event held in San Martino.

December : La Scala opera season opens with great fanfare in Milan.

Places to Stay

Central Italy conjures up the quintessential classic Italian accommodations that we all dream about: the Italian villa perched high above the rolling Tuscan hills of chianti or a seventeenth-century castle set above panoramic views that afford you miles and miles of horseback riding pleasure. Sounds too good to be true? Hardly! There are many companies that specialize in just this sort of accommodation.

Rentvillas is the largest vacation home rental company in Italy. It is an example of one of the many companies that specialize in a complete rental service of villas, ancient restored castles and charming stone farmhouses in Tuscany. But the service doesn't stop there. There is a comprehensive and informative, color picture-filled catalogue of the elegant, historic and gracious accommodations that she offers in Veneto, Tuscany, Umbria, Lazio, Apulia and Sicily. You can choose to spend your holiday exploring the Tuscan countryside by day and relaxing in front of a roaring medieval castle fire by night or opt for an elegant, stylish urban apartment in Florence that is close to the heart of the city. Either way, you areassured of personalized service that fits your needs. At peak season, which extends from April through October, you can rent a splendid country residence for an average cost of $1250 per week for 3-4 people. This price includes all the amenities of a country manor and then some. An apartment in a metropolitan area will be approximately $1000 per week for 1-3 people. Country living requires a car.

Cooking Vacations in Italy

The purpose of this section is to acquaint you with a few of the lesser known culinary vacation schools that deserve merit. Certainly there are many schools to list, and quite a number of these boast "star chefs" and cookbook authors. It is not my intent to promote an already well known school but to offer a more moderately priced yet thoroughly enjoyable alternative in different regions of Italy. This is a delightful way to learn more about the Italian culture. Through cooking and on conducted tours you often can talk first hand to cheese makers, vintners, and pasta makers while learning the history of the region. The cost for one-week cooking classes and accommodations is between $3000-$4000. This does not include airfare but may include meals, excursions and ground transportation to/from the airport.

La Cucina Al Focolare – Reggello, Tuscany

Located in a converted 15th century friary, which produces its own Chianti and olive oil, this school overlooks the Valdarno

Valley on the outskirts of Florence. I have had the pleasure of speaking to this staff and found them to be effusive in their love for Tuscany. As a chef by profession, I believe I would find this cuisine, the school and its surroundings to be the most desirable way to spend a week in Italy. They offer a week-long course in Tuscan cooking, wine tastings and tours through the outdoor markets and towns of the Tuscan countryside. Participants work side-by-side with the top local chefs and the resident sommelier. A wood-burning oven and rotisserie are used to learn the Tuscan way of cooking pizza, foccacia, meats and game.

Italian Neighborhoods in the United States

If you can't manage a trip to Italy in the near future, then treat yourself to the next best thing by visiting an Italian neighborhood in or near your city. You can get the flavors and culture and many products of Italy without spending a lot of money. These Italian sections developed during the late 1800's and early 1900's when many poorer Italians relocated to America because of their homeland's starving economy and the dreams and promises of a more peaceful and prosperous life. These are a fiercely proud, close knit, hard working race of people who made a good life for themselves and their families despite the language, cultural, and socio-economic barriers existing for immigrants. This list of "Little Italys" is not meant to be all inclusive but more a representation of Italian sections across the nation. You'll notice the majority of people opted to settle on the east coast.

Boston, Massachusetts: The North End

Bordered by Commercial Street and the J.F. Kennedy Highway, this area is surrounded by brick and stone warehouses and the docks of Boston's old harbor. Packed in the narrow, small streets are an abundance of red brick and painted houses, restaurants and trattorias, cafe bars, shops and a seemingly never-ending selection of Italian food shops. The blending of residential and commercial works well here. This Italian section has many religious processions.

New York, NY: Little Italy

Mulberry and Mott Streets make up the heart of this Italian section, affectionately dubbed "Little Italy." Located south of

Houston Street (pronounced Howston) and butting against Chinatown, this area was originally a stronghold of southern Italians, particularly Neapolitans, Calabrians and Sicilians. Full of cafes and espresso bars, religious stores, little shops, wonderful restaurants and small specialty food stores. In the latter, you will find shop owners hanging their freshly-made mozzarella, rolling out their country loaves of bread, stuffing their sausages and pinching off pieces of home made dough to make the many shaped pastas. As in Boston, these Italians are strongly tied to their religious heritage and hold many processions in the streets of "Little Italy."

Philadelphia, Pennsylvania: South Philly

Bounded by Front, 20th, Washington and South Streets, this is very noticeably a working class neighborhood. People recognize this Italian section from the movie Rocky. Cafes and espresso bars abound. The heart of this area is the Ninth Street Italian Market where you can by anything Italian – from fresh produce and imported cheeses to clothing and shoes. In the fall and winter you can smell the delicious earthy aroma of roasting Italian chestnuts. Full of great restaurants, trattorias and food stores, this section also indulges in colorful and festive religious processions.

Pittsburgh, Pennsylvania: Bloomfield/"The Strip"

Located on Liberty Avenue and Pennsylvania Avenues, this section also includes "The Strip." Though it began as a mixture of many regions of Italy, Bloomfield is now composed of Abruzze people. You can see this influence in the shops where typical Abruzze products and foods are sold. The patron saint of this region, Saint Rocco, is honored in August by the festival to attend. The area offers good restaurants, cafes and a few excellent Italian food shops.

San Francisco, California: North Beach

Built around Washington Square in the north section of town, this Italian area is large and convivial. Jam-packed with cafes and authentic espresso bars and their well trained baristas, this Italian section tends to be a haven for the writer, the neighborhood resident and the tourist alike. Composed of northern and southern Italians, a tour of the area offers a huge variety of food shops, kitchen-ware shops, trattorias, and obscure little shops on upper Grant Street that offer handmade clothing and leather coats, unusual fabrics, eclectic jewelry and kitschy vintage wear that will delight the browser. The area's 150,000 residents share space with the commercial tenants. It borders San Francisco's Chinatown.

Recipes

I am including two recipes that my mother used to serve on summer nights. This was considered a "light" meal in our household. She would put together an antipasto with whatever was in the kitchen but the core ingredients were the red peppers that my father roasted over coals, her garlic and dill pickled string beans, oven-roasted new potatoes, and dry cured olives. All this was drizzled with balsamic vinegar and sprinkled with hard boiled eggs that were put through a fine sieve.

Pasta with Clams and Tomatoes

serves 6

8 beefsteak tomatoes, cut in half and squeezed of their seeds

4 cloves garlic, peeled and minced

1/2 cup dark green extra virgin olive oil

1 bunch basil, chopped

1 teaspoon salt

2 tablespoons fresh oregano leaves

3 tablespoons Italian parsley, chopped

3 tablespoons dark green extra virgin olive oil

1 clove garlic, peeled and minced

4 dozen small clams, cleaned

1 lemon, juice only

1/2 cup white wine

2 pounds linguine

Cut tomatoes into small cubes and mix with garlic, and let marinate in 1/2 cup oil, basil, salt, oregano and parsley for about half an hour at room temperature.

Put a pan of water on for your pasta. When water comes to boil, add pasta and cook according to manufacturers directions.

Drain well but do not rinse. While pasta is cooking, heat remaining olive oil in saut pan. Add minced garlic and clams. Shake pan quickly for about one minute then add white wine and lemon juice and shake pan once more, then cover to steam the clams for about two minutes. Remove lid and add marinating tomato mixture. Shake pan again to disperse sauce and cook for 3-4 more minutes. Toss with drained pasta.

Mixed Berries with Ricotta Creme

serves 6

My mother made this recipe with her Easter ricotta pie filling, which we all loved, and fresh berries that are available during summer. This is also good with wedges of winter pears, slices of star fruit, circles of navel oranges and bananas.

1 quart strawberries

1 quart raspberries

1 quart blackberries

3 cups ricotta cheese

1/2 cup powdered sugar

3 ounces bittersweet chocolate, chopped

1/2 orange zest only

3/4 cup toasted almond slivers

6 sprigs mint

Combine berries in a large bowl. Place ricotta and sugar in a processor and mix until smooth, or mix by hand. Remove from the processor and stir in the remaining ingredients. Serve half cup of berries per person. Top with a good sized dollop of the ricotta creme. Garnish with mint sprig.

Summary

I hope you realize that, to truly experience life as an Italian, you must succumb to the lure of its culture, the dominating force of its antiquity, the contagious mood of romance in the air and the passions of its people. Forget your phones, your newspapers and your television – leave these at home and surrender yourself to the gentle, persuasive rhythm that flows like a current in Italy.

Indulge in an espresso and engage in the idle cafe chatter with the locals. You may find yourself caught in Italy's magic spell and may never want to leave.

JAPAN

Introduction

The cuisine of Japan is shaped by its four distinct seasons and by regions. It is a cuisine that first and foremost delights the senses – in Japan, the eyes, nose, and palate feast along with the stomach. The essence of Japanese cuisine is based on various elements of taste, cooking techniques, and the use of the freshest seasonal ingredients.

Geography

Japan (the land of the rising sun) is composed of four main islands, stretching north to south: Hokkaiko, Honshu, Shikoku, and Kyushu. It also includes the islands of Okinawa and around 4,000 smaller islands. The whole of Japan would fit inside the state of California. The capital is Tokyo.

A Mini-Glossary of Japanese Dishes

Korokke **:** Deep-fried and breaded croquettes, often consisting of mashed potatoes and minced meats.

Nigirizushi **:** Often called finger sushi because of its shape; seasoned cold Japanese rice shaped like a finger is topped with a variety of ingredients, including slices of raw fish. The hotness comes from wasabi, Japanese green horseradish.

Okonomiyaki **:** A giant savory pancake cooked right in front of you on a hot plate. You choose the ingredients and make it yourself.

Sashimi **:** Slices of raw fish.

Shabu-shabu **:** Thinly sliced beef and a variety of vegetables are dipped into a bubbling broth and quickly cooked. A selection of special dipping sauces are used.

Tempura **:** A delectable variety of seafood and vegetables are deep-fried in a crispy, light batter.

Tonkatsu **:** Fried breaded pork cutlets served with a sauce.

Yakitori : Various parts of chicken and vegetables threaded on bamboo skewers and grilled over charcoal. During cooking, it is flavored with either salt or brushed with a mildly sweet soy sauce.

Japanese Products by Mail Order

Nancy's Specialty Market

PO Box 530

Newmarket, NH 03857

To order a catalog: (800) 688-2433, Orders only: (800) 462-6291

Nancy's offers an international selection of dried foods, spices, books, and utensils. Their Oriental (Thailand, Vietnamese, Japanese, Chinese) selection is expansive. Japanese items include everything from wakame, kuzu powder to make silky sauces, noodles such as udon, soba and somen, a large variety of soy sauces, tea, miso (fermented soybean paste), *Japanese Cooking A Simple Art* for the low price of $29.95, and even some tableware, such as multi-colored bowls. Nancy, herself, is currently recommending Myron's #1 Yakitori Sauce, an all natural, low-sodium sauce made by a small Massachusetts company.

Well-Known Japanese Product Lines

Most of these products can be found at local supermarkets or gourmet specialty stores.

Kikkoman : Kikkoman is most well known for its soy sauces. They even offer a lite (low-sodium) version. Many sauces, such as Tonkatsu (for deep-fried pork cutlets) and stir-fry sauces are also made by Kikkoman, as well as instant clear broth and miso soups.

Marukan & Nakano : Marukan and Nakano are both known for vinegars, mainly rice vinegar and seasoned rice vinegar for making sushi.

S & P : S & P is number one for seasonings and spices. Look for their authentic Japanese curry powder.

House : Offers a great variety of instant foods and soups.

Nisshin : Nisshin sells a wide selection of instant ramen.

Sho Chiku Bai, Gekkeikan & Hakutsuru **:** All famous makers of sake (rice wine).

Aji no Moto **:** One of the many makers who sell instant dashi (Japanese fish stock) granules.

One Famous Japanese Dish: Sukiyaki

Nobody really seems to know the origins of *sukiyaki*. One theory is that in the old days farmers slipped a little flesh into the vegetarian diet imposed by Buddhist strictures by grilling (*yaki*) meat on a plowshare (*suki*.) In 1873, Emperor Meiji declared that beef was acceptable for consumption, and from that time on it became part of the Japanese diet, although traditional dishes continue to use small quantities of meat.

Sukiyaki, called *gyunabe* during the Meiji era (1868-1912), is beef and vegetables lightly simmered in a sweetened sauce, served with a raw egg as dipping sauce. It is eaten year-round.

As with many traditional Japanese dishes, the method of making sukiyaki differs from area to area. Kanto (the Tokyo area) sukiyaki is made by simmering the beef and vegetables in a prepared sauce, while in Kansai (Kyoto-Osaka area), the sauce is made in the pot as you cook.

All you really need with sukiyaki, which is quite filling, is a bowl of freshly cooked Japanese rice, some Japanese pickles, and green tea and fresh fruit to finish the feast.

MEXICO

Covering the bottom third of North America and made up of thirty-one states and one very large capital, Mexico is probably the best neighbor a food-lover could have, when you consider the natural bounty of this rich and varied country. That's no doubt what the Spaniards thought when they landed on the shores of the Yucatan in 1521, much to the dismay of the Aztec, Maya, Zapotec and other natives populating this vast stretch of land. Hernan Cortes and his crew set the stage for three centuries of Spanish rule which finally started to unravel in 1810, when a village priest, Miguel Hidalgo, uttered his famous *grito*, or cry: "Mexicanos! Viva Mexico! Viva la Independencia!" The ensuing hundred years were filled with invasions (most notably from the

U.S.) and fitful leadership, whereas the dawn of the twentieth century saw the beginning of the Mexican Revolution in earnest, with the likes of Pancho Villa duking it out with his countrymen. When the dust had settled, the Mexicans were in control, but hardly united. This was, after all, a country comprised of three distinct groups: native peoples, the descendants of the Spanish and *mestizos*, the result of intermarriage between the first two.

The melding of cultures contributed significantly to the melding of foods and food preparation in Mexico, often referred to as *mestizaje*, or "mixing." Corn, a staple for over 4,000 years, is the backbone of the diet. The kernels are softened in water and lime and then ground and fashioned (most commonly) into tortillas. Protein-rich beans and an infinite variety of chilies round out this holy trinity of Mexican cookery. The Spanish liked what they saw in Mexico and added a few things of their own, among them domestic animals, sugar and cheese. Mexican cuisine is further enhanced by an incredible array of fruits

and vegetables which seem to taste better in Mexico than anywhere else: tomatoes, squash, sweet potatoes, avocado, coconut, pineapple, papaya and prickly pear cactus, to name several of the best. Herbs and spices also flavor the pot: cinnamon, clove, anise and cumin are all frequently-used spices, while cilantro, thyme, marjoram and the pungent *epazote* are popular herbs.

Good ingredients certainly count for a lot, but the Mexicans are also gifted cooks and seem to know how to give a dish that extra zing that makes it special. A simple salsa Mexicana is taken to new heights with a touch of cilantro and lime, while a complex mole sauce is always heavenly thanks to over thirty carefully-chosen herbs and spices which are added in and left to slowly simmer in the pot. Whether it's humble *tacos de pollo* or a regal *cochinita Pibil*, the Mexican kitchen is filled with honest, flavorful food which is prepared in a host of interesting ways.

The Mexican Diet

The Mexican table is filled with an assortment of foodstuffs. Sauces, soups and stews are common and expected, while preparations range from a quick-fry to slow roasting. The following is a list of key elements in the Mexican diet.

Corn: most commonly used for tortillas, the warm, flat rounds which accompany or enhance many a dish. Also used for tacos (tortillas stuffed with chicken, beef, fish or cheese) and tamales (steamed and stuffed with meat or vegetables).

Chilies: used both fresh and dried, it's the white veins and seed pods that are the hottest part and pack a punch. Mexicans like to distinguish between heat and flavor, something that can be lost on the untrained palate. Popular varieties of chilies are jalapeno, poblano, serrano, guajillo, chipotle, pasilla, habanero, ancho, mulato and cascabel.

Beans: they run the gamut from lentils to kidney beans and fava beans and are found in many soups and stews. Small beans are often served *refrito* (refried in lard, tasty but heavy) or *de la olla* (boiled and served in a light broth).

Tomatoes: the essential ingredient for a tasty salsa Mexicana and also used in sauces for both fish and beef dishes. Tomatillos are small green tomatoes encased in a stiff husk – they're more tart and often used for a kicky tomatillo salsa which is laced with spicy chilies.

Fruit: mango, papaya, coconut and pineapple are all eaten fresh as well as used in sauces and desserts. Nopales (prickly pear cactus paddles) are sauteed and eaten as a vegetable of sorts but can also be found sweetened in desserts.

Special ingredients: flor de calabaza (squash blossoms) are used in everything from soups to sauces. Huitlacoche is a small, dark fungus (!) which grows on a corn stalk and is surprisingly creamy and delicious. Crepas de huitlacoche (huitlacoche crepes bathed in a dreamy cheese sauce) are a singularly Mexican treat. Romeritos and epazote are two pungent herbs which add a special zest to fish, beef and chicken dishes. Pepitas (pumpkin seeds) are used in sauces, most commonly in pipian, which is used to top many chicken dishes.

Regional Cuisines

It stands to reason that a country as large as Mexico would have a variety of regional cuisines. Some of the best can be found in the states listed below.

Puebla: two hours south of Mexico City is where the first mole sauce was prepared. As the legend goes, an order of nuns was asked to prepare a special dish for a visiting dignitary. Unsure of what would constitute a worthy dish, the nuns literally emptied out their pantry and filled a pot with a combination of herbs, spices and chocolate, over thirty ingredients in all. Left to simmer for several days, the resulting thick, sweet *mole* sauce was served over turkey at the royal feast. Today, mole is most commonly served over chicken. "The nuns are the best cooks in Mexico," says Francisco Cisneros, chef at *Guaymas* restaurant in Tiburon, California. Anyone who has ever tasted a good mole sauce would have to agree. Coffee is grown in Puebla, a nice accompaniment to the area's many unique desserts, especially *camotes,* a sweet potato confection. Pastry shops are as common in Puebla as churches, no small feat since there are said to be over 300 churches in the city of Cholula alone. Your meal is likely to be more attractively presented in Puebla than anywhere else in Mexico, since this area is known for its *azulejos,* or glazed blue and white pottery and tiles.

Yucatan: the land of the Maya is a welcome relief for anyone tired of chilies. Many Yucateco sauces are fruit-based, chief among them a sauce made from brick-red annatto seeds (*achiote*) and flavored with Seville oranges, pepper, garlic and cumin. This sauce is spread over chicken (*pollo pibil*) or pork (*cochinita pibil*), the meats are then baked in a banana leaf, and the result is delightfully good. Pack a picnic and trek to the ruins at Chichen Itza for a meal in an unbeatable setting.

Veracruz: fish is the dish of choice in seaside Veracruz, a busy port filled with salty folks who love life and a good meal. Any fish dish *a la Veracruzana* means it'll be topped with a sauce of tomatoes, olives, capers and chilies. Exotic fruits (guanabana, mamey, chirimoya) and coffee are also grown in this fertile region. Care for a taco? tamale? enchilada? It's bound to be filled with fish while you're in Veracruz.

Oaxaca: you might want to drink your dinner while you're in Oaxaca. Coffee is grown in this state and is usually prepared *a la olla,* which means it's laced with sugar and cinnamon and left to simmer in a large pot for hours. The resulting brew will definitely perk you up. Heartier sorts will gravitate to the region's mescal, a very sober cousin of tequila. Hungry folks should try anything topped with *mole Oaxaqueno,* a sweeter version of the Puebla original thanks to the addition of bananas. The Oaxacans are rightfully proud of the bounty of their vast state, which also includes beautiful *artesania* (hand-carved wooden animals and the black pottery of San Bartolomeo de Coatepec are especially nice) and lyrical Zapotec dances.

The Market

El mercado (the market) is a key part of Mexican life, a big deal with the emphasis on BIG. Cities throughout the country are blessed with markets that are a combination of food hall, discount store, meeting place and social club. These markets are often found in the city center, and most cities of any size have one primary market and several lesser markets. Foodies traveling through Mexico should add the mercado to their list of requisite stops: some of the best can be found in Oaxaca, Guanajuato, Toluca and Mexico City.

On a recent trip to Mexico, I visited the market in Toluca with Gabriel O'Farrill, chef of *Los Danzantes,* a stylish Mexico City restaurant where the accent is on nueva cocina Mexicana. While the market is open every day of the week, Friday is the market day. An infinite number and variety of stalls are spread out over many square blocks next to the central bus station. A new Wal-Mart has opened up across the way, but don't even think about it: you're in the right place.

What will you find at the Toluca market? People for starters, and lots of them. A sea of humanity courses between rows and rows of food, clothes, trinkets, gadgets, games and more. Tables are piled high with the reddest tomatoes and the pinkest strawberries you've ever seen, while buckets are filled with beans of every color, size and shape. Young boys peer into tubs of hot oil as they fry gigantic pork rinds. Shiny fish and swirly sausage compete for your roving eye, while hawkers do their best to sell you a bowl of soup or a plate of stew. This experience is not for the faint of heart, nor is the food for the faint of stomach. Tripe and potatoes chopped on a super-smooth tree trunk and then deep-fried? Chef O'Farrill didn't have a bite (neither did I), but it was sure fun to watch.

Strolling through a Mexican market lets you see first-hand the bounty of the land and its many uses. Among my favorite things: *charales*, tiny river fish which are fried crisp, making for a sorta-fishy chip; *piloncillo*, hunks of sugar cane candy which are used to sweeten cafe de olla ("piloncillo is especially common at wakes," says O'Farrill – "all the calories in that sugar help give people strength"); mango *manila*, small, super-sweet mangoes; and some of the biggest, reddest and juiciest watermelons I've every seen. This last item gives O'Farrill the opportunity to share a tale with me: "Watermelons are indigenous to Mexico," he tells me, "and they're also how we got the colors of our flag. During a hot and bloody battle in Chilpancingo (the capital of Guerrero state) in the 1820s, the fighters took a break and cooled off with some watermelon. When they sliced into it and took note of the bright green, white and red tones, they decided those would be the colors of our new flag." Viva Mexico!

An Interview with Patricia Quintana

Noted cookbook author and chef Patricia Quintana has written nearly a dozen books on the food of her fabled country. Several of them have been published in English, among them "*Mexico's Feasts of Life*," which discusses family celebrations (birthdays, weddings and religious holidays) and the foods surrounding them, and "*The Cuisine of the Water Gods*," covering both coastal and central Mexican cookery. This well-traveled chef studied in Europe under Bocuse, Troisgros and Guerard before returning to her native land and opening her own cooking school, where she taught for ten years. A passion for the foods and flavors of Mexico prompted her to start writing and sharing her favorite recipes. Quintana recently partnered with the Sheraton Maria Isabel in Mexico City to develop "Sabores de Mexico," a combination Mexican food fest and folkloric ballet (courtesy of the Ballet Folclorico Nacional de Mexico) now being offered in the hotel's Cafe Pavillon. I had the good fortune of being in Mexico City for opening night of this new dinner extravaganza and took a few moments to chat with the chef.

"What we're trying to do here is to preserve the special dishes of the repubic," says Quintana. "Whether it's Yucatan, Veracruz or the heart of Mexico, we are working with different ingredients and the stories behind them." As if to prove her point, one of the better appetizers on this new menu is the *tacos sudados en canasta estılb Diego Rivera.* "This is an idea I got from an article I read about fifteen years ago. Lupe Rivera, Diego's sister, told the story of how her brother loved steamed tacos. Although he painted all day long, he would always take a break to eat these little steamed tacos which were served piping hot in a basket. Now we've got them on the menu." Quintana is keenly aware of integrating the old with the new. "We're taking the stories of Mexico and presenting them in a new way by creating dishes with simple, nice and direct flavors. If you eat here, you'll be able to remember what you ate because it3 straightforward and easy to understand."

Quintana shared her views with me on a number of things. On food as ritual: "Since prehispanic times, food has been a ritual. Through food you create a way to celebrate. That's what holidays are about: surrounding yourself with friends and family and creating a menu of feelings. It3 a way to understand the concept of gathering." The role of food: "That's what the markets are all about. It's a gathering. You go to eat, you go to buy, you go to meet people. It's a way of communication." Mealtimes: "We favor the *comida* (late lunch) over *sena* (supper). We like to start with a big breakfast and then have lunch later in the day. Most people can4 have three big meals and then go to sleep – especially not with the altitude of central Mexico! So we focus on the midday meal."

Some of Quintana's keenest observations were on the role of regional cuisines: "Oaxaca has a rich ethnic heritage, a fusion of the native peoples, the Spaniards and the French after that. You can see it in how they handle corn tortillas and the moles, with their varying tints and types. The Yucatan also has an ethnic cuisine which is very European-influenced – you can see it in the Dutch cheeses and how they are used. Veracruz includes the food of eight distinct regions in the state, from the interior to the coast. There's much of a Mediterranean influence here which you can see in how the fish and meats are grilled. And then there's Puebla, which combines aspects of the surrounding states plus the influence of the Spaniards after the conquest and that of the convents. Two of our main dishes come from Puebla: *chiles en nogada* (stuffed Poblano chilies) and *mole Poblano*. The moles were greatly aided by the spice trade, which brought us peppercorns and sesame seeds from Asia, among other ingredients. Moles are so unique: different consistencies, sweet or not, even a variety of chilies. A mole Poblano is completely different from a mole Oaxaqueno. It has to do with color, spices and seasoning and how they2e combined and prepared."

Quintana is understandably excited about "Sabores de Mexico." "This is like my first restaurant. I'd always wanted to have a restaurant but couldn't find the right place. As a consultant here, I get to manage the fusion of the cultures in the food and combine it with the dancers and what they mean to our heritage. I feel as passionate about the dancers as I do about the food!"

Anyone looking for the essence of Mexico in one night need look no further than the Sheraton's "Sabores de Mexico." This is one food and dance experience which is as much substance as style and makes for a delightful evening. Best of the best on Chef Quintana's winning menu are the *camarones empulcados* (shrimp sauteed in mescal and pulque), the *tamal del Istmo de Tehuantepec* (a moist tamale stuffed with perfect mole chicken) and everything on the dessert cart (don't miss the chocolate torte or the lemon mousse). As if this wasn't enough, the best margaritas in Mexico City can be found right here: whether it's a margarita mixed with *tamarindo y mango, flor de jamaica* or *Grand Marnier con limon*, this is a sip you shouldn't miss.

Sabores de Mexico is featured in the Cafe Pavillon of the Sheraton Maria Isabel, Mexico City, from Tuesday through Sunday at 8 PM. Dinner is served until 1 AM; the Ballet Folclorico's hour-long show begins at 9:30 PM. Rates at the Sheraton Maria Isabel are USD $189 to $249 per night; check for special weekend and seasonal rates, an excellent buy.

Recipes

The following recipes are from Francisco Cisneros, chef at Guaymas Restaurant in Tiburon, California.

Chiles en Nogada (Stuffed Poblano Chilies)

Serves Six

12 poblano chilies

Stuffing:

1/4 C. cooking oil

1 whole chicken boiled in salt water, onions, celery, carrots and garlic

1 white onion, finely chopped

3 garlic cloves, peeled and roughly chopped

4 oz. brown sugar

4 bay leaves

4 oz. raisins

2 oz. vinegar

1/2 bunch cilantro, chopped

4 oz. blanched walnuts, chopped

1/4 tsp. black pepper

3 T. tomato paste

Sauce:

2 lbs. cream cheese

1/2 lb. goat cheese

1 C. sour cream

8 oz. blanched walnuts

1/2 tsp. nutmeg

1/4 T. granulated sugar

Garnish:

pomegranate seeds

cilantro

Roast, clean, peel and devein chilies, making sure to slice them along one side only so they can be reconstructed after they are stuffed. Remove meat from boiled chicken and chop. Saute onion and garlic until they are soft. Add chicken, raisins, sugar, walnuts, pepper and bay leaves and saute for a few minutes. Add vinegar, cilantro and tomato paste and cook for 15 minutes. Cool mixture. Stuff chilies with cooled mixture, reheating them in the oven prior to serving. To make the sauce, blend together sauce ingredients and heat oven to medium heat. Pour sauce over heated chilies and garnish with pomegranate seeds and cilantro.

Don Cacahuate ("Mr. Peanut")

Serves Six

Blend for marinade:

4 oz. achiote paste

2 C. vegetable oil

3 cloves garlic

Marinate 6 double breasts of chicken in this mixture.

Peanut-Serrano chile sauce:

2 C. unsalted roasted peanuts

2 C. soybean oil

2 fresh Serrano chilies

1 bunch cilantro, rinsed

1 tsp. dijon mustard

juice from 1 lemon

salt and pepper to taste

In blender, add oil, garlic, cilantro and chilies and blend; add peanuts, then blend. In a bowl, fold mustard, lemon juice and salt and pepper into this mixture.

Mesquite grill the chicken breasts. Onto a round plate, pour the peanut-Serrano chile sauce, place a chicken breast, lightly brush with the sauce and garnish with slices of lemon, cilantro and fresh radish.

Huachinango Entomatado (Snapper in Tomato Sauce)

Serves Two

2 oz. tomato-chile butter (see recipe below)

10 oz. fresh snapper filet

1/2 white onion, cut into wedges

4 medium mushrooms, sliced

1/2 tomato, seeded and cubed

salt and pepper to taste

1/4 chile pasilla

2 scallions, sliced into rings

1/2 C. seafood stock or clam juice

1 jalapeno pepper, seeded and cut into julienne strips

1 garlic clove, chopped

2 oz. olive oil or soybean oil

Heat oil in saute pan. Season snapper filet with salt and pepper. Sear snapper on both sides (about three minutes on each side). Add onions, mushrooms, scallions, chile pasilla, salt and pepper and saute for three minutes over high heat. Add garlic and 2 oz. of the tomato-chile butter and saute for another minute over high heat. Add the stock or clam juice and continue cooking over high heat for three more minutes (sauce will thicken slightly). Snapper should be cooked throughout. Add tomatoes and cook one more minute.

Serve over a banana leaf cut to fit the plate, garnishing with a radish rosette and fresh lime wedge.

Tomato-chile butter:

1 lb. unsalted butter

3 pickled jalapeno peppers, seeded and chopped

2 oz. tomato paste

1/3 bunch cilantro, chopped

salt and pepper to taste

Using a food processor, add butter and soften, then add the remaining ingredients and blend until consistent mixture is formed.

The following recipes are from cookbook author and consulting chef Patricia Quintana, and they are featured at the "Sabores de Mexico" dinner/show at the Cafe Pavillon of the Sheraton Maria Isabel in Mexico City.

Flautas Jaliscienses (Jalisco-Style Flautas)

Makes 20 flautas

20 corn tortillas

2 1/2 C. vegetable oil

For the potato flautas:

2 large potatoes, peeled and boiled in salted water, drained and mashed

1 C. Oaxaca cheese or firm yellow cheese, cut into thin strips

For the chicken flautas:

2 chicken breasts, cooked in salted water with onion and garlic; remove chicken from bone, chop

1 medium onion, finely sliced into rounds

1 T. vegetable oil

For the green sauce:

4 C. water

7 green tomatoes (tomatillos), without husks

1/2 white onion, chopped in half

3 cloves garlic, peeled

3 Serrano chilies

1/2 C. cilantro

1/4 C. onion, finely chopped

1/8 C. cilantro, finely chopped

1/2 Hass avocado

Salt to taste

For the red sauce:

4 C. water

1 1/2 tomatoes

1 medium onion, sliced into rounds

3 cloves garlic, peeled

2 Chipotle chilies, fried but not charred

Salt to taste

Topping:

1 C. creme fraiche

1/4 C. sweet whipping cream

3/4 C. cream cheese, crumbled

For the potato flautas: heat corn tortillas. Place a small amount of the potatoes and cheese in the center of each tortilla and roll them tightly. For the chicken flautas: combine the loose chicken with the onion and oil; season to taste. Place a small amount of the mixture in the center of each warm tortilla and roll them tightly. For the green sauce: boil the water and add in the tomatillos, onion, garlic and chilies. Cook for 30 minutes; remove from heat, drain and reserve the liquid. Let the tomatillos cool. Blend the cooked ingredients in a food processor along with the onion, cilantro and avocado. Season to taste. If the sauce is too thick, add back some of the reserved liquid.

For the red sauce: boil the water and add the tomatoes, onion, garlic and fried chilies. Cook for 25 minutes; remove from heat, drain and reserve the liquid. Blend the ingredients in a food processor and season to taste. Add back some of the reserved liquid to thin the sauce. Presentation: heat the oil in a large frying pan, but not too hot. Fry the flautas until they are golden, turning them carefully. Drain on an absorbent paper towel. Place the flautas on a large serving dish. Alternately top with green and red sauce. Combine the creme fraiche and sweet whipping cream and drizzle it over the flautas. Top with crumbled cream cheese.

Ceviche Acapulqueno (Ceviche Acapulco-Style)

Yield: 16 servings

For the fish:

2 lbs. red snapper fillets, chopped into small chunks

The juice of 8 large lemons

Salt to taste

For the vinaigrette:

1 medium white onion, finely chopped

2 Serrano chilies, finely chopped

1 1/2 large tomatoes, finely chopped

3/4 C. green olives (stuffed with pimento), finely chopped
1/8 C. parsley, finely chopped
1/4 C. cilantro, finely chopped
2 1/2 C. ketchup
1 can V-8 juice, approx. 12-oz. size
1 C. olive oil
1/2 can jalapeno chilies, finely chopped (approx. 4-oz. size)
1/8 C. Worcestershire sauce
1/2 tsp. chopped oregano
Salt to taste

Preparation: In a large glass dish, place the fish and cover it with the lemon juice and salt. Marinate for 15 minutes; remove half of the liquid. Combine the ingredients for the vinaigrette, add to the fish and cover. Marinate for three hours in the refrigerator. Serve in individual goblets and top with chopped cilantro. Optional garnish: place a small skewer of olives, avocado and pickled carrots next to each goblet.

PHILIPPINES

History

Sitting at the very edge of South-East Asia, a country twice colonized and twice liberated, the Philippines has absorbed influences from East and West, land and sea, and its food and culture reflect them all.

In the beginning there was rice and so, of course, there is rice still. In fact, for all but the wealthiest, rice is the main food eaten three times a day and everything else is simply a condiment.

Then come the fruits of the sea. The Philippines may be a mere two-thirds the size of neighboring Indonesia, but it consists of 7,107 islands with the longest discontinuous coastline in the world. Fish and seafood by definition supply the principal and favorite source of protein. Prior to their contact with other cultures through trade and conquest, the 80 or more ethno-linguistic groups of this island cluster shared certain cooking techniques and flavor preferences, many of which are still found today despite layers of external influence.

Early Filipinos cooked their food minimally by roasting, steaming or boiling. The freshest of fish was made into kinilaw, "cooked" by immersion in vinegar and salt with ginger, onions and red peppers.

Flavors and Ingredients

With notable exceptions, Filipino cooks and eaters still show a distinct preference for sour and salty flavors. Sinigang, lightly boiled fish in a sour stock with vegetables and fish sauce, typifies the foundation layer of Filipino cuisine. The sources for these flavors go well beyond vinegar and salt. Numerous unripe fruits such as tamarind, mango and guava provide sour power as well as the tiny kalamansi, a citrus halfway between an orange and a lime, which is sour even when ripe. For salty flavoring, Filipinos rely on patis or fish sauce, bagoong or shrimp paste, and, with the arrival of the Chinese, soy sauce.

The first set of foreign influences on Filipino cuisine came from Chinese traders who ultimately settled there. Eager to eat the food of home, they introduced stir-frying and deep frying. Noodles and soy products became indispensable to the food vocabulary. But local cooks incorporated indigenous ingredients and their own preferences into foods of Chinese origin. Thus pansit, saut%d noodles, are incomplete without a squirt or two of fresh kalamansi. And many types of lumpia, the Filipino version of spring rolls, are dipped in a sauce that consists simply of crushed garlic and vinegar.

With the Spaniards came an entirely new range of ingredients and dishes. Thick, rich stews, sausages, and dishes emphasizing meat and dairy products, they remain a luxury item today. Many show up on the table only at Christmas or fiesta time and are quickly spotted because they retain their Spanish names — relleno, mechado, pochero, leche flan. Adobo, perhaps the best known Filipino dish, is a product of Spanish influence. In Spanish cuisine, adobo refers to a pickling sauce made with olive oil, vinegar, garlic, thyme, bay leaf, oregano, paprika and salt. Filipinos selected their favorite flavors — vinegar, garlic, bay leaf — along with peppercorns and, more recently, soy sauce, used it for a stewing sauce for chicken and/or pork, and gave it the Spanish name.

And finally came the Americans with their all-pervasive culture and cuisine. Whereas the Spaniards reserved education for the elite, the American colonists set out to educate the entire population. Within a generation, not only did Filipinos speak English, they became consumers of American products – Wrangler wearers, Marlboro men, Coca-cola consumers, and burger freaks.

But today's Filipino is likely to want chopped onions, garlic and soy sauce in his burger. Fried chicken, that specialty of the American deep south, will not be breaded, but marinated in soy sauce, vinegar and garlic before it is fried.

All of which goes to show that you can add to a people's range of choices, but you can't keep their culinary identity down. Through rich and tangled web of food influences, the Filipino palate asserts itself again and again.

Sulu carries approximately 15 cookbooks or books about food. Most of these relate to the Philippines, but Sulu's scope includes other South-East Asian countries as well. Related interests covered include health and the natural sciences. Unfortunately their catalogue does not list prices so you will have to call in and ask.

Philippine Expressions

Recipes

Sinigang na Isda (Fish Sinigang)

Sinigang can be made with fish, pork or beef. Most commonly it is made with a fresh-water fish called bangus which is now available in many cities in the US. A medium sized fish, it is simply chopped in pieces and boiled – head, tail and all. But bangus is bony, so for those who would rather do without, we recommend salmon or rock cod. This recipe is adapted from one used by the Sulo Restaurant in Alameda, California. Modify the degree of sourness to suit your own taste.

1/2 cup or more lemon or lime juice (to taste) (or 1 cup or more green tamarind*, crushed and cut into two or three pieces)

5 cups rice water, the water left over from washing your rice

1 cup finely sliced onion

1/4 cup fresh ginger julienned

2 cups sliced tomato

1 large or two small daikon* (Chinese radish), peeled and sliced thinly on the diagonal

2 pounds bangus, salmon or rock cod steaks or filets

2 Tablespoons patis* (Filipino fish sauce)

2 bunches of spinach, cleaned and stemmed

Chopped scallions for garnish

If you would rather not have the chipped shells and seeds of tamarind in the final product, tie the tamarind loosely in a piece of cheesecloth which you can remove later. Simmer wa ter, lemon or lime juice or tamarind, onion, ginger, and tomato lightly for one-half hour. Add water if it appears to cook away too quickly. Add daikon and simmer for 10 more minutes. Add fish and cook for another five to 10 minutes, until the fish is cooked through. Remove tamarind bundle at this point and add patis. Add spinach and cook just until soft. Garnish with chopped scallions. Serve with rice and a small bowl or cup for the broth. Pass additional patis at the table.

Lumpia Shanghai

There are many types of lumpia, the Filipino version of China's spring rolls. Some are heavy on vegetables. Others are made with chicken or fish. For our version of Lumpia Shanghai we turned to Vicki Valdez, owner of – what else? – The House of Lumpia in San Francisco.

3/4 pound lean ground pork

3/4 pound shrimp, finely chopped

1/3 cup water chestnuts, chopped

1/3 cup onions, finely chopped

1 teaspoon salt

1/2 teaspoon pepper

1 teaspoon soy sauce

2 eggs

30 to 35 lumpia wrappers*

In a medium bowl, combine pork, shrimp, water chestnuts and onions. Mix them well. In a smaller bowl, beat eggs. Add salt, pepper and soy sauce and beat again. Add to meat mixture and mix thoroughly until ingredients are well blended. Separate wrappers. Place one tablespoon of mixture at one end of wrapper. Roll tightly halfway. Fold over left and right ends of wrapper and continue rolling. Brush end of wrapper with water to seal.

Deep fry in moderately hot oil for 20 minutes until golden brown and crisp. Drain on paper towels. If you wish to serve them in bite-size pieces, cut each lumpia diagonally into three pieces with a sharp knife. Serve hot with a sweet and sour sauce or garlic vinegar or a choice of either.

Sweet and Sour Sauce

1/4 cup vinegar

1/4 cup sugar

1/4 teaspoon salt

1/2 cup water

2 Tb. catsup

2-3 drops hot pepper sauce

2 teaspoon cornstarch dissolved in 1 Tb. water

In a small pan combine vinegar, sugar, salt, water and catsup. Boil for two minutes. Add hot pepper sauce and corn starch. Stir well to blend. Cook for 3 more minutes at medium heat.

Garlic Vinegar Sauce

1/2 cup vinegar, preferably coconut or palm

2 cloves of garlic, smashed

Salt to taste

Mix it all together and set it out for dipping.

Adobo Pork Chops

Adobo can be made with pork or chicken or a mixture of the two. Most home cooks use pork butt cut into bite-sized chunks and stewed. Nick Mendoza, chef/owner of the Banaue Restaurant in Daly City, California, likes to use pork chops because they are more tender and cook quickly. He leaves out the traditional bay leaf and peppercorn and substitutes lemon juice for vinegar.

8 pork chops – 1/2" thick

2 cloves garlic, smashed and chopped

1 Tablespoon onion chopped

Juice of one lemon

1/4 cup soy sauce

Pour just enough cooking oil into a large skillet to coat the bottom. Heat the oil and sear the pork chops, approximately 3 minutes per side.

Add garlic and brown lightly. Add onions, lemon juice, garlic and soy sauce, turn heat down and cover. Simmer for 5 minutes.

Reduce the sauce as much as you like. Nick likes his adobo dry; others like it with plenty of sauce to go with their rice.

Fried Chicken Manong Style

Emil De Guzman spent years living with and advocating the rights of the manongs – the first generation of Filipino immigrants who worked the fields and filled service industry positions up and down the west coast. He learned their cooking secrets and his passion for food continued though times and careers changed. This is an adaptation of his version of fried chicken which includes rosemary and parsley - not exactly Filipino herbs. But with or without rosemary, you'll have to agree that Colonel Sanders would never recognize the dish.

1 cup soy sauce

1 teaspoon sesame oil

Juice of one lemon

2 generous Tablespoon ginger, sliced thin and lightly smashed

1/2 head garlic, peeled and minced

1 small bunch parsley, chopped fine

1/4 cup fresh rosemary, chopped

1/2 teaspoon pepper

1 chicken cut in pieces, skinned, washed and dried thoroughly

Mix soy sauce, sesame oil, lemon juice, ginger, garlic, parsley, rosemary and pepper. Place chicken in marinade using shallow bowl or plastic bag and turn the chicken to insure it is coated. Marinate chicken overnight, turning several times.

Remove the chicken from the marinade and wipe lightly to remove herbs, ginger and garlic. Heat approximately 1/8" to 1/

4" of oil on high. Fry 8 minutes to a side to achieve a crispy brown layer. Lower fire to medium and continue frying for another 20 to 30 minutes keeping close attention to avoid blackening or burning.

RUSSIA

Geography

Russia, stretching from eastern Europe across Asia to the North Pacific Ocean, is as diverse as it is vast. It is nearly twice the land mass of the United States, with a population of 150 million. Large plains cover much of the land, with a number of mountain ranges in the eastern and southern regions. The Ural Mountains serve as a natural boundary between European and Asian Russia.

The country's coastline stretches nearly 37,000km along the Arctic and Pacific Oceans, with Baltic, Black and Caspian seas inland. Russia boasts innumerable rivers and lakes, steppes and forests, swamps and tundra. The harsh continental climate and tough terrain leave large parts of the country uninhabited.

Nearly three quarters of Russians live in urban areas. In addition to the greatly varied terrain and climate, there is much diversity in the Russian populace. While the majority of the population is ethnically Russian, there are over 100 ethnic groups that constitute the minority. It is no wonder then, that Russian food is greatly varied, with its fair share of ethnic and regional crossover. In this article, I will concentrate on the traditional food of European Russia.

Food

The Russian meal is not simply about food, it's an event, a celebration. Even an informal meal can become a festivity with a string of dishes punctuated with toasts, stories and laughter. Russian hospitality is a long-standing tradition and a source of pride for the host. A guest in a Russian home is invariably showered with drinks, refreshments, and more often than not, a full meal. Russians are prone to dropping by unannounced, and the hosts will always rise to the challenge of quickly (and creatively!) assembling whatever ingredients are at hand into a beautifully presented spread. When my Moscowite friend gave his mother an hour's notice of our impromptu visit, she greeted us with cake fresh out of the oven, brewed tea, and an assortment of finger foods. We were not allowed to leave until we tried one of everything, with our hostess apologizing profusely for not having more food to offer. A visit is incomplete without a proper gathering around the table, no matter what the occasion.

The first course is typically an assortment of salads, pickles, and cured savories called "zakuski", which loosely translates to "accompaniments", eaten along with shots of vodka. Much like Spanish tapas or Mediterranean meze, these appetizers are small tastes of a variety of dishes. Zakuski could be as simple as smoked meats, cured fish, caviar and marinated mushrooms, or more elaborate dishes such as vegetable salads. Salted herring under a thick layer of shredded beets, carrots and walnuts is called " sel'odka pod shuboy" which literally translates to "herring under a fur coat". Despite its intimidating name, this is a very tasty dish. A cooked eggplant salad, "baklazhanaya ikra" is also very popular. Similar to Romanian "gvetch", eggplant is stewed with carrots, onions, garlic and tomatoes, and served chilled. A cold salad of potatoes, beets, pickled cabbage and onions called "vinegret" is a Russian classic, as is "salat olivier", a potato salad with eggs, peas, pickles and meat. Many Russian salads are dressed with mayonnaise or sour cream, and are hearty enough to be eaten as a main course.

Soup is always part of the dinner menu. A soup course offers a variety of vegetarian and meat- or fish-based soups. The most well-known Russian soup is "borscht", a tangy dish that gets its sweetness from beets and tartness from sour cream. Borscht is exceptionally versatile – it can be vegetarian or meaty, served hot or cold. Everyone seems to have their own recipe for this wonderful soup, but the more authentic versions always include beets, cabbage, potato, and carrot, with the meat-based broth made with beef. Another common soup is "shchi", a hearty cabbage soup. Ingredients can vary somewhat, but it is typically made of cabbage, potato, onion, herbs, and optionally, beef and dumplings. Much like borscht, it is usually served with a dollop of sour cream and a slice of hearty rye bread.

Russian entrees run the culinary gamut, from stews to stuffed vegetables to fried fish and meat. Many main courses are accompanied by thick, flavorful sauces, and are served with buckwheat or potatoes. Mushroom sauces are particularly popular, and tend to go well with many dishes. "Kotlety Pozharskie" are ground chicken cutlets prepared with lots of butter. While not exactly dietetic, these cutlets are fluffy and melt in your mouth. Dumplings filled with meat or potatoes are called "Pelmeni". The meat filling, which is often made of ground pork, is encased in thin, light dough. I especially love serving pelmeni with a dip made of sour cream, scallions and dill. "Golubtzy" are cabbage leaves stuffed with rice and beef, and roasted in tomato sauce. Stuffed cabbage tends to be a labor intensive endeavor, but well worth it. A number of dishes, such as beef stroganoff and chicken kiev have trickled into the western culinary vernacular over the years. Although these dishes have lost their exotic edginess, it's good to see that they represent Russia's contribution to international palates.

No meal is complete without lingering over cups of strong tea and sweets. Even large meals are usually followed by a dessert course, which, much like the savory assortment of zakuzki, consists of a sweet assortment of cookies, candies, and cakes. Rich layered tortes are composed of sweet butter creams and nuts in between sheets of cake. Candy is often just as rich, made of nuts, marzipan, dried fruit or wafers dipped in dark chocolate. A variety of candy and cakes can be found in most Russian food stores, but the tastiest desserts are homemade. "Vareniki" are dumplings filled with fruit or sweet cheese. Not only are they delicious, but they are easy to make at home.

"Medianyk" is a wonderful honey cake, and "Medianyky" are honey cookies, based on the same recipe. A fresh fruit compote is the perfect summer dessert, but can also be made from dried fruit off-season. Cherries, apples, and stone fruit are best in this dish, and berries can be added to enhance the flavors. Compote can also be poured over vanilla ice cream or sweet crepes. I can't think of a better way to end a wonderful meal. And just when you think you can't possibly eat one more bite, you will be talked into having one last cup of tea.

Recipes

Vinegret (vegetable salad):

6 red potatoes
5 medium beets
3 large carrots
2 cups pickled cabbage
1 medium red onion
1 cup peas (canned or frozen)
1 bunch parsley, chopped
1 1/2 cups mayonnaise
Salt and pepper to taste

Boil the potatoes and beets in their skin until tender (about 45 minutes). In a separate pot, boil carrots until tender (about 20 minutes). Drain the cooking liquid and let vegetables cool about 15-20 minutes before peeling (the skins should come right off when the vegetables are at room temperature). Dice the cooked vegetables by hand. Protect your hands from beet juice stains handling beets with plastic wrap or rinsing hands every few minutes. Squeeze excess liquid out of the cabbage. Combine the diced vegetables with the rest of the ingredients in a large bowl. Season to taste with salt and pepper. Serve chilled. Note: For best results, refrigerate salad over night or 4-6 hours before serving.

Shchi (Cabbage Soup)

3 quarts beef stock (or water for vegetarian version)
4 tablespoons butter or olive oil
1 large or 2 medium onions, grated
2 large carrots, grated
1/2 head cabbage, coarsely shredded
1 parsley root, shredded
3 large potatoes, peeled and cut in ½ inch cubes
½ cup tomato sauce
Bay leaf
Fresh herb parcel (parsley, dill)
Salt
Pepper

Melt the butter in a sauce pan set over high heat. Add the onions, carrots, and parsley root, reduce the heat to moderate, and cook for 8 to 10 minutes, or until they are soft but not brown.

Pour the meat stock or water into a 4-quart pot and bring to a boil. Lower the heat immediately to medium and add cabbage. After 10-15 minutes, add potato, bay leaf, and onion mixture. Simmer over medium heat until the potatoes are almost soft (10-15 minutes). Add tomato sauce, herb parcel and salt and pepper to taste. Remove bay leaf and herbs once soup is ready. Serve hot with dollop of sour cream.

Kotlety Pozharskie (Ground Chicken Cutlets)

4 slices fine white bread with crusts removed

¼ cup of whole milk

2 pounds skinless, boneless chicken breasts

8 tablespoons of softened, unsalted butter (1/4-pound stick)

1 tablespoon salt

1 teaspoon freshly ground pepper

2 cups fresh white breadcrumbs

6 tablespoons of unsalted butter, cut into small bits (same amount of clarified butter can be used)

In a small bowl combine the slices of bread and ¼ cup of milk. Soak the bread for about 15 minutes. Squeeze out and discard any extra liquid. Cut the chicken into small pieces and grind them through the finest blades of the meat grinder twice. Combine ground chicken and soaked bread, and grind through again. With a large wooden spoon (or with your hands), gradually incorporate 8 tablespoons of softened butter, salt and pepper and continue to beat until the mixture is smooth. Dip your fingers into cold water and shape the mixture into 6 oval patties, each about 1½ inches thick. Roll the patties in the bread crumbs, coating them thoroughly.

Melt 3 tablespoons of butter in the pan. Place over moderate high heat and when the butter is hot, add the patties. Fry about 5 minutes on each side, turning them over with a spatula. Add remaining butter as necessary. The patties are done when the crusts are golden brown and the inside is cooked through. Serve immediately.

Vareniki (sweet dumplings)

5 cups Unbleached all-purpose flour 1 ts Salt 2 tb Butter 1 cup Evaporated Milk; 1/2 c Water, as needed In a food processor, combine the flour, salt, and butter, stirring a few times. With the machine running, add liquids until a ball forms. Allow to rest for a few minutes and then process until smooth. Place the dough in a lightly oiled bowl and cover for about 30 minutes. (The dough can be made one day ahead, wrapped in plastic and refrigerated; be sure to bring dough to room temperature before rolling it out.) Place a fourth of the dough on a floured work surface, covering the rest with a towel. Roll the dough evenly into a circle, until it is about 1/8-inch thick. With a 3-inch cookie cutter or glass, cut into rounds. Place 1 Tb of the filling on one round and place another round on top, sealing them tightly with your fingers or a fork. Place dumplings on a floured cookie sheet and cover with a towel. Repeat this process with the remaining dough. Use as little flour as possible in this process to avoid tough, heavy dough. Gently drop varenyky into 4 quarts of boiling water, in a wide pot, making sure they're not crowded. Boiling them in batches of 15 is best. Stir gently and cook for 3 to 4 minutes—don't overcook. Drain in a colander and place in a lightly buttered serving bowl. Sprinkle with powdered sugar before serving.

Medianyk (Honey Cake) 4 oz Butter 4 large Eggs 14 oz Honey 14 oz Unbleached All-Purpose Flour (about 3 cups) 1/2 ts Ground Ginger 1/2 ts Ground Nutmeg 1/2 ts Ground Cloves 1 ts Cinnamon 2 ts Baking Powder Separate the eggs and let stand at room temperature. Cream the butter, and add in yokes one at a time, beating well. Mix in the honey. Sift the flour, baking powder, and spices and add to the butter mixture. Whip the egg whites until stiff. Gently fold in the egg whites into the batter. Preheat the oven at 350F. Pour the batter into a buttered loaf pan. Bake until firm on top and a toothpick inserted in the center comes out clean, about 1 hour. Cool in the pan for 10 minutes before removing the cake to cool on a wire rack.

Bibliography

Auguste, E.: *Escoffier Cook Book: A Guide to the Fine Art Cookery,* New York, Crown, 1969.

Bryson, McDowell: *Concierge: Key to Hospitality: A Training Manual,* New York, Wiley, 1992.

Charles, G.: *International Dictionary of Food & Cooking,* Chicago, Fitzroy Dearborn, 1998.

Clark, Mona: *Interpersonal Skills for Hospitality Managers,* London, Chapman Hill, 1995.

Cracknell, H. L.: *Escoffier: The Complete Guide to the Art of Modern Cookery,* New York, John Wiley, 1979.

Donald, M.: *Customer Service in the Hospitality and Tourism Industry,* Englewood Cliffs, Prentice Hall, 1994.

Elio, C.: *The Hospitality Law Desk Reference,* Miami, Southern Beverage Journal, 1994.

Gisslen, Wayne: *Professional Cooking,* New York, Wiley, 1999.

Hubert, B.: *A Host of Opportunities: An Introduction to Hospitality Management,* Chicago, Irwin, 1996.

Jarvis, R.: *Business Accounting for Hospitality and Tourism,* London, Chapman and Hall, 1995.

Judi, Radice: *Restaurant & Food Graphics,* Glen Cove, PBC International, 1994.

Marjorie, E.: *Careers in Travel, Tourism, and Hospitality,* Lincolnwood, VGM Career Horizons, 1997.

Michael, John: *Principles of Hospitality Law,* London, Cassell, 1999.

Nancy, N.: *Choosing a Career in Hotels, Motels, and Resorts,* New York, Rosen Pub. Group, 1997.

Norman, G.: *Hotel, Restaurant, and Travel Law: A Preventive Approach,* Albany, Delmar Publishers, 1993.

Robert, C.: *Cases in Hospitality Marketing and Management,* New York, John Wiley, 1997.

Rocco, M.: *An Introduction to Hospitality Today,* Orlando, Educational Institute, 1998.

Rosemary, E.: *Managing Employee Relations in the Hotel and Catering Industry,* London, Cassell, 1995.

Rosenzweig, J. E.: *Organisation and Management,* New York, McGraw Hill International, 1963.

Sherman, Barry: *Telecommunications Management,* New York, McGraw Hill, 1995.

Thomas, F.: *Introduction to Management in the Hospitality Industry,* New York, Wiley, 1995.

Timothy, R.: *Cases in Hospitality Management: A Critical Incident Approach,* New York, Wiley, 1995.

Vallette, J.: *The International Trade in Wastes: A Greenpeace Inventory,* Washington, Greenpeace, 1989.

Walden, Richard: *Genetic Transformation in Plants,* England, Open University Press, 1988.

Waller, Keith: *Improving Food and Beverage Performance,* Oxford, Butterworth-Heinemann, 1996.

Ware, Richard: *How to Open Your Own Restaurant: A Guide for Entrepreneurs,* New York, Penguin Books, 1991.

Wendy, B.: *Elegant Hotels of Europe,* Glen Cove, PBC International, 1994.

William, H.: *The Chef's Guide to Practical Restaurant Cookery,* New York, Van Nostrand Reinhold, 1988.

Zupan, J.M.: *The Distribution of Air Quality in the New York Region,* Baltimore, Johns Hopkins University Press, 1973.

Index

□□□